ARGUMENTS AND ICONS

Arguments and Icons

Divergent modes of religiosity

HARVEY WHITEHOUSE

OXFORD
UNIVERSITY PRESS

*This book has been printed digitally and produced in a standard specification
in order to ensure its continuing availability*

OXFORD
UNIVERSITY PRESS

Great Clarendon Street, Oxford OX2 6DP

Oxford University Press is a department of the University of Oxford.
It furthers the University's objective of excellence in research, scholarship,
and education by publishing worldwide in

Oxford New York

Auckland   Cape Town Dar es Salaam   Hong Kong   Karachi
Kuala Lumpur Madrid Melbourne Mexico City   Nairobi
New Delhi Shanghai Taipei Toronto
With offices in
Argentina Austria Brazil Chile Czech Republic France Greece
Guatemala Hungary Italy Japan South Korea Poland Portugal
Singapore Switzerland Thailand Turkey Ukraine Vietnam

Oxford is a registered trade mark of Oxford University Press
in the UK and in certain other countries

Published in the United States
by Oxford University Press Inc., New York

ISBN 0-19-823415-5

Antony Rowe Ltd., Eastbourne

Dedicated to Danny

ACKNOWLEDGEMENTS

Much of the material in this volume has gone through a series of incarnations as seminar and conference papers, and some of it has been published in journals. I have, as a consequence, accumulated many debts.

For their stimulating and constructive comments on earlier drafts of many parts of this volume, I should like to thank those attending my departmental seminar presentations at the London School of Economics (1991), the Universities of Oxford and Manchester and the Queen's University of Belfast (1993), and the Universities of St Andrews and Edinburgh (1996), as well as my fellow participants at conferences of the European Society for Oceanists in Nijmegen (1992) and Copenhagen (1996), of the Association for Social Anthropologists in Oceania in Hawaii (1996), and of the European Association for Social Anthropologists in Oslo (1994) and Frankfurt (1998). My attendance at overseas conferences was generously funded by the Queen's University of Belfast and the British Academy.

A series of workshops in Paris, organized by Carlo Severi and funded by the CNRS, and two workshops on anthropological studies of Christianity, organized by Fenella Cannell and Maia Green at the University of Manchester (1997) and the London School of Economics (1998), also provided invaluable opportunities to discuss aspects of this volume and I am indebted to all the participants at these meetings.

I am grateful also to the NIDevR for funding my archival research for this book in 1996, at the Australian Archives, the Pacific Manuscripts Bureau, and the National Library in Canberra, and the Mitchell Library in Sydney. I should like particularly to thank Chris Ballard, Ian Keen, and Hank Nelson for their invaluable guidance in relation to this work. I also benefited greatly from Ton Otto's bibliography of archival material on Manus, which he kindly made available to me in advance of its publication. Some of the ethnography presented in this volume also derives from my fieldwork in Papua New Guinea as a doctoral student, funded by the Economic and Social Research Council. For this material, I am, as ever, in the debt of my many friends in the field, especially the people of Dadul, Sunam, and Maranagi.

I am grateful to the Royal Anthropological Institute of Great Britain and Ireland and to Oceania Publications for permission to reprint in this volume my own material previously published as articles in *Man*, the *Journal of the Royal Anthropological Institute*, and *Oceania*. I should also like to thank the Anthropological Society of Oxford and the Anthropological Association of Ireland for permission to reprint in this volume my own material previously published as book reviews in *JASO: The Journal of the Anthropological Society of Oxford* and the *Journal of the Anthropological Association of Ireland*.

In relation to each chapter of this volume, there are particular individuals to whom I owe a special debt of gratitude, for commenting at length or in writing on earlier drafts. I benefited greatly in this way from the generosity of: Marcus Banks, Bob Barnes, Maurice Bloch, Simon Harrison, Ingjerd Hoem, and Howard Morphy (Chapter 1); Pascal Boyer, Sini Cedercreutz, William Christian Jr, Simon Harrison, Michael Houseman, and Carlo Severi (Chapter 2); Alfred Gell, Tim Ingold, Tom Lawson, and Gilbert Lewis (Chapters 3 and 5); Pascal Boyer, Justin Barrett, Simon Harrison, Michael Houseman, Stephen Hugh-Jones, Tom Lawson, Carlos Mondragon, Carlo Severi, and Eduardo Viveiros de Castro (Chapter 4); Mark Burnett, Fenella Cannell, William Christian Jr, and Chris Marsh (Chapter 7); Steve Mithen (Chapter 8).

An entire draft of the manuscript was read and commented on by Pascale Bonnemère, Tony Crook, Bob McCauley, and Brian Malley. Any remaining errors are mine, of course, but there would have been many more without the help of Pascale and Tony, whose expert knowledge of key ethnographic cases provided a valuable corrective on several points. Likewise, Brian's critical sharpness and Bob's unrelenting rationality, precision, and candour helped me to avoid some particularly embarrassing mistakes.

Of the two anonymous reviewers for OUP, only James Laidlaw subsequently revealed his identity to me. He brought to his report on the manuscript impressive breath of learning and intellectual clarity, from which I have profited greatly. The other reviewer, whose identity I have not been able to divine, also provided many extremely helpful suggestions, to which I have tried to respond (however inadequately).

CONTENTS

FIGURES

Introduction

This book distinguishes two fundamentally contrasting sets of politico-religious dynamics which may be dubbed 'doctrinal' and 'imagistic' modes of religiosity.[1] Modes of religiosity constitute *tendencies* towards particular patterns of codification, transmission, cognitive processing, and political association. The imagistic mode consists of the tendency, within certain small-scale or regionally fragmented ritual traditions and cults, for revelations to be transmitted through sporadic collective action, evoking multivocal iconic imagery, encoded in memory as distinct episodes, and producing highly cohesive and particularistic social ties. By contrast, the doctrinal mode of religiosity consists of the tendency, within many regional and world religions, for revelations to be codified as a body of doctrines, transmitted through routinized forms of worship, memorized as part of one's 'general knowledge', and producing large, anonymous communities. These fundamentally contrasting dynamics are often to be found within a single religious tradition, where they may be associated more or less strongly with different categories or strata of religious adherents. For instance, the religious practices of social élites and literati may have a noticeably 'doctrinal' character, whereas 'little traditions' (Redfield 1955) and 'cults of the little community' (Werbner 1977) are often more distinctively 'imagistic'. However pronounced the tendencies towards one or other mode of religiosity may be within a particular field of religious activity, they remain tendencies and nothing more. Even the most iconoclastic doctrinal traditions incorporate certain properties of the imagistic mode and vice-versa, not least because doctrines themselves may evoke multivocal imagery and because ritual symbolism is often crucially augmented by doctrine-like discourse. Having said that, the distinction between doctrinal and imagistic modes of religiosity corresponds to empirically significant trajectories, and this book attempts to explain why.

Demonstrating the empirical productivity and explanatory value of the theory of modes of religiosity requires a delicate balancing of the pressures to substantiate and to generalize a set of claims. The strategy

---

[1] These concepts were developed in my earlier monograph, *Inside the Cult* (Oxford University Press, 1995).

adopted in this volume is to focus heavily on a small number of exceptionally well-documented religious traditions in Melanesia. A comprehensive substantiation of my argument, even if restricted to Melanesian examples, would necessarily run into many volumes, because there are a great many distinct cults, sects, and religious denominations in Papua New Guinea alone. To extend these arguments further still, to religious traditions all around the world, would require a massively greater body of data, and place me in the position of a reckless trespasser on the regional specialisms of others. By focusing on just a few case studies, however, I hope to demonstrate the explanatory *potential* of the theory of modes of religiosity. That is the aim of this book. What follows is not intended as a contribution to the ethnographic record, of Melanesia or anywhere else, but as a theoretical treatise which, though it happens to be illustrated by (and therefore oriented to) Melanesian examples, I hope will be taken up and extended by others in relation to a broader range of materials.

An initial aim of this volume is to show that the Melanesian traditions examined gravitate strongly towards one or other of the two modes of religiosity, or towards both but within readily distinguishable domains of operation. More generally, it is suggested that the doctrinal mode was unelaborated in pre-contact Melanesia, whereas imagistic practices were well established in many parts of the region. By contrast, certain varieties of missionary Christianity tended towards a purely doctrinal mode of operation and often acted to suppress imagistic forms of both Melanesian and European origin. Thus, Papua New Guinea has recently been the site for a dramatic confrontation between divergent modes of religiosity. Only in the light of this confrontation is it possible to explain many of the recurrent features of new religious movements in Melanesia, including distinctive patterns of interaction between doctrinal and imagistic fields of activity.

If modes of religiosity constitute general tendencies towards the coalescence of particular transmissive, cognitive, and political features, then it must be because these features are mutually reinforcing. A major part of this volume is devoted to the formulation of these interconnections. It must be emphasized, however, that there is nothing deterministic about these arguments. Modes of religiosity do not always coalesce and their component features, where they tend to become pronounced, must always be the outcome of multiple, historically contingent causes. Imagistic and doctrinal modes nevertheless may be regarded as clusters of features that tend to coalesce, all else being equal. As such, they constitute relatively robust cultural models that, once established, often endure in more or less elaborated forms for centuries, and even for millennia.

How modes of religiosity came into being in the first place, at various times and locations, is a complex question. On the basis of archaeological evidence, it is tentatively suggested in this volume that the imagistic mode first appeared among Upper Palaeolithic hunter-gatherers through processes of religious experimentation that turned out to be highly adaptive in conditions of intensified competition for resources, not least because they fostered forms of especially intense local cohesion, facilitating more effective forms of group defence. The doctrinal mode appears to have been invented very much later, precipitated by the advent of writing technologies just a few thousand years ago. The emergence of the doctrinal mode was likewise portentous, paving the way for processes of colonization, missionization, and indigenous struggles for independence.

The Theoretical Context

In *Inside the Cult* (Whitehouse 1995: 197), I distinguished thirteen contrasting features of doctrinal and imagistic modes of religiosity respectively. Inevitably, there was a certain arbitrariness in the enumeration of thirteen features, rather than ten or twenty. Nevertheless, any method of carving up the component elements of doctrinal and imagistic modes of religiosity is likely to evoke contrasts already identified in established theories of religion (see Whitehouse 1995: 203–17). Among previous theories of direct relevance, Max Weber's (1930; 1947) varied distinctions, for instance between routinization and charisma, and between 'World religions' and 'traditional religions', stand out as perhaps the most pioneering and influential. Such models have arguably informed all subsequent attempts to differentiate between modes of religiosity, including: Ruth Benedict's (1935) contrast between 'Appolonian' and 'Dionysian' religious modalities; Ernest Gellner's (1969) distinction between urban and rural religious syndromes within his 'pendulum-swing theory of Islam'; Jack Goody's (1968; 1986) dichotomy between the relatively rigid orthodoxies of literate religions and the more mutable, innovative character of non-literate religions; Victor Turner's (1974) opposition between universalistic 'fertility rituals' and particularistic 'political rituals'; I. M. Lewis's (1971) contrast between 'central' and 'peripheral' cults; Richard Werbner's (1977) distinction between 'regional cults' and 'cults of the little community'; Fredrik Barth's (1990) contrast between wide dissemination of the religious teachings of Balinese gurus and the much more localized, fragmentary dissemination of ritual imagery in Melanesian cults of initiation. All these theories had already

identified the co-variation of at least two of the features listed in my original model. Moreover, in the voluminous literatures on the history of
world religions, great and little traditions, religious phenomenology, sects
and cults, and in various related fields of research, it is also possible to
find illuminating discussions of the coalescence of certain features of
doctrinal and imagistic modes of religiosity.

Such scholarship has produced a massive body of data and a wide variety of models and insights of indisputable importance and originality.
Nevertheless, nobody seems to have tried to bring together within the
ambit of a single theory all the features which, taking the existing literature as a whole, appear to be interconnected. Moreover, the unique role
given to cognitive processes in my approach is crucial to understanding
the coalescence of other features within doctrinal and imagistic modes of
religiosity.

It has long been appreciated that the proliferation of doctrine may lead
to the development of large, expansionary religious communities, the
members of which could not possibly all have met but nevertheless experience a sense of common identity. It is similarly well established that
ecstatic forms of ritual action are capable of producing intense cohesion
among small groups of religious adherents. Sociological theories of this
divergence in the course of the twentieth century have been heavily influenced by quite antique (although often very brilliant) scholarship, especially that of Emile Durkheim and Max Weber. But we have not advanced
very much beyond the seminal insights of these early theorists. In some
ways we have backtracked, by failing to pursue and build upon their most
promising insights.

Cohesion is not explicable in purely sociological terms, for it is always
in important respects an emergent *psychological* property. Durkheim's
seminal work on the relationship between ritual and social cohesion was
marred by a principled aversion to the use of psychological perspectives
in the analysis of social phenomena (e.g. Durkheim 1952: Book 1). But, in
any case, nineteenth century psychology was not sufficiently developed to
lend support to Durkheim's symbolist project, or to the (often neglected)
intellectualist thread that ran through *The Elementary Forms of the
Religious Life* (1915). One aim of this book is to show that certain
'cutting-edge' theories in cognitive psychology have profound implications for social theory in general, and the comparative study of religion in
particular.

If we are to understand the various ways in which people come to feel
united or to regard themselves as sharing a common identity, we are obliged

to make certain assumptions about human memory. At the very least, we must assume that people remember certain emblems, historical representations, attitudinal stances and stereotypes, experienced events, ways of behaving, and a great variety of other phenomena that are used to define the character, boundaries, and relations of social categories and groups.

The relevance of memory for social theory was first substantially explored by Halbwachs (1925; 1950), whose work has recently been revisited in a spate of fresh scholarship on 'collective' and 'social' memory.[2] By and large, this literature focuses on the ideological content of memory, and the political dynamics of repression, forgetting, selective recall, decay/distortion, and alternative discourses about memory. At the heart of many studies is the question of who controls representations of the past, and to what ends. The central thrust of my argument goes in the opposite direction. Instead of asking how political organization and ideology help to mould people's memories, I am asking whether universal features of human memory, activated in different ways, might be said to mould political organization and ideology. The former question is both obvious and valid and has deservedly become a fashionable topic for debate. The question with which I am concerned is less obvious, but the two questions, and the divergent approaches which they imply, are by no means incompatible.

Episodic and Semantic Memory

My starting point is a distinction made by psychologists between 'semantic' and 'episodic' (or 'autobiographical') memory (Tulving 1972). Episodic memory refers to mental representations of personally experienced events, conceptualized as unique episodes in one's life. Semantic memory refers to mental representations of a general, propositional nature. For instance, the knowledge I have concerning road signs, the history of anthropological theory, how to behave in a restaurant, and what happens in the story of Little Red Riding Hood, are all expressions of my semantic memory. Within psychology, these two types of memory have tended to be studied and theorized quite separately.[3] Nevertheless, the

---

[2] An informative introduction to this literature is provided by Connerton (1989) and Fentress and Wickham (1992). Moreover, in the field of Melanesian studies, highly sophisticated discussions of memory and cultural transmission have recently been published (e.g. Küchler 1994; Munn 1995).

[3] As Bloch points out (1995), episodic memory has been examined extensively in relation to theories of personal identity, whereas such issues have seldom been addressed in regard to semantic memory (where the principle focus of interest has been in retention and recall).

two types of memory are processually connected. According to Cohen (1989: 114–15): 'Semantic knowledge is derived from episodic memories by a process of abstraction and generalization.' This point requires closer examination.

On the basis of my semantic knowledge of the world, I know that the process of getting a haircut at a barber's shop involves a standard sequence of events which include: entering the premises, making myself known to the barber, perhaps being invited to sit in a designated area to wait my turn, proceeding to a different chair for the hair-cutting, putting on a gown, seating myself, keeping my head still, finally inspecting the haircut with the aid of mirrors, removing the gown, undergoing the brushing procedure, paying, and leaving. These episodes occur in a fixed sequence, giving my knowledge of 'how to behave in a barber's shop' a firm overall structure. Psychologists usually refer to such structures as 'schemas'.[4]

The first time I had my hair cut at a barber's shop (presumably as a young child), I almost certainly did not know how to behave, and had to be guided through the procedure by experienced adults. I may already have formed schemas for certain elements of the experience, such as entering and waiting (which of course feature in schemas for going to doctors, dentists, and many other providers of services). But certain elements would probably have been new to me (the donning and removing of the gown, the requirement to keep my head still, the inspection and brushing procedures, and so on). Elements of my first visit to the barber's shop which could not be attached to existing schemas for receiving a service would initially have been remembered as unique personal experiences, and thus encoded in episodic memory. Through repeated experiences of visiting the barber's shop, however, the once-novel elements would come to be expectable in the context of a specialized barber's shop schema. I can no longer recall my first episodic memories of visiting a barber's shop, but my semantic knowledge for how to behave in barbers' shops generally, could not have been constructed without them. This is what Cohen means when she says that semantic knowledge is 'abstracted' from episodic memories.

Nevertheless, the concept of 'abstraction' is somewhat vague. In

---

[4] In the case of detailed event structures of the type I have just described, these are also commonly referred to as 'scripts'. The term 'schema', however, has a wider application, being used to describe a variety of types of knowledge, ranging from simple typological classifications of objects to complex but recognizable strands of philosophical theorizing. For the sake of simplicity, I shall keep to the general term 'schema'.

mentally reconstructing a particular visit to a barber's shop ten years ago, I must draw on the common elements of numerous experiences; I do not recall details peculiar to a single episode, such as the barber sneezing or talking about the cost of car insurance. Such specific things, because they are not recurrent, are not part of my barber's-shop schema. Likewise, the exact posture of the barber as he holds up the mirror (unless this posture was distinctive and repeated) would not stick in my mind. Thus, in visualizing this phase of the visit, I know that the posture I attribute to the barber is imagined rather than remembered, even though the holding up of the mirror, at least as a type of event, is indeed remembered correctly. As Cohen points out: 'The most important prediction from schema theory is that what is normal, typical, relevant, or consistent with pre-existing knowledge will be remembered better than what is unexpected, bizarre, or irrelevant' (1989: 72). Thus, semantic memory consists of the common denominators of a series of episodic memories, along with invented details that fit with the schema but are not experienced as authentic or definite recollections of individual episodes.

On this basis, we might expect episodic memories to possess relatively short life spans. To some extent, this is true. I remember my last visit to a barber in considerable detail, including elements extraneous to my barber's-shop schema. Visits to the same barber more than a year ago, however, are indistinguishable, my knowledge being largely based on semantic rather than episodic memory. But what about the enduring memories people have of certain events that occurred many years ago? Most people can recall a vast array of unique episodes in their lives, which tend to have a distinctive emotional salience and/or set of sensory associations. These sorts of memories seem to pose a problem to schema theory: unique aspects of events should be forgotten because they are irrelevant to existing schemas, and the first occurrences of subsequently repeated events should be dissolved into the melting pot of semantic memory.

One area of study which might shed light on this anomaly concerns itself with a special type of episodic remembering, known as 'flashbulb memory'. This term, coined by Brown and Kulik (1982), refers to vivid and detailed recollections of emotionally arousing events that radically violate existing schemas. Following a close investigation of this phenomenon, Wright and Gaskell (1992) argue for a 'cognitive processing loop' that would account for both episodic and semantic memory. Presented with an event, the cognitive apparatus searches for a suitable schema, on the basis of which to cue appropriate understandings and responses. If no relevant schema is found immediately, the search is repeated. In the case of events which substantially conform to existing schemas, the searching is rapidly concluded and the event assimilated to existing knowledge. Any details of such an event that are extraneous to existing schemas are assigned to a sort of mental waste-disposal system the contents of which remain accessible for a time but gradually drain through the bottom of the container, after which point they are lost (forgotten) entirely. By contrast, events which substantially violate existing schemas set off a frantic and prolonged search for relevant schemas, vainly trying to match all sensory inputs (randomly selected in the absence of schematic criteria for relevance) to semantic knowledge. An unsuccessful search eventually leads to the encoding of an entirely unique schema, incorporating a variety of irrelevant details, which is one of the hallmarks of 'flashbulb memory'. By this reasoning, young children, who are continually encountering events for which no schemas are available, should 'lay down' a great many vivid memories which could still be recalled in adulthood. Wright and Gaskell argue, however, that most of the unique schemas encoded by young children are effectively cut off from the developing structures of semantic knowledge because childhood retrieval cues rapidly become obsolete. In this way it is possible to account for episodic and semantic memory systems, as well as for the phenomenon of 'childhood amnesia', within the ambit of a single model.

A drawback of Wright's and Gaskell's theory, however, is that their 'cognitive processing loop' does not incorporate one of the apparently crucial recurrent features of flashbulb memory, which is the emotional excitation that accompanies encoding. I have argued elsewhere that recent models in neuroscience, and particularly the theories of the Nobel Laureate Gerald Edelman,[5] support many of Wright's and Gaskell's principal hypotheses about the relationship between episodic and semantic memory, and at the same time establish affective and sensory processes firmly at the core of these memory systems (Whitehouse 1996c). What is suggested is that the establishment of schemas depends on emotional reinforcement—in biological terms, the substantial and co-ordinated replication of populations of neuron firings selectively reinforced by biochemical emissions from the brain's affective centres in the limbic system. Semantic memory results from the strengthening over time of such repertoires, such that the organism is able to classify and model experiences on the basis of common features, in other words, to develop schemas for recurrent experiences. Episodic memory, by contrast, results

---

[5] For a clear introduction to Edelman's theories, see Edelman (1992).

from the massive biochemical reinforcement of novel repertoires. In the case of flashbulb memory, considerable emotional and/or sensory stimulation occurring in conjunction with novel patterns of neurological activity occasioned by a surprising or unfamiliar event produces unique schemas that incorporate a wide variety of vivid inputs. Such memories of distinct episodes may endure a lifetime, both because repetition of the surprising event is unlikely and because, even if a substantially similar event is experienced, the traces left by the first will have been so strongly reinforced by excessive emissions from the brain's emotional centres that the original set of representations will retain much of its salience, detail, and uniqueness.

Memory and Modes of Religiosity

One of the central characteristics of the doctrinal mode is the frequent repetition of both ritual and dogma. Many of the ceremonies performed, for instance, in the holy places of doctrinal religions, along with the reciting of texts, prayers, and liturgical formulae, are encoded in *semantic memory*. Routinization is directly connected to the style of codification: the implicational logic of doctrinal systems, expressed in language (sacred texts, sermons, theological debates, and so on), can only exercise a continuous and stable influence on people's attitudes, beliefs, and actions if it is frequently reviewed. The processing of religious materials in semantic memory has important sociological implications.

An Anglican layman asked to recall the chain of events at a Sunday service five years ago will be able to provide a rich and detailed account of what happened on the basis of liturgical schemas but will probably not be able to recall the singular episode. Aspects of the particular occasion in question which are not included in general schemas will have been forgotten (unless, of course, the excluded elements were shocking and emotionally arousing—as would probably have been the case if, for instance, the vicar had suffered a heart attack during Holy Communion or members of the congregation had been struck down by falling masonry). Thus, the particular identities of members of the congregation are not specified in liturgical schemas. When describing the behaviour of worshippers in a church service, our Anglican informant will not visualize real, flesh-and-blood people, but a mass of fictitious, anonymous others enacting the rites in unison. Schemas of this type form the cognitive underpinnings of universalistic ideology or, indeed, any conception of a community whose members are not individually specifiable. Religious identity, in the doctrinal mode, is primarily conferred on the basis of presumed commonalties in the thought and behaviour of anonymous others, a state of affairs which is only conceivable with reference to semantic knowledge.

By contrast, the rituals and images of the imagistic mode are primarily encoded in episodic memory. In many societies, religious life is focused around very infrequent, traumatic ritual episodes. Rites of initiation, for instance, commonly involve the terrorizing and torture of novices and the challenging of everyday knowledge through the partial transmission of esoteric revelations. Similar patterns may be identified in a variety of ideologically distinct religious systems (from climactic forms of millenarism to diabolical cults). The elements of shock and arousal entailed in such contexts produce enduring episodic memories, and even classic flashbulb experiences (e.g. Herdt 1989: 115). If you ask participants to describe what occurred in a given ceremony of this type several years afterwards, their accounts will not be based primarily on semantic knowledge. On the contrary, we would expect to be told exactly who the participants were, along with many peculiar details of their behaviour. Common identity among religious adherents in the imagistic mode is fundamentally particularistic, based on lasting episodic memories of undergoing the traumatic lows and ecstatic highs of sacred events together with a specifiable group of individuals. The longevity and intensity of such memories corresponds to the strength and inviolability of the cohesion which they engender. These issues are explored in depth in the chapters which follow.

Durkheim's concept of the 'elementary forms' of religion fully acknowledged the cohesion engendered in imagistic practices. But because Durkheim could not (and famously did not want to) identify the cognitive underpinnings of these practices, he tended to generalize them to all religious traditions, thereby overlooking the qualitatively different trajectory of the doctrinal mode.

Many scholars after Durkheim have rather uncritically adopted his conception of the relationship between ritual and cohesion. But this has often been done in a way that projects the mnemonic properties of doctrinal religion on to the sorts of imagistic practices with which Durkheim and many of these later scholars were really concerned. This problem was especially apparent during the structural-functionalist era when all rituals were presented in ethnographic texts as general schemas ('they do this' and 'they believe that'), a discursive technique which became known as the 'ethnographic present'. It is a curious irony that, whereas certain post-functionalist texts have seriously advocated synchronic analysis of 'traditional' society, despite admitting its inapplicability to complex 'historical' societies (Goody 1977), it actually makes more sense to describe Christian rituals in the ethnographic present and tribal initiation rites in the past tenses. After all, the former are locked into the ahistorical schemas of semantic knowledge and the latter, by contrast, cognized as historically situated episodes.

Before proceeding any further, however, an area of potential misunderstanding must be anticipated and dealt with. Semantic and episodic memory are universal features of human cognition and, indeed, are common to the cognitive systems of many other species. In consequence, there is no such thing as a religious tradition that does not depend for its transmission on both semantic and episodic memory. All varieties of Christianity operate in the doctrinal mode, although they may also incorporate imagistic practices. Some of the more iconoclastic forms of Christianity, however, more or less effectively suppress the expression of imagistic forms. For instance, I will describe tendencies in that direction within early Protestantism in Europe and missionary Christianity in Melanesia. But no matter how successfully the imagistic mode is excluded, Christians everywhere will have enduring episodic memories for at least some religious experiences (and probably for a great many). Likewise, as we shall see, certain cults of initiation are highly imagistic and unconnected to any sort of thoroughgoing doctrinal tradition. Nevertheless it would clearly be untrue to claim that all the religious ideas and actions entailed in such initiation rites are encoded exclusively in episodic memory. On the contrary, all forms of human action utilize elements of semantic memory, and some of the component features of even the most infrequent and traumatic rituals evoke familiar schemas. These may be borrowed from non-religious contexts: for instance, washing procedures, conventional styles of address and comportment, and standard forms of sharing and consuming foods (even though all such tasks may be modified in the ritual setting and certainly envisaged as different from the profane activities upon which they are modelled). Likewise, very irregularly performed rituals may incorporate sequences (or elements of sequences) found in much more frequently repeated rites.

Clearly, episodic and semantic memory are ubiquitous. Nevertheless, these principles of cognitive processing have different ramifications in doctrinal and imagistic modes. Everything hinges on how systems of memory are linked to patterns of identity-formation. In the doctrinal mode, much of what defines one's religious identity (for instance, in the case of a Christian, regular church attendance and knowledge of the life and teachings of Christ) constitutes a set of representations encoded in semantic memory producing imagined, anonymous religious communities. By contrast, the most valued revelations and forms of collective identity in the imagistic mode cannot be understood primarily with reference to a person's semantic knowledge. Religious imagery, and its multivocal resonances, are largely remembered as extremely intense, life-changing episodes, through which enduring and particularistic social bonds are forged.

Summary of the Book

Chapter 1 provides an introduction to the indigenous religions of Papua New Guinea, many of which are founded on imagistic practices. Particular attention is focused on initiation, in so far as certain aspects of these rites serve to illustrate the general nature of religious experience and revelation in various regions of pre-contact Melanesia. Like all imagistic practices, initiation rituals evoke a sense of surprise, presenting novices with a radically new understanding of the cosmos, or at least of certain of the mechanisms through which it is reproduced. Such experiences tend to be associated with intense affective states and often also with forms of sensory stimulation. In initiations, novices are commonly terrorized, but most existing explanations for this dimension of the rites establish generalities only at the cost of adequate engagement with the cognitive and affective processes entailed in ritual performance. I propose an alternative approach, which links the intricate psychological dynamics of Melanesian religion to the political structure and ethos of indigenous communities, including the characteristics of localized cohesion and inter-group raiding and warfare. Central to my exposition is the argument that cognitive shocks, coupled with states of mortal terror (and other emotions) produced the enduring episodic memories upon which solidary and enduring face-to-face relationships were substantially based in pre-contact Melanesia.

Whereas the central revelations of Melanesian initiation rites are transmitted through rare and secretive climactic rituals, those of missionary Christianity are publicly disseminated via orations and texts, according to a routinized regime of sermonizing and liturgical ritual. In Chapter 2, I examine the process of missionization in Papua New Guinea, arguing that it introduced a radically new conception of religion, and also of patterns of political association.

The practices of the early missions were dominated by the doctrinal mode of religiosity, in which the performance of repetitive ritual was inextricably bound up with universalism, centralization, and hierarchy. It has long been recognized that the missionization of Melanesia contributed to the enlargement of indigenous conceptions of humanity, partly through the spread of universalistic ideas entailed in Christian teaching. I argue that a more crucial (and hitherto neglected) factor is that identity-conferring ritual came to be remembered in the form of general-izable schemas for repetitive Christian rituals.

Unlike the rare and traumatic imagistic practices of local fertility cults and systems of initiation, which were remembered as distinct episodes, the routinized practices of the mission station established scripts for 'how to be a Christian' in which the actual participants were not specified in ritual schemas. This made possible the conceptualization of anonymous, 'imagined' communities. In due course, missionary practices contributed to the establishment of new religious movements, under indigenous lead-ership, dominated by the doctrinal mode of religiosity.

Routinization in new indigenous religions, just as in the missions, tended over time to become monotonous, opening the way for periodic splintering whereby local factions reactivated imagistic practices in temporary outbursts of climactic ritual. As a result, some large-scale movements in Papua New Guinea came to encompass two domains of operation: that of the mainstream orthodoxy, dominated by the doctrinal mode, and that of the sporadic and localized splinter group founded on imagistic practices. An unintended consequence of this has been that the cohesion evoked in splinter-group ritual has tended to be projected on to the mainstream community, rejuvenating commitment to the movement as a whole and establishing its enduring role in the formation of microna-tionalist groupings. The implications of this for the political future of Papua New Guinea are briefly examined, showing that existing theories of the relationship between indigenous religious movements and nation-alist struggle need to be modified.

In Chapters 3 to 6, the main characteristics of the two modes of reli-giosity are examined in closer detail, with particular reference to four case studies: Baktaman initiation in inner New Guinea, the Taro cult of north-ern Papua, the Pomio Kivung of East New Britain, and the Paliau Movement of Manus and its environs.

Chapter 3 focuses on contrasting styles of codification and transmis-sion in doctrinal and imagistic modes of religiosity respectively. The mainstream institutions of the Paliau Movement and the Pomio Kivung, heavily modelled on missionary Christianity and exemplifying the various features of the doctrinal mode, rely on orally transmitted, argument-based rhetoric for the spread of religious ideology. In such traditions, the persuasiveness of ethical and cosmological representations depends to a large extent on their overall coherence, achieved through the ordering of dogma in strings of implied questions and answers (or 'implicational logic'). The adoption of this principle of codification facilitated the spread of both movements across wide areas. Ideas that could be communicated orally or in texts were readily transported by patrolling leaders and their representatives. Koriam (the founder of the Pomio Kivung) and Paliau were able to establish headquarters where a managerial tier of patrolling officials received much of their training. These links between doctrinal codification and the scale and hierarchical, centralized structure of the Paliau Movement and the Pomio Kivung are explored in detail.

Alongside this discussion of codification and transmission in the doctrinal mode, I construct a contrasting analysis of imagistic practices using material on Baktaman initiation and the activities of Taro cultists among the Orokaiva. In the latter contexts, virtually no attempt was made to communicate religious ideas as bodies of doctrine. Revelations were codified in iconic imagery, transmitted primarily through the choreography of collective ritual performances. Religious representations were structured as sets of revelatory images connected by loose (and somewhat fluid) thematic associations, rather than as cohering strings of logically connected dogma. These imagistic practices did not produce leaders, partly because the source of religious insights was the collectivity (i.e. the group of ritual actors) rather than an individual conduit for the divine. Moreover, they could only be spread through contact between groups of people and never by patrolling mediums, prophets, or messiahs. The particular initiation rites of local Baktaman groups were in any case shrouded in secrecy and no attempt was made to spread them more widely. In the case of the Taro Cult, imagistic practices did spread between contiguous groups in chains of contact transmission, but as they travelled, these practices mutated dramatically (in contrast to the homogenization of doctrinal traditions that can be centrally orchestrated).

Chapter 4 examines the implications of contrasting regimes of codification for debates about religious 'order'. Ron Brunton's argument, that anthropologists have tended to exaggerate the orderliness of Melanesian religions, is modified and extended through a discussion of the cognitive foundations of divergent modes of religiosity. The doctrinal mode, imported to Melanesia by Christian missionaries, is organized around dialogical, implicational, narrative, and binary schemas which, in conjunction with certain mechanisms for the reproduction of orthodoxy, produce a high degree of coherence, stability, and uniformity of religious belief. In contrast, the imagistic mode, indigenous to Melanesia, emphasizes analogic resonances and multivocality rather than logical integration; the dynamic is towards creative elaboration rather than faithful repetition and the production of local differences rather than regional homogeneity. I argue that what anthropologists have tended to exaggerate is not the intellectual productivity of indigenous Melanesian religions but the extent to which they incorporate styles of codification and cognition prevalent in the doctrinal traditions of European experience (especially Christianity).

Chapter 5 focuses on the psychological underpinnings of divergent patterns of political association. The cognitive implications of extensive routinization in the Paliau Movement and Pomio Kivung are closely explored, both in regard to the reproduction of logically integrated bodies of doctrine and the conceptualization of large, diffusely united communities. Routinization is also linked to the affective quality of worship, characterized by sober self-discipline. In stark contrast, the imagistic practices of Baktaman initiation and the Taro cult stimulated intense emotions and sensations which, along with cognitive shocks engendered in ritual activity, produced a very distinctive mnemonic process, adapted to conditions of infrequent transmission. Drawing on recent studies of 'flashbulb memory', the psychological dynamics of localized group cohesion are examined.

Chapter 6 focuses on what can happen when the two modes of religiosity occur within a single religious tradition as relatively discrete but interacting domains of thought and action. In the case of the Paliau Movement and the Pomio Kivung, imagistic practices are expressed in sporadic outbursts of climactic ritual and spirit possession, triggering revelations through the iconicity of collective performances. The cohesion generated within each local ritual community is periodically projected on to the mainstream movement, having the effect of rejuvenating support for the doctrinal programme. In the absence of such a process the routinized mainstream movement would be more fragile, forever threatening to collapse in the face of impatience and low morale.

Chapter 7 argues that the patterns of interaction between modes of religiosity in Melanesia have as much to do with the history of Christianity in Europe as with Melanesian pre-history. In the Pomio Kivung and the Paliau Movement, and other similar traditions, there is a

tendency for doctrinal and imagistic modes of religiosity to become estab
lished as readily distinguishable domains of activity. In part, this i
explained by the fact that some pre-contact Melanesian religion
provided models of purely imagistic practices, operating in the absenc
of, and therefore subsequently distinguishable from, a doctrinal mode o
religiosity. An equally important factor, however, is that missionar
Christianity, as a set of doctrinal practices, tended to suppress or exclud
the imagistic mode, whether derived from European Christianities o
from Melanesian cults. Consequently, the meeting of religious tradition
of Melanesian and European origin amounted to a confrontation betwee
two starkly opposed styles of codification, transmission, and politica
association. This raises the question of why missionary Christianity wa
largely denuded of imagistic dimensions.

My answer to this is that missionary Christianity was profoundl
influenced, albeit indirectly, by processes that began during th
Reformation. Reformed Christianity was highly adapted to rapid an
wide dissemination, largely because of its central preoccupation with th
establishment of purely doctrinal forms and the elimination of imagisti
ones. The hostility of certain early Protestant preachers to imagistic prac
tices has recently been described by one historian as a sort of 'logocentri
iconophobia' (Collinson 1977). I argue that these extraordinary develop
ments in both Protestant and Catholic Reformations provided radicall
new models for subsequent varieties of Christianity which were crucial t
the development of evangelical missionary projects.

Chapter 8, which concludes the volume, attempts to broaden the scop
of the argument by considering the possible role of modes of religiosit
in processes of political evolution. The chapter begins by examinin
evidence that some hunter-gatherer populations in the Upper Palaeolithi
possessed a variety of imagistic practices. The development of the doctri
nal mode occurred much later, as part of the establishment of templ
complexes in both the Old and New Worlds. The role of literacy in thi
crucial transformation is considered in some detail, with reference t
arguments put forward by Jack Goody and Ernest Gellner. It would seem
however, that, although literacy may have been a precipitating factor, o
even a necessary condition for the independent invention of the doctrina
mode of religiosity, the presence of systems of writing was not essentia
to the spread of doctrinal models, as our Melanesian examples als
demonstrate. Discussion must therefore focus crucially on the socia
conditions of transmission rather than on technologies of inscription.

This topic is addressed through a reformulation of Victor Turner' portrayal of the sequential emergence of three types of 'communitas'. The first of these is existential or spontaneous communitas, a sort of revelatory sensation of the 'brotherhood of Man', which Turner believed was engendered in moments of liminality, whether in tribal initiation rites, Muslim pilgrimages, or any of a range of other specific religious activities. Turner regarded this state as logically and historically prior to normative communitas, established through routinized expressions of the original epiphanic experience. Turner argued that the normative phase was followed by ideological communitas, codifying spontaneous revelations as a corpus of doctrine. I argue, however, that spontaneous communitas does not occur in tribal rituals, including the Ndembu initiation rites studied by Turner, and that a more appropriate starting place is normative communitas. Normative communitas may be regarded as the crucial development that transformed the tribal societies of human prehistory into large-scale, centralized, and hierarchical states. Ideological communitas followed, in so far as the potentiality of universalistic themes was realized in specific doctrinal regimes, and Turner's spontaneous communitas must be regarded as the end rather than the beginning of these transformations, resulting in some cases from the interaction of imagistic and doctrinal modes of religiosity.

1

Indigenous Religions of Papua New Guinea

In view of the extreme diversity of religious ideation and practice in Papua New Guinea it is clearly difficult to provide anything resembling a 'balanced' overview of the indigenous religions of that country. Nevertheless, in the context of this book, one of the greatest parameters of variation is of relatively limited relevance—namely, the representational/cosmological content of different religious traditions. It need not concern us here that people in one village might distinguish eight classes of spiritual agency and the people of another village only two, or that in one region the dead are left to rot in the bush, whereas in another they might be partially decomposed, dismembered, and certain body parts worn as decorations. This kind of diversity is not at issue, at least not directly, because I am primarily concerned with the ways in which religious ideas are (and have been) codified and transmitted, the general psychological processes activated, and the relationship of these things to patterns of political association. This last sentence condenses the central concerns of the whole volume, and requires some preliminary unpacking.

Styles of codification and transmission are closely linked to the structuring of religious representations, especially the ways in which they are interconnected. For instance, Christian doctrine in all its various forms is organized as a system of interconnected rhetoric, and its persuasiveness rests quite substantially (at least for many people, much of the time) on its logical coherence and integration. In traditions of this type, religious ideas have to be transmitted orally, for instance as teachings, sermons, prayers, and theological discussion, whether or not they are also set out in sacred texts.

In Papua New Guinea, this method of codifying, organizing, and

Most of the text for this chapter was first published in the *Journal of the Royal Anthropological Institute* (NS), 2(4): 703–715, under the title 'Rites of Terror: Emotion, Metaphor, and Memory in Melanesian Initiation Cults' (Whitehouse 1996d).

transmitting religious conceptions has been substantially elaborated through the efforts of missionaries and also those involved in the establishment of party politics, whose ideologies are likewise disseminated as a corpus of logically persuasive, doctrine-like policies. Prior to contact, the religions of Papua New Guinea were substantially founded on rather different principles of codification and transmission. As Trompf puts it: 'Formal, doctrinal instructions into the nature and attributes of the spirit-powers have been rare in Melanesia: one "feels into" one's cosmos and its inhabitants through an organic process, with paradigmatic moments of disclosure into cultural secrets at initiations, until one knows what to *do*, rather than possess speculative knowledge for its own sake' (1991: 14, Trompf's emphasis). Trompf's remarks capture something of the character of the indigenous religions of Papua New Guinea. Nevertheless, his concept of 'feeling into one's cosmos' is too vague. This chapter attempts to penetrate more deeply the nature of revelatory experience in much of pre-Christian Melanesia.

The most widely recurring features of ritual life indigenous to Papua New Guinea include initiations and fertility rites, funerals, divinations and seances, puberty rites,[1] weddings, magical rites, sorcery, and a host of ceremonial activities that have a celebratory character (often connected with group achievements such as a peaceful victory over exchange partners or a bloody victory over one's enemies). Of these, initiation and fertility rites in general tend to produce particularly elaborate and revelatory forms of religious experience.

The *Concise Oxford Dictionary* defines 'revelation' as 'the act or an instance of revealing, especially the supposed disclosure of knowledge to humankind by a divine or supernatural agency.' This process of disclosure is a central focus of attention in initiatory ordeals, as we shall see, but it is of lesser significance in many other forms of indigenous ritual. An obvious example of non-revelatory rites would be those forms of magic that are stored, shared, bartered, and generally treated in much the same way as tools and weapons (see J. F. Weiner 1991: 27). The purpose of such rites is ostensibly instrumental rather than revelatory. But the same is broadly true of weddings and puberty rites because people are not

---

[1] I am here following Allen's crucial distinction between puberty rites and initiation rites: 'initiation rites, whether performed at puberty or not, differ from all other *rites de passage* in that those who have passed through constitute a clearly defined social group. Puberty rites, like other individual *rites de passage*, are a social recognition of an acquired status and its associated rights and privileges, not an induction into a social group' (1967: 5–6).

expected to come away from these ceremonies with a new awareness of the structure of the cosmos and their place within it. It is true that such phenomena as puberty rites and weddings constitute *rites de passage*, and thus mark a transition from one phase of life (i.e. location in the society/cosmos nexus) to another (Van Gennep 1965 [1908]). Yet this is primarily a transition of one's status, not of one's 'state of knowledge'. Newlyweds do not generally possess a 'deeper' comprehension of religious matters than courting couples, and the same is frequently true of adolescents before and after puberty rites.[2] In initiations and fertility rituals, huge amounts of labour and material resources are often invested in the process of triggering enduring religious revelations in the minds of novices. By contrast, mortuary rites and exchange ceremonial, like weddings, are not primarily directed at triggering religious revelations, even though they are often deeply moving and costly occasions. The vast amounts of energy and wealth that may be directed into mortuary rites[3] and ceremonial exchanges[4] are intended primarily to reflect glory on the deceased/donor, and his relatives/faction, rather than to open up new forms of religious experience and understanding.

Initiation rites (along with a variety of fertility rituals that may incorporate initiatory themes[5]) are prototypically about religious revelation and this sets them apart, at least in very broad terms, from certain other forms of ceremonial in Papua New Guinea. The focal concern of fertility and initiation rites is commonly the reproduction of the cosmos, especially of humans, crops, and game, and the regeneration of their sources of sustenance (primarily rainwater and sunshine). Natural cyclical processes of renewal are envisaged in many parts of Papua New Guinea as occurring through the intervention of extranatural agencies (gods,

---

[2] For instance, Maschio (1994) describes how Rauto puberty rites, far from evoking new cosmological understandings, merely act out pedestrian, everyday occurrences in the domestic round. Although Maschio speaks of this as a sort of 'initiation', these rites do not confer group membership or transmit memorable revelations. Moreover, 'initiates really do not receive formal acknowledgement during the rite that they have come into a completely new stage of social being; neither are new social and sexual responsibilities really taught to or imposed upon them by elders at this time. In fact the initiates sometimes cannot even remember the simple *ikit* that are taught to them in the ritual' (1994: 107).

[3] For instance, among the Tolai of New Britain (T. S. Epstein 1968: 26–7), or the Trobriand Islanders (A. B. Weiner 1992: 92–4).

[4] For instance, the Hagen *moka* or Enga *tee* (A. J. Strathern 1971, Meggitt 1974, Feil 1978).

[5] A good example would be the fertility ritual of the Waina-Sowanda culture area known as *ida* or *yangis* (described by Gell 1975 and Juillerat 1992; 1996), which entails a sort of initiation (Juillerat 1992: 106).

ancestors, or whatever), periodically set in motion through the performance of rituals. Initiation provides one of the most widespread and important contexts for these types of rituals.

Initiation rites are found in all regions of Papua New Guinea and, although not every community performs them, 'all or most Melanesians know of neighbouring communities that practise some form of the rites' (Allen 1967: 4). There are some regions where practically every community practises rites of initiation (for instance, parts of inner New Guinea and the Sepik region) and a few where such practices are rather less frequent (notably parts of the New Guinea highlands).

Although systems of initiation are by no means ubiquitous in Papua New Guinea, certain focal elements of indigenous religiosity may be said to coalesce in traditions of this type. Similar elements recur in ceremonial complexes that have nothing to do with initiation, and examples of this (in the form of new religious movements and 'cargo cults') are examined very closely in Chapters 3 to 6. Nevertheless, if we are looking for a syndrome of typologically similar institutional forms that are both widespread and exemplify the revelatory character of Melanesian religions, systems of initiation provide an excellent starting place.

Initiations as Rites of Terror

Several monographs, each focusing in detail on a particular local complex of initiation rites in Papua New Guinea, have been published in recent years (e.g. Barth 1975; Tuzin 1980; Herdt 1981); there are also books devoted to the comparative analysis of initiation rites across a number of New Guinea cultures (e.g. Allen 1967; Barth 1987, Herdt 1982; 1984). Taken in conjunction with a vast array of journal articles and chapters that deal with Melanesian initiation, it is clear that there is now an abundance of scholarly material on this topic. At first blush, this literature reveals a bewildering diversity of cosmological themes and institutional arrangements. But behind this variability there are certain recurrent features, one of which is the extreme fear that initiation often evokes in the hearts of novices. The traumatic nature of these rites demands close attention because, in understanding that, we can begin to grasp the general nature of revelatory religion in much of Papua New Guinea.

It would not be unduly fanciful to describe many initiatory practices in Papua New Guinea as 'rites of terror'. Following a hair-raising account of ritualized penis-bleeding among the Ilahita Arapesh, Tuzin observes that the whole ordeal 'is carefully and successfully designed to inspire maximum horror in its victims' (1980: 74). Barth describes how a Baktaman novice was so terrified by the ordeals of initiation that he defecated on the legs of his elders and had to be excluded from the group of boys being initiated (1975: 56). In his analysis of Orokaiva initiation Schwimmer (1973: 177) approvingly cites Chinnery's and Beaver's (1915) claim that a function of the rites is to instil 'absolute and lasting terror in the candidates'. In his discussion of Bimin–Kuskusmin initiation, Poole likewise emphasizes the terror of novices, observing that 'the piercing of the nasal septa and the burning of forearms . . . created the most trauma, producing overt signs of physical and/or psychological shock in six cases' (1982: 144). In Iatmul villages, Bateson (1936: 131) describes a competitive ethos among initiators of different moieties to establish which group could be the most sadistic in its treatment of novices. Examples could easily be multiplied, but I propose to focus initially on a single case.

The principal dynamics of 'rites of terror' may be identified in the initiation system of the Orokaiva of northern Papua. Schwimmer (1973) divides these rites into several phases which do not necessarily occur in a fixed sequence. One phase entails the isolation of novices in a hut where, for several months (Iteanu 1990: 46), they observe a taboo on washing but are generally well treated. During a second phase, the novices are herded together in the village, blinded by barkcloth hoods, and brutally attacked by senior men who assume the guise of spirits described as *embahi*. In the course of this ordeal, novices are gradually corralled on to a ceremonial platform. Then there follows a much longer period of seclusion. According to Iteanu, this second seclusion lasts for between three and seven years, during which time the novices must not be seen or heard beyond their place of confinement, on pain of death (1990: 47). During this period, novices learn to play sacred instruments (flutes and bullroarers). Schwimmer's third phase concerns the *début* of the novices, decked out in full dancing regalia. The novices enter the dancing ground in a dense phalanx, brandishing mock spears and stone clubs. A fourth phase involves the presentation of 'homicidal emblems' or *otohu*, at which time aged warriors recite the names of men they have killed in battle, before *otohu* are fastened to the foreheads of the novices. There is a final phase which is not included in Schwimmer's summary, but which Williams and Iteanu regard as indispensable. This phase entails, among other things, the distribution of amassed wealth. Iteanu stresses the fact that novices are responsible for sharing out cuts of pork from a lofty platform, not unlike the one to which they were earlier driven by the *embahi*.

All ethnographers of the Orokaiva have stressed the terrifying nature of the *embahi* ceremony. The early accounts of Chinnery and Beaver (1915), further enriched by Williams (1930: 181–3), convey a sense of the real panic induced in the Orokaiva novices, and the anguish of parents who are witnesses to their suffering. Moreover, as Iteanu more recently observes, there is always a risk that some children may not survive the ordeal (1990: 46). Any thoroughgoing analysis of the ceremony clearly needs to take into account its traumatic and life-threatening character. A problem with many existing approaches to the interpretation of this kind of ritual is that they fail to show how the complex conceptual and emotional aspects of initiation are interconnected.

Existing Approaches to Rites of Terror

Bloch has recently used Orokaiva initiation to elucidate what he calls the 'irreducible structures of religious phenomena' (1992: 4). His starting point is that there is a universal recognition of the biological processes of birth, maturation, reproduction, physical deterioration, and death which characterize the life cycles of humans and many other species. Social groups, however, are not subject to this kind of process; they have a notional permanence which is unaffected by the arrival and departure of particular members. In a Durkheimian spirit, Bloch argues that ritual provides a way of conceptualizing a timeless social order. Through the caricature and violent negation of biology and process, ritual affirms the transcendent authority of society, represented in the timeless order of the ancestral world.

According to Bloch, the *embahi* ceremony among the Orokaiva brings into focus an image of transcendental permanence through the symbolic destruction of earthly vitality. The hooded novices are like pigs, in so far as their persecution by the *embahi* is construed as a hunt, and they are herded on to a platform which is associated with butchery. With some ingenuity, Bloch argues that pigs represent the biological aspects of humans. Pigs are the only other species of large mammal indigenous to Papua New Guinea, and the similarity of their reproductive characteristics is therefore especially significant. They are also uniquely associated with humans by virtue of their integration into social life. They are referred to as 'children' and their deaths are mourned. Bloch maintains, therefore, that pigs represent the vital or bodily aspects of people.

The *embahi*, by contrast, are like birds. Bloch argues that the feathers, movements, and vocalizations of the *embahi* have strong avian connotations. According to Bloch, the bird is symbolically the mirror image of the pig. Birds are linked with an immortal extraterrestrial existence beyond the village world of vigorous activity, birth, and ageing. Avian imagery provides a way of conceptualizing the sacred or spiritual side of humanity, which is somehow the opposite of corporeal, transformative experience. In the *embahi* ceremony, the pig-like aspects of the novices are 'killed' by the bird-like ancestors. All that remains of the novices is their sacred, transcendental character. This is nurtured during the period of seclusion, away from the vitality of village life, where (appropriately enough) the novices are said to 'grow feathers'.

The ritual could not end at this point, because the aim of initiation is not to 'kill' the novices, but to deliver them back into village life as changed persons. This is not simply a matter of recovering the vitality which was earlier beaten out of the novices by the *embahi*; it is also a matter of conquering that vitality, of bringing it under transcendental control. This enables Bloch to account for the triumphant and militaristic tenor of the *début*. The brandishing of spears and clubs, the conferral of *otohu*, and the climbing of the platform in the guise of hunters and butchers rather than prey, publicly declare the new role of initiates as killers rather than victims. They are reinstated in the village, the life cycle, and the production process, but they are now more bird-like, more sacred than before. In keeping with Hertz's image of the 'social being grafted upon the physical individual' (1960: 77), transcendental authority is seen as penetrating more deeply into the fleshly, vital body of the initiate. This is a process which will continue through life until finally, at death, the corporeal shell is utterly consumed.

Bloch's re-analysis of Orokaiva initiation emphasizes certain ideological implications of ritual violence. According to this approach, the most important effect of the *embahi* ceremony is that the novices are symbolically killed or, more precisely, their vitality is negated so that they become purely transcendental beings. The jubilant return of the novices, which Bloch describes as 'rebounding violence' (1992: 6), is a way of conceptualizing and instituting a political order which is subject to ancestral authority.

A problem with Bloch's interpretation, as applied to the *embahi* ceremony or Papua New Guinea initiation rites in general, is that it does not capture very much of the conscious experience of participants. According to Bloch, *embahi* violence is part of a bifurcation process, as cognitively simple as it is ideologically powerful. In the context of this irreducible core of religious thought, the terror of Orokaiva novices seems to be superfluous, a mere side-effect of the particular choreography which happens to be involved. One gets the impression that an equally satisfactory result could be achieved in the *embahi* ceremony by symbolically killing the novices *without actually frightening them*. I will try to show that this is not the case. But before we can understand the role of terror, it is first necessary to appreciate that many of the cognitive processes involved in Papua New Guinea initiation rites are themselves rather disconcerting, and may not fit very easily with the principle of 'rebounding violence'.

Bloch's hypotheses about the symbolic value of birds and pigs are not substantially derived from Orokaiva statements. This is wholly justifiable in principle, and would be true of any thorough interpretation of the symbolic value of these animals. Whatever understandings are cultivated through the use of porcine or avian imagery in Orokaiva initiation, they are not substantially transmitted in language. Williams commented at length on the absence of exegetical commentary attaching to Orokaiva ritual (e.g. 1928: 175–6) and Schwimmer supports his observation that novices are not given verbal interpretations of initiatory symbolism (1973: 177). Even if they were, that would not be the end of the anthropological quest for meaning, as Gell (1980) and Sperber (1975) remind us, but in the case at hand virtually the entire burden of cultural transmission rests on the ritual acts themselves.

Bloch suggests that the revelations of Orokaiva initiation are iconically codified. In his interpretation, the physical and behavioural characteristics of pigs are concrete metaphors for human characteristics. Thus, under certain circumstances, the killing of pigs would imply the destruction or negation of porcine qualities in the sacrificer, in a manner which parallels the symbolic killing of novices behaving like pigs. *Contra* Bloch, however, novices are not treated in a way that makes them like pigs in general, but in a way that specifically makes them like *wild* pigs. The 'hunting' of novices by numerous *embahi* connotes the collective wild-pig drives for which the Orokaiva are renowned (Williams 1930: 45–7; Schwimmer 1973: 143). This technique of hunting frequently involves the members of several villages, who set light to the tall blade grass to drive wild pigs and other animals into the hands of their pursuers. The novices in initiation who are similarly herded and hunted do not, therefore, resemble domestic pigs, as Bloch assumes, but *wild* pigs. Domestic pigs are, indeed, anthropomorphically cognized by virtue of their integration into social life, but the case of wild pigs is rather different. If wild pigs are like people, then this has nothing to do with images of the village world of physical activity, maturation, death, and so on; as Iteanu observes, it is because they are like alien and dangerous human enemies who, prior to pacification, were likewise killed and eaten if encountered in the forest (1990: 37). In so far as novices appreciate that their senior kinsmen are treating them like quarry and thus repudiating their former nurturant, protective roles, this is likely to stimulate confusion and strong emotion. What sense novices make of all this has never been comprehensively explored by ethnographers of the Orokaiva, but knowledge of other New Guinea religions encourages us to be wary of a simplistic understanding of iconicity.

Bloch's interpretations of porcine and avian imagery in Orokaiva initiation are generated by a highly original and ambitious theory, but this theory seems to bypass much of the intellectually challenging and emotionally stimulating aspects of Melanesian religious experience. For example, if it is argued that the 'core' understandings cultivated in the *embahi* ceremony are fetched from everyday knowledge, then it is hard to see how initiation might engender revelatory experiences. According to this theory, things that one already knows about pigs and birds are dramatically re-presented in ritual performance. If there is a sense of 'revelation' then it is presumably rooted in an appreciation of the hierarchical relationship between corporeal aspects of humans (their porcine qualities) and immortal ones (their avian qualities). This in itself is unlikely to be particularly surprising or impressive since it is a pervasive aspect of discourse in religious communities everywhere and not simply an outcome of ritual. This is affirmed by the way Bloch construes iconicity in initiation: that pigs reproduce, mature, and die is known independently of ritual; but so too is the notion that birds do not seem to age and die, the fact that they move in spaces where human bodies cannot go, and so on. Pigs and birds are accorded these attributes independently of ritual action and so these attributes are re-presented rather than invented in the *embahi* ceremony, at least according to my reading of Bloch.

Yet there is also a strand to Bloch's argument which seems to deny the iconicity of avian imagery by suggesting that immortality is only 'thinkable' as a result of binary logic in which images of the 'other world' are constructed out of contrasts with the perceptible, physical world. As he puts it, this is a process by which 'a mirror-like alternative existence is set up' (1992: 20). A sense of the revelatory character of ritual is thereby rescued, but at a theoretical premium. The recourse to binary or digital codification makes it appear that the 'transcendental' emerges as an artefact of the ritual process, rather than of everyday experience. The idea that people's everyday perceptions of birds could imply a world outside biological process becomes theoretically burdensome rather than useful.

It seems to me, however, that these problems do not arise if iconicity is seen to operate in a way that conflicts with everyday attitudes and assumptions. It then becomes possible to explore the revelatory character of initiation rites without seeking refuge in digital operations which reduce religious concept-formation to a very simple thought (for instance, that pigs are to birds what bodies are to spirits).

It is necessary to put the Orokaiva material on one side for the moment, and to look at Melanesian initiation systems which have been more comprehensively studied. Some especially impressive work has been done by Fredrik Barth among the Baktaman of inner New Guinea, where the power of iconic codification, or what Barth calls (following Bateson 1972) 'analogic' codification, lies in the cultivation of paradox, mystery, multivocality, and secrecy.

Barth has shown that Baktaman initiators entertain ambivalent attitudes towards wild male pigs. On the one hand, wild pigs frequently damage gardens and are therefore inimical to the prosperity of crops and banned from initiation ritual. On the other hand, their ferocity and virility (not least the vital service they provide in impregnating domestic sows) exemplify desirable qualities in men. Barth describes how a group of novice warriors carried into battle the mandible of a wild male pig that they had just killed in the act of copulation. Following the success of this raid, the mandible was introduced to the male cult, but an ambivalent attitude to wild boar persisted to the extent that the bones of other specimens were still debarred from the temples.

What Bloch has to say about pigs among the Orokaiva might equally be said about pigs among the Baktaman. In both environments, pigs are the only large mammals, both the wild and domesticated animal is valued for its meat, and in behavioural and physiological terms their resemblances to human beings are much the same in both societies. There is, however, no reason to privilege the connection between pigs and ideas of vitality, or biological process. The attitudes of the Baktaman towards wild pigs, in the context of everyday life, focus primarily on their destructive habits: 'Baktaman men seem to regard themselves as involved in a continuous war with the wild pigs; they spend hours in the men's houses describing their depredations in detail, discussing their habits and individual idiosyncrasies, speculating on their location and next move' (Barth 1975: 39). A novice confronted with a relic of this public enemy in the context of a fertility cult is likely to experience confusion, and a sense that wild pigs are not the kind of creatures one might suppose. As Barth puts it: 'An aura of mystery and insight is created by dark hints that things are not what they appear. That ignorant assumptions are negated by guarded knowledge is the very stuff of mystery cult' (1987: 33).

A clue to the meaning of the mandible is likely to be picked up by the novice in contemplating the aggressiveness and virility of wild male pigs. In addition to mulling over the paradoxical character of this revelation, the novice is likely to associate the mandible with other items of temple sacra: the bones of ancestors, and the blackened ceiling of the cult house which in turn connotes the blackened vine used to tie the novices together—an even more explicit image of male solidarity (Barth 1975: 67). Above all, the first encounter with the pig mandible will be associated with the tortures and privations of third-degree initiation, which are among the most terrifying of all Baktaman rites. But here I am jumping ahead of myself.

It is not only in the Baktaman case that porcine imagery lends itself to the cultivation of ideas about masculinity and spirituality. Among the Ilahita Arapesh of the Sepik region, initiators use pig incisors to lacerate the glans penises of novices as part of an act of purification and sacralization. Here, it is an attack by a pig rather than by a bird which makes the novice more like an ancestor, and less like a worldly, polluting being (Tuzin 1982: 340–1). At a later stage of initiation, Tuzin claims that Ilahita Arapesh novices are ritually transformed into pigs, as a result of gorging on pork during the phase of liminality (Tuzin 1982: 344).

The point is that the analogic or iconic principle operates in New Guinea initiations in such a way as to confound everyday understandings, and to emphasize the multivocal and multivalent character of revelation. This process is resistant to expression in language, and certainly does not emerge out of a simple digital operation, nor out of a straightforward representation of everyday understandings.

Where I part company with Barth over his approach to analogic codes is at the point where he turns to psychoanalysis to incorporate the affective quality of ritual symbolism, and to account for patterns of variation in time and space. Drawing on Noy's (1969; 1979) classification of the operations of primary process, Barth tries to identify the unconscious generative mechanisms which might produce incremental changes in the feelings, insights, and performances entailed in initiations. It seems odd that Barth should wax Freudian, given the grounds of his aversion to Lévi-Straussian structuralism. Some twenty years ago, he wrote: 'One may be justifiably unhappy about a method where structures or patterns must be constructed merely with a view to make all the pieces fit together and without opportunity for falsification at any stage. The naive question of how much of these thoughts have actually been thought by the actors concerned can be raised . . . but not resolved in such a structuralist framework' (1975: 213). A more recent quotation will show that Barth's views on the matter have not changed substantially: 'I feel intuitively committed to an ideal of naturalism in the analytical operations I perform: that they should model or mirror significant, identifiable processes that can be shown to take place among the phenomena they seek to depict' (1987: 8).

Nevertheless, Barth's appeals to Noy, and ultimately to Freud, seem to violate his empiricist instincts. For, as we shall see in the Chapter 3, Barth's insistence on the unconscious nature of culture change is nowhere supported by examples of such transformations. In fact, all the evidence of culture change adduced in Barth's publications on the Baktaman are shown to have been consciously introduced.

The psychological effects of initiation ritual in Papua New Guinea are far more wide-reaching than any analysis of the cognitive processes entailed in analogic communication could encompass. Psychoanalytic theory, however, presents only one of a range of possible ways of understanding the emotional impact on novices. Another approach, that has the advantage of seeking to establish the conscious experiences of participants, is suggested by social psychological studies of attitude-change among the victims of terrorism. Such an approach is elaborated by Donald Tuzin in his analysis of Ilahita Arapesh initiation, and his conclusions are worth quoting at length:

Under certain conditions the victim of extreme terror, by virtue of what may be called coerced regression, experiences love and gratitude toward, and deep identification with, his persecutors. During the ordeal, of course, the novice's attitudes are at best highly labile; but immediately following it, the initiators drop their razors, spears, cudgels, or what have you, and comfort the boys with lavish displays of tender emotion. What resentment the latter may have been harbouring instantly dissipates, replaced by a palpable warmth and affection for the men who, moments before, had been seemingly bent on their destruction. As their confidence recovers itself, the novices become giddy with the realization that they have surmounted the ordeal. If there is an element of identification disclosed in this remarkable transformation—and I do not know what other interpretation to place on it—then the terror component may well be essential if the cult, and indeed the society itself, is to continue in its present form. (Tuzin 1980: 77–8)

Tuzin's analysis is quite plausible and, unlike the theory of 'rebounding violence', it goes a long way towards accounting for the terrifying nature of initiatory ordeals. But, as with Bloch's approach, the 'love-of-the-oppressor' paradigm does not take proper account of the multivocality and multivalence of religious imagery. The alternation between cruelty and kindness in Ilahita Arapesh rites would presumably have the same effect on the novices without the complex imagery of the male cult.

F. E. Williams would probably have sympathized with Tuzin's approach. The image which he held in mind throughout his analysis of the *embahi* ceremony was one of public school 'ragging' rather than terrorist violence, but he preceded Tuzin in stressing the way that novices come to identify with their oppressors (Williams 1930: 197). In so doing, Williams sought to redress what he saw as an imbalance in Chinnery's and Beaver's approach, which emphasized the educational value of terror. According to Chinnery and Beaver, *embahi* violence produced in the novices a 'receptive . . . frame of mind' (1915: 77). This constitutes one of the earliest attempts to explain the use of terror in Papua New Guinea initiation, but the line of reasoning it suggests has been among the most neglected.

The Cognitive and Political Implications of Rites of Terror

In seeking to bring the cognitive side of Orokaiva initiation rites, exemplified in Barth's theory of analogic codification, into harmony with their affective aspects, and especially the terrifying nature of the *embahi* ceremony, I am inclined to return to Chinnery's and Beaver's hypothesis. The terrifying ordeals of initiation are, indeed, a form of education in so far as they transmit a body of revelatory knowledge that is consciously turned over in the minds of initiates for years to come, and may well accompany them to the grave. When a Baktaman novice first realizes that he is (in some sense) being made into a virile, aggressive pig—a warrior and a father—he is not only struck by the absurdity of his previous assumptions about pigs, but he associates this revelation with the terrifying and agonizing experience of being beaten with stones, whipped with nettles, and dehydrated almost to the point of death. This combination of cognitive and emotional crises produces long-lasting and poignant memories. As Herdt points out, such memories provide focal imagery for subsequent reflection (1989: 115), and this is how the 'fans of connotations of sacred symbols' (Barth 1987: 31) are elaborated. Initiation rites produce a patterned screen of representations and feelings against which later insights and revelations are projected.

The vividness and detail of people's memories of initiation rites are related in part to the surprising and unexpected nature of revelation and in part to the high level of emotional arousal. For instance, it is relevant that Baktaman esoteric knowledge is surprising, but the reversal of every-day assumptions about wild male pigs is not in itself sufficiently impressive to produce long-lasting memories. Psychologists have suggested that surprising events are remembered in greater detail if they are also emotionally arousing (e.g. Christiansen and Loftus 1991). Moreover, at least three studies suggest that the detail of people's recollections increases directly with the intensity of emotion at encoding (see Christiansen 1992: 287). The longevity of such memories is very striking, as has been demonstrated by victims' detailed and closely matching recollections of atrocities in concentration camps, forty years after these camps were closed down. There is also some evidence that recall of disturbing or traumatic experiences actually improves with time (Scrivner and Safer 1988), in contrast with other sorts of memories which may be subject to decay (Cohen 1989: 156–9). We shall return in much more detail to the role of memory in Papua New Guinean religious traditions in subsequent chapters.

Now, the *political* implications of initiatory traumas reside partly in the nature of the moving and long-lasting memories that they evoke, and partly in the contrived circumstances of transmission. The religious understandings cultivated in initiation ritual derive from collective performances, and can only be disseminated among neighbouring groups, or through the displacement of whole populations. As Barth points out (1990), this helps to explain the fragmentary, localized character of many religious traditions founded around initiation rites. The traumatic nature of these rites, and the secrecy surrounding them, generate intense solidarity among participants, as many writers have observed (e.g. Barth 1975: 223, 245, 251; Lindenbaum 1984; Feil 1987: 231; Godelier 1991: 294). This experience of solidarity is linked to courage in war, as the foregoing discussion clearly demonstrates. Warfare, as I pointed out earlier in this chapter, is conducive to the autonomy of small local groups (see also Modjeska 1982).

All these factors encourage a highly fragmented political landscape composed of small, boundary-conscious ritual communities, standing in relations of hostility or rivalry. Internally, the emphasis is on cohesiveness and solidarity. If there is also an egalitarian ethos among adult males, this may be linked to the conditions of religious transmission, and in particular to the fact that revelations are not mediated by leaders. In the context of initiation, crucial insights are inferred by participants in a process subjectively experienced as personal inspiration. Nobody comes forward to impart the wisdom of the ancestors, for this wisdom is elusive to oral transmission. Religious instruction is, therefore, a matter of collective revelation, rather than a transaction between teacher and pupils (cf. Barth 1990). Admittedly, the authoritarian behaviour of initiators instantiates a striking imbalance of power (cf. Tuzin 1980: 73–4), but once the metamorphosis of the novices is complete, the camaraderie engendered in their common experience of liminality is extended to their initiators. In a real sense initiators and novices undergo the experience together and share its dramatic consequences (Tuzin 1980: 78). When it is over, they are closer than before, both in status and identity.

People undergo particular initiation rites once in a lifetime. They may participate in or witness such rites again, but never as objects of the performance. In these conditions of infrequent transmission, it is vital that the original impact of the experience endures in memory. An important quality of people's memories of initiation rites is that they are unforgettable, vivid, and haunting. Their potency is a concomitant of the uniqueness and emotionality of the situation which gave rise to them. The cohesion generated among initiates is lasting, but it is also difficult to generalize or extend. This is another factor contributing to the politically bounded character of initiation systems and it is best understood in terms of its impact on memory. What is encoded is a set of very particular events, experiences, and responses. In the case of initiation, these recollections are tied to the actual historical context in which the events occurred. What this means, among other things, is that actual persons inhabit these memories. This is very different from the memories that people have for highly repetitive rituals, involving schemas for general sequences of actions that might be performed by anybody and not a specific set of people (see Chapter 2). Thus, the political and religious community which initiation creates is fixed forever in the minds of novices. The bonds of solidarity, once forged cannot easily be revoked or extended. They encompass those people who actually endured the terrifying experience together, and separate them forever from the rest of humanity.

Rites of terror may be seen as part of a nexus of psychological and sociological processes in which specific dimensions of concept-formation, feeling, and remembering are linked to the scale, structure, and political ethos of social groups. Social anthropologists have long appreciated that intense emotional states are a crucial element of the nexus, but (as in the sample of interpretations surveyed in this chapter) these states have not been related to the complex conceptual processes that are engendered in terrifying rituals. An advantage of focusing on the integrity of emotion and conceptual complexity, via a close analysis of the workings of memory, is that it impels us deeper into the ethnography at the same time as it forces us to generalize. This is one of the main goals of the present volume.

2

From Mission to Movement

Most of the earliest European settlers in Papua New Guinea were missionaries and for many indigenous villagers even up to the present time, the most enduring and intensive links with European culture have been mediated by proselytizing Christians.[1] The latter were by no means exclusively white; indeed, many early missionaries were Polynesians and, later, Melanesians from the more heavily Christianized areas. But whether or not the carriers of these diverse 'Christianities' were themselves ethnically European, the mode of religious transmission they established was fundamentally alien to most Papua New Guineans. My principal concern in this chapter is not with the thematic differences between indigenous and Christian cosmologies but with a set of fundamental contrasts in the nature of their transmissive characteristics.

Christianity codifies its revelations primarily as a body of doctrines. Its mode of transmission is repetitive, involving continual sermonizing and liturgical ritual. Worship is public and the intricacies of religious dogma are broadcast openly to all who would listen. I will argue that these factors are related to the way in which Christianity instantiates a vast, diffusely integrated Christian fellowship, bound to an elaborate ecclesiastical hierarchy, incorporating elements of centralization at various levels.

The spread of Christianity in Papua New Guinea produced radical changes in the way representations of 'community' were conceptualized.

Most of the text for this chapter was first published in the *Journal of the Royal Anthropological Institute* (N.S.), 4(1): 43–63, under the title 'From Mission to Movement: the Impact of Christianity on Patterns of Political Association in Papua New Guinea' (Whitehouse 1998).

[1] Of course, planters and traders preceded missionaries in many parts of Papua New Guinea, but it was missionaries who led the way in establishing close and long-term relations between Europeans and indigenous peoples. Much of the colonial administration of the region was effectively undertaken by the missions: the introduction of 'hygienic' practices and 'tidy' villages, the interpretation and dissemination of government laws and policies, and the provision of basic education and training (enabling the export economy to exploit indigenous labour more effectively). In all these areas, and many others too, missionaries were the leading intermediaries between Western and Melanesian social systems.

In particular, the forms of cognitive processing entailed in the remembering and enactment of Christian ritual enabled people to identify with large, anonymous communities, governed by centrally regulated orthodoxies. This was a necessary condition for the development of indigenous movements promoting 'micronationalist' programmes.

Modalities of Codification

In order to win converts and maintain the faith or commitment of those raised within its churches, Christianity relies to a very great extent on the power of the Word. To be sure, the iconography of Christian art and architecture, the ethos and aesthetics of its melodies, rituals, clothes, body practices, and other non-verbal elements all contribute to the distinctive character of Christianity as a whole, and of its myriad different churches, sects, and cultic off-shoots. But the Word stands out among other transmissive modalities because it supplies crucial aspects of the *meanings* of all of them. No Christian ritual, no painting, no hymn, no statue, no altar, no posture in church—in fact, no aspect of Christian culture in general—can be adequately understood without reference to a body of ideas codified in language. This is by no means true of all religions, including many of those in pre-contact Papua New Guinea (as we saw in the last chapter).

Words are powerful in Christianity because they are used rhetorically to bind together a set of absolute presuppositions through the logic of question and answer (Collingwood 1940). Codes of etiquette, differences of status, and many other factors may restrict the arenas within which questions about Christian doctrine may be posed and by whom, but Christian cosmology is structured around sequences of questions and answers, rhetorically expressed in the Gospels, sermons, and a range of other forms of language-based transmission. We may pick any topic at random, and the answers to our questions (however naive they may be) spring readily to mind. Why did Christ allow himself to be crucified? To atone for the sins of humanity. Why is humanity sinful? Because God endowed humanity with an ability to choose between good and evil. How can we choose to be good? By following the example and teachings of Christ. What are the teachings of Christ? And so we could go on and on, choosing between a wide variety of possible questions in response to each answer, and answers in response to each question. All questions, however, would eventually lead us back to absolute presuppositions beyond which further enquiry is impossible.

This is not to suggest that Christian orthodoxies are perfectly integrated logically. Contradictory absolute presuppositions, entailed, for instance, in the problem of theodicy, present a serious challenge to the faith of some Christians. Other absolute presuppositions, such as the Catholic doctrine of transubstantiation, may contradict common sense rather than each other. The simplest (and no doubt the commonest) policy is to convert problems into absolute presuppositions. How can a benevolent and omnipotent God allow the innocent to perish in natural disasters? A typical answer is that this is God's inscrutable will, and all further questioning is ruled out. Moreover, logical weaknesses can be converted into personal moral victories to the extent that the faithful can overcome or deny their doubts.

Nevertheless, the persuasiveness of Christianity rests to some extent on the plausibility of its absolute presuppositions and the comprehensiveness with which it supplies answers to all possible questions that connect them. This is an indispensable element in the revelatory character of Christianity. The process of accepting particular absolute presuppositions (for instance because they accord with deeply held values or ontological commitments) and the process of constantly recapitulating the strings of questions and answers through which they are integrated, is a prerequisite of what Christians describe as 'faith'. Faith may appear to spring from other sources and the way it is codified may be taken for granted, but without its system of interlocking rhetoric, Christianity could not exist or, rather, would be a very different kind of religion.

An alternative modality of codification is presented by some of the indigenous religions of Papua New Guinea, as we saw in the last chapter. For instance, within many fertility and ancestor cults, particularly those based on systems of initiation, language plays only a supporting role in the transmission of religious insights. Revelations often take the form of iconic imagery, triggered by the peculiar artefacts and choreography of collective rituals. In the case of initiation rites, novices typically discover that their assumptions about certain familiar phenomena are substantially false, that processes of reproduction, growth, and decay are constituted in ways that invert and otherwise contradict what is implied or asserted in everyday discourse. It follows that such cults, and their revelations, are secret. The uninitiated (usually women and children) ostensibly live in ignorance of the esoteric mysteries of nature, and only initiates come close to understanding the dynamics of cosmic renewal.

The contrast between styles of codification in Christianity and Melanesian fertility cults could, of course, be exaggerated. Even the most iconoclastic forms of Christianity possess imagistic features, including considerable emphasis on sensory and emotional stimulation and multi-vocal imagery, in at least some areas of transmission. Moreover, many of the traditional rituals of Melanesia are associated with quite elaborate exegetical traditions, often taking the form of a corpus of esoteric mythology (see Poole 1982; Young 1983; Harrison 1990). Nevertheless, Melanesian myths are seldom presented in the discursive format characteristic of Bible stories, or related to a broader, argument-based discourse. Moreover, knowledge of indigenous ritual exegesis tends to be restricted to ritual experts, so that the transmission of revelations to most adherents has to occur through the ritual process itself. In Christianity, by contrast, the Word occupies a position of pre-eminence because all image-based transmission is ultimately rooted in verbal and textual rhetoric. It is true that within all Christian traditions, pictorial, monumental, and other visual images play a crucial role in religious experience, but these trans-missive features depend for their meaning and revelatory potential upon doctrine and narrative. Thus, whereas Christian rituals possess meaning only in the light of doctrines, stories, and other verbal and textual mate-rials, the iconic imagery evoked by many traditional Melanesian rituals is a source of meaning in its own right, which may or may not be success-fully embellished through oral transmission.

Early Missionization and the Politics of Memory

There is abundant evidence that, from the viewpoint of Melanesians encountering Christianity for the first time, the ideas and behaviour of missionaries presented little that was recognizably 'religious'. A common early response to missionary efforts was to agree to instruction or baptism merely in the hope of acquiring Western goods. As Wetherell puts it: 'Young people turned to the missionary, not because he was thought a safer guide to heaven than the village sorcerer, but because he had such things as fish-hooks' (1977: 165). Or, as one beleaguered missionary observed in 1936: 'I have known people to come up and ask for tobacco . . . but never for the gospel' (quoted in Wetherell 1977: 159).

In the anthropological literature, this type of response to missioniza-tion has sometimes been attributed to 'Melanesian pragmatism' (Barker 1990b: 173). It seems to me, however, that there was nothing specifically Melanesian about this pragmatism towards early missionaries. Confronted with the sudden appearance of aliens bearing wealth and wielding power of a nature and magnitude previously unknown, what community would not seek to tap some of these resources, whether in

Melanesia or any other part of the world? What throws the Melanesian response into relief, and gives it the appearance of a particular form of 'pragmatism', is the fact that it was hitched to a lack of indigenous understanding of the central aim of the missionaries, which was to transmit a corpus of textually codified doctrine. Missionary writers themselves often complained that 'the natives attached little value to mere dogmas' (Koskinen 1953: 92), but what few European observers, even up to the present time, have seriously considered is that the very nature of doctrinal religion was initially unintelligible to (rather than 'undervalued' by) the tribal peoples of Melanesia. For the latter, the packaging of revelations in rhetorical strings of question-and-answer transmitted in sermons and holy books was quite alien, and consequently the religious purposes of missionary work were more or less inscrutable. Christianity was therefore: ' "quite beyond their comprehension, just as were the sermons of repentance, justification by faith, holy living and dying, spiritual regeneration and the like" . . . Before the conversion of the natives could take place, something had to happen that could make their minds more susceptible' (Koskinen 1953: 22–3 who quotes Henderson 1931).

The first task of missionaries in Melanesia was to establish a common tongue, to learn local languages and to teach European ones, as a means of providing indigenes with access to the Gospel, and of course to a variety of psalms, hymns, and prayers. Having achieved a degree of fluency in local dialects, missionaries proselytized from the pulpit, and presented potential converts with the basic, routinized format of the liturgy. After years of listening, reading, rote-learning, and participating in church services, villagers were baptized and described by their missionary teachers as 'converts'. But in many regions there is evidence that the transmissive styles of Christianity remained mysterious, particularly for the older population.

In his erudite history of the Anglican church in Papua New Guinea, Wetherell describes how many elders initially reacted to missionary teaching with 'withdrawal, passive resistance, and occasional feeble rearguard challenge . . . Most elders did not resist with words but affected a wooden unconcern for the *tawaroro* [Christian church] . . . A few old people on Dobu said, "Our minds are dark: we do not understand; the children will understand, but we cannot" ' (1977: 159–60). Thus, much of the energies and resources of the missions throughout Papua New Guinea came to be directed into the conversion of *children* through the provision of a lengthy education. But this too presented problems, of which perhaps the greatest was truancy. A somewhat more effective strategy, adopted by several early missions, was to remove children from their villages and install them in boarding schools where their lives could be regulated according to a fixed, almost monastic regime. Wetherell describes the daily routine for such children as follows: '[The children] rose at six in the morning, sang a hymn and said a short service, and worked in the garden till breakfast at eight. After Matins, school took up the morning from nine until midday. The afternoon was divided between recreation and outdoor work; Evensong at 5.30, dinner at 6.00 and bed at 9.00' (1977: 166).

Such regimes obviously facilitated extensive exposure to the general themes of Christian dogma (transmitted orally and through Bible-reading), the routinized liturgy and other rituals, the hierarchical character of the church, the sombre ethos of worship, and some sense of the scale of world religion. A similar strategy of converting individuals separated from their village environment was adopted with adults employed as labourers at mission stations and their associated plantations. When schoolchildren and labourers who had experienced Christianity in such a sustained fashion eventually returned to their villages, they brought with them a set of understandings that were crucial to the political destiny of Melanesians.

The ideological content of these new understandings was, in one sense, of little relevance. At any rate, from the viewpoint of the present argument, it makes no difference that these people were converts to Christianity, rather than to Islam, Judaism, Hinduism, or any other doctrinal religion. What mattered was that the returnees were capable of conceptualizing the social world, and their place within it, in a radically new way. This process must be understood at least partly in terms of people's experiences of routinized worship at school and in the mission station.

There can be little doubt that mission Christianity strove to routinize worship far more extensively than was usual in the lives of church-going Europeans during the same period. As Koskinen observes: 'Church discipline was generally very severe. Attendance at divine service became compulsory. Prayer meetings were frequent . . . The Sabbath became the pivot around which the activities of a converted community revolved, with not only church meetings, but also family assemblies, best clothes and special meals' (1953: 35–6). The emphasis on routinization, strict adherence to doctrinal orthodoxy, and rigid forms of discipline based on the Decalogue (Koskinen 1953: 35–6), was intended to instil what some missionaries described as a 'Christian habit of life' (Barker 1990b: 175). The attempt to establish daily 'habits' and routines at the mission station was premissed on the same folk theory of memory, so popular in Europe during the late nineteenth and early twentieth centuries, that promoted collective rote-learning in schools. Groups of children chanting in unison were expected to encode and remember knowledge more 'deeply' and enduringly than was possible by any other means. The continual repetition of Christian liturgy and other rituals, like the collective recitation of strings of utterances in the classroom, no doubt served to establish in the minds of converts a truly unforgettable repertoire of schemas for 'how to be' a Christian.

Familiarity with the routinized practices of the mission station helped to establish membership of a community of Christians extending indefinitely beyond the horizons of the natal clan or village. Through their involvement in life at the mission, Melanesian converts acquired general schemas for participation in church services, mealtime rituals, classroom routines, and other repetitive sequences of events. These schemas consisted not of memories of specific ritual episodes but of ideal models for the performance of different types of activity. As each mission station took in new residents or visitors and bade farewell to others, the throng of faces at each church service continually changed. Consequently, people's memories of these rituals did not specify the unique identities of participants. The political implications of this cannot be underestimated. The Christian community, as constructed through people's memories of routinized activities, evoked in its schemas throngs of anonymous, unidentifiable worshippers—a mass of imaginary persons. One's identity, as part of this community, was conferred on the basis of presumed commonalties in the schematic and behavioural patterns of people one had never met, and did not even need to meet in order to be united with them (however diffusely) in a common fellowship of Christian worshippers. Having acquired this fundamentally new conception of community, it was possible to grasp a range of universalistic Western discourses, not only those of the missions but of the colonial order more generally, and of some of the large-scale indigenous movements that subsequently became established.

The fact that early missionization set this process in motion is in no sense a 'new' observation. For instance, Hogbin writes: 'Every [Christian] church asserts its universality, and those who belong to it offer the same kind of prayers to the one Deity. A mission native may continue to believe for many years that his chief obligations are to the members of his own society, but a basis is now provided for broadening the concept of brotherhood until it embraces not only the inhabitants of neighbouring settlements but also strangers' (1958: 182). To this, Barker adds: 'Christianity, particularly in the early missionary stages, introduced its followers to an enlarged and vastly complicated world—indeed, cosmos . . . [and the missionaries] introduced islanders to a language within which Christians could speak about their enlarged social and spiritual community' (1990a: 16).

Thus, the effects of early missionization are well known. What is new about my argument concerns the means to this transformation. For the above commentators, the enlargement of indigenous conceptions of community was partly a result of encountering the universalistic themes of Christian ideology. Nevertheless, as I have attempted to show, Melanesians were not initially in a position to grasp universalistic ideas, any more than they were able to recognize as 'religious' practices based around humdrum behavioural repetition, reading, and sermonizing. Universalistic ideology only made sense once the capacity for conceptualizing large anonymous communities had been established. Before something so abstract could be codified in dogma, it had to have some conceptual reality and this occurred through the mnemonic effects of routinized, identity-conferring ritual. Once the conceptual basis for an enlarged, potentially international conception of humanity was in place, Melanesians were well on the way to adopting new forms of political association. Often this occurred, however, not at the mission station but through the establishment of new religious movements under indigenous leadership.[2]

Christianity and Indigenous Movements

Christian doctrine, as taught by missionaries, was not a particularly 'contagious' body of representations in Melanesia (Whitehouse 1995:

---

[2] It should be acknowledged that missionary activity in some regions, even up to the present time, has been limited and sporadic, and the evangelist's dream of universal religious routinization in Melanesia is far from having been achieved. Largely for this reason, there are still many peoples who do not experience a sense of belonging to a 'world religion' or a nation, or any such large anonymous community. Nor has the experience of extensive Christianization everywhere given rise to routinized indigenous movements. In many cases, church orthodoxies have been only slightly modified, so that the appellation 'indigenous movement' hardly seems applicable. A case in point might be the Catholics of Karagur village (Kairuru Island, East Sepik Province), of whom Smith has observed: 'Though there was no organized cargo cult in Koragur during my sojourn, some apparently have found convenient employment for their energies in the intense and ritualistic pursuit of a regimen of Catholic prayer and religious observance to which they attach extravagant hopes and expectations' (1980: 45). Thus, the dividing line between mission and movement is far from clear, and the arguments presented here might be taken to apply not only to named 'movements' but also to a range of indigenized versions of Christianity that have instantiated new forms of political association.

ch. 7). In the first place, it was not substantially rooted in cosmological assumptions that Melanesians regarded as plausible or relevant. It did not seem to cohere as a total system, except in the minds of its experts (primarily an educated clergy). When members of the laity asked questions, they often received incomplete or contradictory answers, and many came to believe that crucial explanatory elements in the religious scheme were being kept hidden by missionaries, perhaps for nefarious reasons (such as the desire to reserve 'space' in heaven for white people, to the exclusion of Melanesians). Different denominations offered conflicting visions of religious truth and correct ritual procedure, and there appeared to be no reliable basis on which to select one vision over another.

The success of many large-scale politico-religious movements in Melanesia, such as many of the more enduring 'cargo cult' associations, lay in their capacity to avoid many of these pitfalls by making available to all a coherent body of doctrine, the authority of which was guaranteed by virtue of the apotheosis of the movements' leaders and the confinement of their followings to geographically distinct regions. These new movements were highly routinized, encompassing large 'imagined' communities just like the missions. But their evangelical programmes were more effective in transmitting and maintaining doctrinal orthodoxy. All these movements were centralized and hierarchical, being modelled on forms of organization observed in the missions and in colonial government. Many of those appointed to positions of authority within such movements had lived in mission stations or in similar circumstances, and were therefore already capable of envisaging the possibility of large, anonymous communities.[3] Through the routinized practices of these movements, all their members developed a new conception of 'community' as well.

The emphasis on routinization in large-scale, indigenous, religious movements was no less extreme than in many early missions. It even incorporated elements of military practice, such as roll calls, marching, drilling, and parading (e.g. Mead 1956; Schwartz 1962; Lawrence 1971). Punctuality became virtually an obsession in these movements, with whistles, bells, and other loud signals continually announcing that it was

---

[3] Paliau himself had comparatively little direct experience of Christian practices prior to the establishment of his movement (Maloat 1970). It was largely through his work as a police officer that he became acquainted with the dynamics of the doctrinal mode. Similarly, experiences of working for the police and armed forces clearly shaped the careers of other new religious leaders, such as Tommy Kabu (Steinbauer 1979: 29–32) and Yali (Lawrence 1971: 117–26). Thus conversion to Christianity was not the only stimulus to the political transformations described in this chapter. It was, however, arguably the most influential for the vast majority of rank-and-file followers of the new large-scale religious movements.

time to perform another round of daily rituals, meetings, or practical tasks. Many new ritual forms were introduced, including idiosyncratic church services, the placing of offerings to ancestors, attendance at frequent meetings, and various forms of recitation and prayer. The highly repetitive character of the new rituals distinguished them from indigenous practices and linked them inextricably to those of church and mission. Through the performance of such rituals over time, followers came to conceptualize a basis for unity across a wide area, enabling them to recognize common identity with anonymous others they had never met. This radically new conception was thoroughly incorporated into the aspirations of these new movements: self-government, salvation, 'modernization', and 'development'. All such movements were expansionary, or at least they tried to be, and claimed that their dogmas transcended ethnic differences.[4]

In terms of their universalistic orientations, these movements were inspired by Christianity but the leaders were markedly more successful than most missionaries in transmitting a coherent, plausible, and persuasive body of doctrine. Through creative and selective synthesis of already popular ideas and assumptions, these new movements established doctrinal orthodoxies that were both persuasive and accessible to large numbers of people. The reproduction of these orthodoxies over time occurred through the attendance of all members at regular local meetings, modelled on Sunday schools and Bible-reading classes. Such meetings were directed and led by carefully selected officials, generally well schooled in the limits of their movement's orthodoxy, and cautious of innovation and heresy. The speeches of local officials reiterated the body of doctrine in schoolroom conditions, usually on a daily basis and seldom less frequently than twice a week. There were elements here of rote-learning on the part of many followers but the effect was also to encourage followers to grasp the logical connections between elements of doctrine, providing all worshippers with a general ethical framework for the interpretation of diverse events. Orators did not simply recite official doctrines, but persuasively revealed the underpinnings of their authority (Whitehouse 1995: 81–4). The aims of such speeches were analogous to

---

[4] It should be noted, however, that some indigenous movements have adapted a hostile stance towards particular ethnic groups. For instance, the Pomio Kivung repudiates certain customs of the neighbouring Tolai, and regards as oppressive the dominance of the latter in commerce and government (Whitehouse 1995: 60–2). Nevertheless, the Pomio Kivung is clearly expansionary, cutting across the barriers of language and culture that formerly divided non-Tolai ethnic groups.

sermons, except that they did not refer to largely inaccessible texts (such as the Bible) but rather to ideas already familiar through other repetitive acts of verbal transmission (Whitehouse 1995: 146).

The Tedium Effect and Localized Splintering

A problematic side-effect of such extensive repetition is that rituals may eventually become boring to some people, especially where competent performance of sacred tasks consists merely of the enactment of entrenched habit. The body goes through the motions automatically and the mind wanders or is numbed by the predictability and familiarity of it all. Even the doctrines, no matter how enthusiastically and creatively they are represented by local orators, are obviously subject to unnecessary repetition. This syndrome has been widely documented in relation to the early spread of Christianity in Melanesia, just as it became a problem in many of the larger indigenous movements. Evidence of this is easy to find in the missiological literature on the Pacific region. Of the Anglican mission, Wetherell observes: 'It was a pedestrian and monotonous move-ment, providing no heady and volatile excitement . . . Many candidates [for baptism] dropped out before the instruction was complete' (1977: 171). Even those who completed the lengthy process of conversion were often subject to the tedium effect, as Koskinen points out: 'disappoint-ment and tedium soon made their appearance . . . The alluring accumu-lation of feeling, carrying all before it, of mass enthusiasm is generally shortlived' (1953: 93). The same points have often been made in relation to the more routinized indigenous movements (e.g. Steinbauer 1979; Otto 1992; Schwartz 1962).

What has tended to happen in Christianized regions of Melanesia is that attempts have periodically been made, typically when the tedium effect has been most acute (see Whitehouse 1995; Schwartz 1962: 286–7), to transform humdrum religious practices into more dramatic, colourful, and even ecstatic ones. Numerous examples of this tendency among early converts to Christianity have been recorded (e.g. Guiart 1951: 82; Koskinen 1953: 95; Wetherell 1977: 179). Stripped of its ethnocentric phraseology, the following observation conveys the gist of what was happening rather well: 'In discouraging and suppressing so many of the innocent interests and activities of the islanders, the missionaries took far too much out of their lives and put far too little back to fill the void . . . When deprived of their dances and games, the natural outlet for their joy of life, the natives soon began to perform them in secret' (Koskinen 1953:

95). In some regions, a sort of *modus vivendi* was achieved by separating the domains of village and mission station, enabling indigenous peoples to move freely in both. For instance, as Barker describes in Uiaku, the village became the locus of more climactic, periodic rituals focused around 'life crises' whereas, at the mission station 'interactions with the divine [continued to] take the form of public Christian worship at regular times. The priest conducts a relatively ornate (high church) service that is disciplined and sober' (1990b: 181). In other regions, the *modus vivendi* has taken other forms, such as the introduction of more 'entertaining' and emotionally stimulating forms of Christian worship, an idea with which early missionaries from several denominations experimented, and which has become particularly apparent with the spread of Pentecostal orders in recent decades (see Trompf 1991).

Within routinized indigenous movements, however, the enlivening of religious experience has tended to involve a rather different trajectory. For instance, it is clear that during periods when the tedium effect has been most acute, small groups of followers of large-scale indigenous movements have tended to break away from the mainstream organizations for short periods of time, in order to perform rituals of a particularly ecstatic nature (a process examined closely in Chapter 6). In contrast with the apparently smooth reconciliation of the mission station and village in Uiaku, splinter groups in indigenous movements have tended to be condemned by mainstream followers and leadership (at least in their public rhetoric). Nevertheless, astute leaders tended to avoid intervention until splinter groups had run their course and their followers could be readily brought back into the fold (Schwartz 1962; Whitehouse 1995).

Whereas large-scale, routinized mainstream movements are modelled substantially on the institutional forms of missionary Christianity, sporadic splinter groups owe their inspiration to indigenous traditions, including the sorts of fertility and ancestor cults discussed in the last chapter. As in rites of initiation, for instance, the activities of splinter groups take the form of highly stimulating and revelatory collective rituals, encoding imagery that is resistant to verbal expression and indissolubly linked to particular transmissive episodes.

An unintended consequence of splintering is often to stimulate commitment to the humdrum rituals and doctrines of the mainstream movement. This is because, unlike the situation described by Barker in Uiaku, the climactic activities of splinter groups are usually based on mainstream ideology. Rather than rejecting orthodox dogma, splinter groups *recodify* it as a body of loosely connected, ritually transmitted metaphors. For instance, in a recent splinter group of a movement known as the Pomio Kivung, mainstream ideas about sin, salvation, and ancestors were expressed through the ritual imagery of a ring, formed of human bodies and physical objects. The ring represented God's elect, and the post at the centre (usually represented by the body of the splinter-group leader) corresponded to a post on which was carved the numbers of the Ten Commandments, and also the central post of traditional round houses which supported the rafters. The community, here connoting the rafters, converged on the leader, who they believed would carry them (shouldering the burden of their sins) to salvation. This kind of imagery was not, however, accorded verbal exegesis. It was triggered by the kinetic, visual, tactile, and auditory properties of ritual performances (see Whitehouse 1995: chs. 4 and 5). Such rituals had the effect of stimulating intense cohesion within the small, face-to-face communities that performed them. Yet this sense of excitement and cohesion was, at least in some cases, projected on to the wider movement after the collapse of the splinter group itself.

Routinized movements, although providing the necessary conditions for *conceptualizing* large (and therefore abstract) communities, are not always capable in themselves of producing intense cohesion for long periods of time. Depending on the revelatory power of their doctrines or policies, such movements may engender a very real and compelling experience of solidarity and excitement for periods of time, but this can wane dramatically with the onset of the tedium effect. Localized splinter groups, however, engender a more enduring excitement, by re-codifying revelations in a surprising, emotionally arousing, and memorable way. Thus, within the Pomio Kivung and other similar organizations in Melanesia, long-term routinization has been punctuated by sporadic splintering, involving the temporary efflorescence of climactic rituals.[5] The memories instantiated by such practices relate to small communities of people who undergo the highs and lows of ecstatic or traumatic ritual together (just as in the indigenous initiation rites discussed in Chapter 1). But because a larger abstract community is now a conceptual reality, these feelings of cohesion and renewed commitment may be projected on to it, with the result that the mainstream movement, over time, is strengthened or rejuvenated.

---

[5] A detailed analysis of these patterns is presented in Chapter 6 (see also Whitehouse 1995: chs. 4 to 6).

The Political Implications of Indigenous Movements

It has often been argued that 'cargo cults' constitute a passing phase in the emergence of Melanesian nationalisms and other pragmatic forms of protest against colonial states.[6] Nevertheless, as I will demonstrate in the following chapters, this impression is misleading.

Firstly, it is only a very visible minority of 'cargo cults' that have the effect of unifying large populations for the purposes of protest. In every case, these are movements dominated by doctrinal transmission and modelled on mission practices. The reason such movements have attracted scholarly attention, and have therefore come to be seen as archetypal cargo cults, is precisely because they are large-scale, enduring, and vocal.

Nevertheless, the vast majority of cargo cults are small-scale and sporadic, many passing unrecorded by anthropologists and government personnel, except as instances of temporary insanity, relegated to footnotes or accorded no more than a line or two in the stilted, unsympathetic prose of government patrol reports.[7] The timing and location of such cults are unpredictable; they are not willingly discussed during intervening periods, and often only in cautious and cryptic whispers when they are enacted; the imagery evoked in their rituals is mysterious and difficult for outsiders to penetrate; their effects are usually localized. Where such activities occur in isolation from a large, mainstream movement, they tend to escape the close attention of European observers, even those who are ostensibly trained to document such occurrences. Occasionally, ecstatic cults spread like waves across a wide area, and these phenomena have a much greater chance of being observed and documented by government officers, missionaries, and anthropologists (examples are examined closely in the chapters that follow). Unfortunately, however, Western commentators are often tempted to identify the 'doctrines' of such cults along with their regionally 'unifying' effects (see Worsley 1957: 65–6; Lanternari 1963), despite the evident non-existence of both.

---

[6] Examples include Belshaw (1950); Bodrogi (1951); Brown (1966); Guiart (1951); Hogbin (1958); Lanternari (1963); Lawrence (1971); Mead (1964); (Morauta 1972; 1974); Rowley (1965); Worsley (1957).

[7] This, at least, is the impression I have formed through archival research on the history of 'cargo cult' activity in East New Britain and through informal discussion with Melanesianists over a number of years. A systematic survey of 'unrecorded' cults, based upon interrogation of missionaries, anthropologists, and government workers, would be very useful although it would, of course, only provide a tentative indication of the extent to which such cults are under-represented in documentary sources.

Whereas many Melanesians rapidly came to understand Christian modalities of transmission imported by Europeans, the latter have had considerably less success in grasping transmissive modalities indigenous to Melanesia. Cults founded on imagistic transmission unite only small, face-to-face communities, often through successive waves of contact-transmission; they do not, in regions where Western transmissive forms have yet to take root, have the capacity to unite large, proto-nationalist communities.

Secondly, the genuinely unifying movements, modelled on missionary Christianity and state formations, do not necessarily shed their millenarian and cargoist themes in exchange for nationalistic and secular ones. It is much more common for both to be sustained in tandem, as alternative and complementary strands of the movement's ideology (see Trompf 1991: ch. 9; Whitehouse 1995: ch. 8; Wanek 1996: part 7). The usual reason why scholars regard hopes of supernatural transformation as transient is because these hopes are manifestly unrealistic, but evaluating the success of millenarian programmes is a highly subjective process. There are many cultists in Papua New Guinea who will point to hard evidence that their leaders' prophesies have been realized, if only partially (Koimanrea and Bailoenakia1983); moreover, failures and delays can always be rationalized, whether people's expectations are pinned on pragmatic or supernatural intervention. In short, there is no compelling reason to think that nationalism will necessarily replace millenarism, nor is there very much evidence that this is in fact the historical trajectory in Melanesia.

Finally, the populations unified by indigenous movements operating in the doctrinal mode are seldom large enough to encompass potential nation-states. Leaders of such movements frequently claim otherwise, but the fragmentation of a country such as Papua New Guinea into a series of tiny states founded around the followers of new religious movements remains an unlikely prospect (cf. Spriggs 1991). If so, it is probably appropriate to describe the unifying social movements of Papua New Guinea as 'micronationalist' (May 1982). These 'micronations', which are all directly or indirectly an outcome of the doctrinal mode of religiosity, constitute the most encompassing political communities in contemporary Papua New Guinea. There is little evidence that they are soon to be transcended by popular forms of pan-New Guinean identity. The leaders of large-scale, routinized movements often participate in so-called 'national' politics but they do so with the interests of their regional micronations firmly in mind, rather than as builders of a national identity coterminous with citizenship in the existing state.

Codification, Memory, and Group Formation

Modalities of codification are clearly linked to patterns of group formation and some of the reasons for this can now be rendered in a more
general, if preliminary, form. Religions such as Christianity that privilege
the Word can be spread quite efficiently across a wide area by just one or
a few religious leaders, whereas revelatory imagery triggered by collective
ritual is much harder to spread, implying the movement of whole ritual
communities, or else a chain-like process of transmission between
contiguous populations (Schwartz 1962; Barth 1990; Morauta 1972).
Even when a set of non-verbal ritual images spreads quite widely, verbal
accounts of their history and origins may not. Indeed, each local ritual
community is typically pitted against the others, developing its own
distinctive versions of the religious tradition. In short, argument-centred
doctrinal systems are comparatively easy to spread as regionally homogeneous traditions, producing large-scale religious communities; ritually
transmitted revelations, if they spread at all, tend to do so slowly and to
mutate quite radically in the process.

In addition to these contrasts in scale and transmissive efficiency, the
two modalities of codification are linked to different dynamics of social
organization. The argument-based discourse of Christianity tends to
confer authority on its individual purveyors (e.g. messiahs, prophets,
disciples, priests, missionaries, and so on). By contrast, ritual imagery is
not mediated by religious teachers, but engendered in collectively transmitted metaphors (cf. Barth 1990). Thus, there is a tendency towards
hierarchical structure in Christian churches, but not in ritually constituted Melanesian traditions. Moreover, in Christianity, the achievement
of coherence and homogeneity of the tradition depends upon the
centralization and delegation of religious authority. In indigenous
Melanesian churches, modelled on Christian transmissive forms, cult
founders tend to be construed as the ultimate earthly source of authoritative dogma and practice. They may address congregations at a central
location, or travel widely to visit the faithful, but it is most common for
the orthodoxy to be filtered through deputized, centrally appointed
officials. From a small group of disciples, it is easy to see in the history
of many such religions the elaboration of ecclesiastical hierarchies,
usually increasing in complexity after the death of the original founder
and the spread of the religion to ever-wider populations. An important
task of such delegated officials is to protect the centrally formulated
orthodoxy from local infractions. Such are the broad organizational

characteristics of Christian churches and indigenous movements modelled upon them.

Thus, the two modalities of codification may be linked to some extent with divergent political trajectories, the one large-scale, centralized, and hierarchical, and the other small-scale, uncentralized, and non-hierarchical. What is less obvious, however, is that these trajectories entail contrasting conceptualizations of community, arising from differences in the frequency of religious transmission and the ways in which these transmissive events are remembered.

Argument-centred doctrinal systems must be reviewed on a regular basis if they are to be recalled accurately. The process of being socialized into such a tradition, or of being converted, involves regular exposure to religious teachings which reveal, over time, a relatively coherent and logically integrated world-view. Even when these systems are quite thoroughly grasped by the adherent, their stable reproduction depends upon regular reiteration. Traditions of this type are, therefore, invariably routinized.

By contrast, traditions founded upon revelatory ritual performances tend to be reproduced through longer cycles of transmission. The revelatory quality of the imagery has to do with the violation of everyday knowledge (see Chapter 1) and, in this rather trivial sense, it could not itself be an 'everyday' experience. But there are much more important points to make about routinized and sporadic forms of transmission, because these variables can profoundly affect the way communities are envisaged.

Psychologists describe recollections of specific events as manifestations of 'episodic' or 'autobiographical' memory. When I remember the resignation of the former Prime Minister, Margaret Thatcher, or a fight which unexpectedly broke out at my local bus stop, much of what goes through my mind concerns a distinctive episode or series of episodes. The same is true of the way people remember revelatory rituals, the specific moments when their understandings about the nature of the world were violated or transformed.

By contrast, experiences of repetitive and predictable events are encoded in what psychologists call 'semantic' memory, a set of scripts or 'schemas' specifying, for instance, how to behave on aeroplanes, in restaurants, or (for that matter) during Christian services. This type of memory does not relate to particular episodes. If you ask a Christian what happened in church on a given Sunday several years ago, he or she will be able to describe the standard sequence of events that occurs at every service, but could probably not recall the actual events on that day.

In the study of religious codification and transmission, the distinction between episodic and semantic memory is of the greatest relevance. The sorts of climactic rituals found in Melanesian initiation systems and cargoist splinter groups are not merely surprising to the participants, in so far as they challenge everyday assumptions, but also emotionally charged. Initiation rites, for instance, are very often intentionally terrifying and traumatic, a characteristic that has puzzled many scholars (see Chapter 1). In religious traditions of this type, revelation combines the violation of semantic knowledge with (often extreme) affective and sensory stimulation. These are precisely the conditions in which enduring episodic memories are activated (Herdt 1989; Whitehouse 1996c). Hence, the maintenance of a religious frame of mind among adherents does not require regular transmission. Indeed, precise repetition of a particular revelatory episode would, at best, be redundant and, at worst, rob the original experience of its uniqueness.

In relation to processes of group formation, it is crucially significant that highly infrequent, emotionally intense religious experiences are remembered as distinct episodes. One's episodic memories encode the specific identities of fellow participants or coevals with whom one underwent the ritual experience. The bonds uniting those who figure in each other's memories of emotionally intense, salient, formative, and revelatory experiences are inherently particularistic. They cannot be extended to others who were not there, and they cannot exclude those who were.

The situation is very different in religions such as Christianity, in which rituals are highly routinized and therefore cognized as general schemas. Not only do repetitive experiences of the liturgy become fused into an abstract formula for 'how to do the ritual' but these schemas do not specify the identities of ritual participants. The congregation kneels, prays, stands, forms a line, receives the Eucharistic Host, and so on, but 'the congregation' is construed as an abstract entity. Individual members of the congregation do not constitute a fixed set over time. As the years pass, worshippers age, their appearances change, younger members grow up, older members die, new people are born into the parish, and others depart. The particular identities of worshippers are therefore irrelevant to liturgical schemas.

In all human societies, there are aspects of daily life which are remembered as general schemas rather than as distinctive episodes. Without schema-based memories it would be impossible to conceptualize anonymous others. One's social universe would consist only of particular persons and the seemingly endless series of episodes in which they figure.

But in some societies, including most (if not all) of those in pre-contact Melanesia, schema-based memories were not generated by activities which defined the *community*. Groups were defined primarily in terms of episodic memories of particular experiences of initiation, raiding, seances, mortuary rites, and other types of sporadic ceremonial activity. In routinized religions, episodic memories may also figure centrally, for instance in people's representations of conversion experiences. Nevertheless, in Christianity and many of the indigenous churches and movements of Papua New Guinea, membership of the religious tradition is based upon presumed continuities in the behaviour of anonymous others, conceptualized in semantic memory as a set of abstract schemas. What Anderson (1983) calls an 'imagined' community is literally that, although not simply in the terms he has in mind, because members of a nation, a world religion, or any other anonymous community *must* conceptualize their bonds at least partly in terms of abstract schemas encoding 'imagined' or fictitious others.

What I have been describing are two contrasting sets of dynamics. On the one hand, we have argument-based verbal and textual codification linked to routinization and the establishment of large-scale, hierarchical, centralized, anonymous communities. On the other hand, we have climactic and revelatory ritual episodes linked to sporadic transmission, intense cohesion, localism, and particularism. Within many religions, both constellations of features interpenetrate in complex ways (this will be the subject matter of Chapter 6). What is of particular interest here is that the transmissive modality of missionary Christianity was not to be found in pre-contact Melanesia. Argument-centred, doctrinal traditions may have become established at various times and locations in Melanesian prehistory, but there is no clear evidence of this. Consequently, Christianity radically transformed not only the transmissive and experiential dimensions of Melanesian religious life but also its political implications.

As a result of this transformation, new indigenous movements began to spread, dominated by the transmissive forms of missionary Christianity. Within many such movements, the tedium effect, associated with extensive routinization, gave rise to periodic localized splintering, involving the reactivation of imagistic practices modelled on indigenous religious forms. Because these splinter groups were operating in the context of broader social movements, however, the cohesion and religious fervour which they engendered was readily projected on to the wider unity, rejuvenating support for mainstream ideology. The enduring popularity of such movements suggests that they have an ongoing role to play in the political destiny of Papua New Guinea. Not only have many such movements pioneered forms of local government and influenced national policy and constitutional reform, but many have campaigned for increasing autonomy as part of a micronationalist vision of (at least partial) secession from the state (Maloat 1970; Koimanrea and Bailoenakia 1983; Wanek 1996). From the universalistic aspirations of early missionaries and the tribal cohesion and parochialism of Melanesians has emerged the prospect of an uneasy compromise that is neither local nor truly national: too large to be based on the face-to-face community of clan or village, and too small to encompass the heterogeneous peoples of Papua New Guinea.

3

Modalities of Codification and Dissemination

This chapter explores in more detail a fundamental divergence in the way religious materials are codified in Melanesia. In new religious movements modelled on the doctrinal practices of missionary Christianity, revelations are extensively codified as doctrine. In two such movements described in this chapter, conversion occurred through the power of the Word, affording opportunities for active proselytism over large areas and the establishment of centralized ecclesiastical hierarchies. In contrast, the mode of religiosity indigenous to Melanesia does not rely on doctrinal codification. In some traditional systems of initiation, for instance, there appear to be strict taboos (backed by formidable sanctions) against the verbalization of religious revelations. Moreover, in a number of more recently established cults, operating in this mode, exegetical accounts are characteristically thin, disconnected, or simply unavailable. Even where people do tend to discuss, or make cryptic allusions to esoteric cult activity, exegetical discourse plays a supporting rather than a leading role in religious transmission and revelation.

These points, as well as the arguments of subsequent chapters, are illustrated most elaborately, although by no means exclusively, with reference to four particularly well-documented religious traditions in Papua New Guinea.

The Case Studies

One of the four case studies is the Pomio Kivung of East New Britain.[1]

This chapter reproduces, in abridged form and with only slight modification, pages 42–52 of the article 'Strong Words and Forceful Winds: Religious Experience and Political Process in Melanesia', published in *Oceania*, 65(1): 40–58 (Whitehouse 1994), and also reproduces extracts with only slight modification from the article 'Memorable Religions: Transmission, Codification, and Change in Divergent Melanesian Contexts', published in *Man* (NS), 27(4): 777–97 (Whitehouse 1992b).
    [1] See Whitehouse 1995; Trompf 1984; 1990a; 1990b; Koimanrea and Bailoenakia (1983), Tovalele (1977); Panoff (1969); and Jeudi-Ballini (1998).

Papua New Guinea

Established in the mid-1960s, this movement continues to flourish today. The Pomio Kivung is a popular Christian-syncretic movement, with millenarian, cargoist, and micronationalist characteristics. Pomio Kivung ritual is directed towards the production of a miracle, in which the ancestors are to be reincarnated in the bodies of white people, conferring upon their descendants all the wonders of Western technology and the supernatural means of endlessly renewing them. The main categories of ritual action are the presentation of offerings to the ancestors in three kinds of temple, the cultivation of moral strength through various meetings and monetary donations, and the endurance of God's punishment for original sin through abstentions and garden rituals. In this oral tradition, all ideas and practices are frequently repeated and their intricacies are widely disseminated within the community.

Another of my case studies is the Paliau Movement of Manus and its environs, extensively studied over a period of some fifty years by a series of very talented ethnographers, including Margaret Mead (1956), Theodore Schwartz (1962), Ton Otto (1992), Berit Gustafsson (1992), and Alexander Wanek (1996). As with the Pomio Kivung, followers of the Paliau Movement have always entertained a variety of cargoist and millenarian expectations. The repertoire of highly repetitive rituals adopted in pursuit of these goals is described in Pidgin as the *Nupela Pasin* (literally 'New Fashion' or 'New Way of Life'), involving a strictly co-ordinated daily schedule of worship, labour, bathing, and recreation. In these routinized conditions of transmission, characteristic also of the Pomio Kivung, the doctrines of the movement have become rigid and standardized. Moreover, both the Paliau Movement and the Pomio Kivung have several ranks of leadership responsible for maintaining the orthodoxy at a local level and for reporting back to (and receiving additional instructions from) the movement's headquarters.

It is often noted (e.g. Mead 1956: 148–61, Schwartz 1962: 225–6, Steinbauer 1979: 68) that the Paliau Movement was triggered by the many upheavals of the Second World War and was, in particular, a response to the experience of close contact with vast numbers of American soldiers who passed through Manus at the end of the Japanese occupation. Nevertheless, the inspiration behind the Paliau Movement clearly lay in the same models that were operationalized simultaneously in Yali's Movement and, later, in the Pomio Kivung—namely, the hierarchical, centralized, language-based, routinized systems of Christianity and colonial administration. In this respect, the Paliau Movement (and all others like it in Papua New Guinea) emerged out of a general, relatively long-term experience of Western institutional forms. Paliau, Yali, and Koriam (founder of the Pomio Kivung) pioneered the establishment of these imported forms among the indigenous peoples of Papua New Guinea, by setting up at different locations some of the first truly popular religious movements operating in the 'doctrinal mode'.

My two other case studies are very different, exemplifying religious life that is dominated exclusively by the more traditional 'imagistic mode'. One of these is the initiation system of the Baktaman of inner New Guinea, described most extensively by Fredrik Barth (1975; 1987), and encountered briefly in Chapter 1. Baktaman religion is essentially a fertility cult performed by men, who are gradually introduced to the secrets of the religion by means of seven successive degrees of intiation. Barth stresses the communicative aspects of initiation and describes the construction of largely non-verbal messages through ritual acts and taboos. A significant portion of Baktaman ritual is only enacted in the context of initiations, and each initiation is performed approximately once every decade. In the intervening period, at least according to Barth, very little discussion of the rites takes place, even in secret between initiates, and the cultural materials are silently stored in memory. The main ritual contexts for applying religious knowledge outside initiations are the rites of worship performed by fully initiated men in three categories of temple.

My final case study is the Taro Cult of Northern Papua, which began in 1914 and persisted in localized and sporadic outbursts until the late 1920s. Although often discussed in the literature on cargo cults (e.g. Worsley 1957: ch. 3), the Taro Cult was not concerned with obtaining Western cargo; rather, as in the Baktaman initiation cult, Taro adherents sought to promote natural fertility by supernatural means.[2] The Taro Cult resembled the Baktaman fertility cult in other respects, for both were dominated by the imagistic mode of religiosity. In the Taro Cult, verbalized doctrine and exegetical commentary were all but lacking and revelations were evoked through techniques of irregular, non-verbal transmission, based primarily on feasts and spirit possession. In both the Taro Cult and the Baktaman intitiation complex, the more ecstatic forms of ritual produced small, cohesive, bounded communities and thus highly sectarian and fragmented regional patterns of political association. This contrasts starkly with the large-scale, unified character of the Pomio Kivung and Paliau Movement.

In terms of the ideological themes of all four religious traditions, similarities are easy to find. For instance, the essence of worship in every case is to be seen in the cultivation of bonds with the transcendental realm for the purpose of securing material benefits for the living. Nevertheless, accounting for the ideological similarities and differences between religious traditions, a massively complex and important task in itself involving (among

---

[2] As the English title of the cult suggests, the principal goal was to ensure abundant crops of the staple crop, taro (an indigenous root vegetable).

other things) minute examination of the accidents and vicissitudes of history (local and international), cannot be attempted here. The task of this volume is rather different: to examine a broad divergence in the form, transmission, cognitive underpinnings, and organizational implications of modes of religiosity.

Doctrinal Revelations

Since its inception in the mid 1960s, the religious ideas of the Pomio Kivung have been extensively codified in language, specifically the orations of inspired leaders and those officials empowered to relay and reiterate authoritative doctrine to grassroots supporters. In every Pomio Kivung community, sermons are delivered on a daily basis (when offerings are removed from the communal Cemetery Temple or *Haus Matmat*), but the most extensive orations are delivered on two afternoons each week in community Meeting Houses or *Haus Kivung*. Every Pomio Kivung community (typically comprising all or most of the residents in a village settlement) has two or three offical orators (*komiti*) who speak at the twice-weekly meetings. Attendance at these meetings is obligatory for all community members, except for sick or menstruating persons.[3] Audiences are seated on benches lining the interior bark walls of the Meeting House, or on the dirt floor. Men and woman are strictly segregated. Orators may sit anywhere in the male section. During the first part of the meeting (one to two hours), the pattern of turn-taking in speeches is flexible. Orators neither speak for equal periods of time, nor do they have to observe a particular order of delivery, but each of them is required to address the congregation at some point. The second part of the meeting, however, is more formalized. Only one orator may speak during this period (the task is allocated on a rota), and the topic is restricted to one of the ten central tenets of Pomio Kivung morality (known as the *Tenpela Lo*, loosely corresponding to the Commandments of the Old Testament). These central tenets are therefore transmitted in five-week cycles.

Orations at community meetings cover all areas of Pomio Kivung cosmology, morality, and political ideology, and bind them together in complex strings of implicational logic (see Whitehouse 1995: chs. 2 and 3). For instance, speeches in the Meeting House commonly focus on breaches of morality in the community, such as squabbles among the teams of women who prepare food offerings which are then dedicated to

---

[3] Prohibitions surrounding menstruation, which are linked to a ban on betel-chewing, derive from the Pomio Kivung theory of original sin (Whitehouse 1995: 56–7).

ancestors in the Cemetery Temple. A typical sin would involve the expression of dissatisfaction over relative labour inputs, especially where one woman is accused by the others, behind her back, of being idle. This constitutes a form of character assassination (in violation of the Ten Laws) and, as such, it undermines the collective goal of Pomio Kivung members, which is to produce a miracle, entailing the return of ancestors bearing cargo. The arrival of cargo is associated with a period of temptation, in which hedonism and megalomania may be freely indulged, but the punishment for such indulgence will be eternal damnation. Only those who are able to resist these seductions of the flesh, by channelling their newfound wealth and power back into the Pomio Kivung, will merit salvation construed as a period of indefinite supernatural bliss on earth, in the company of God and the ancestors. Gossip among cooks is driven by self-centred and vindictive motives, precisely the clusters of attitudes that would lead to misuse of the anticipated cargo (and so to damnation). Only when these sorts of feelings have been eliminated or greatly reduced will the ancestors be ready to deliver the cargoist miracle, confident that the living will survive its many temptations.

Orations on the evils of gossip would necessarily take in these eschatological themes, and by a variety of routes. Another crucial factor concerns the purpose of temple offerings. The material substance of the offering is not what is consumed by the ancestors, but rather the moral sentiments of those who prepare and present it. Attention to the morality of one's behaviour is therefore far more important during the preparation of offerings than at most other times. A satisfactory offering serves to draw the living and the dead closer together, through a combination of bonds of kinship (based on mutual interest and affection expressed in the commensal meal) and of moral or spiritual unity (in which obedience to the Ten Laws excites the approval of the ancestors). The theme of moral fortitude is thus re-encountered in the context of temple ritual. The spirit of the offering (its moral rather than material substance) is received by the ancestors as evidence of the community's capacity to resist temptation. The sullied offering is evidence of the opposite, and consequently delays the miracle. Yet temple ritual adds another dimension to this process of persuading the ancestors. It seeks to consolidate *affective* bonds with the dead, through the medium of food, partly in the idiom of kinship and partly through the cultivation of moral unity. As direct recipients of the goodwill of the living, the ancestors are drawn closer ('enticed') into this world. The readiness of the living to withstand temptation is judged by the ancestors in a rather detached way, by rigorously monitoring behaviour in the community, whereas temple rituals influence the *feelings* of the ancestors by cultivating a pressing desire to reciprocate the nurturant devotion of their living kinsmen and to be reunited with them on earth. Gossip among the cooks who prepare offerings for the Cemetery Temple has to be understood in this context. Gossip renders the offerings the opposite of what they ought to be: they become embodiments of ill will rather than affection; they separate or estrange the living and the dead, rather than bringing them into a closer or more intimate relationship.

Orations at community meetings cover wide vistas of Pomio Kivung ideology. Diatribes against gossip should take in many themes, beyond those which I have glossed over. The whole religious system is integrated by a network of logical paths which orators traverse with practised skill. My point, however, is that language, or more specifically rhetorical argumentation, is the privileged medium of transmission. Pomio Kivung members understand their rituals and other religious activities in terms of a coherent, elaborate, and integrated body of ideas which is most fully represented in oratory.

In the Paliau Movement in and around Manus, as in the Pomio Kivung of East New Britain, language has always been a prominent transmissive modality. Since the establishment of the Paliau Movement immediately after the Second World War, it has possessed a strikingly elaborate, logically integrated, and coherent ideology. In the early days of the movement, Paliau's religious ideas centred on a thoroughgoing revision of Christian doctrine that came to be known as the 'Long Story of God' (Schwartz 1962: 252–8). In the mid to late 1940s, the Story was told on countless occasions by Paliau at a specially constructed meeting house in Baluan, which thenceforth became established as the headquarters of his movement. The Long Story of God began with the creation of Adam and Eve by God, and traced the history of civilization from the Fall to the life of Jesus, and ultimately to the colonization of Papua and New Guinea by government and missions bent on distorting the Long Story of God and thereby maintaining supremacy over native peoples. In conjunction with this Story, Paliau introduced a complex spirit/body dualism in which the 'spirit' component became known as *tingting* (anglicized by Schwartz as 'the *thinkthink*'): 'The *thinkthink* derives from God. It is God in each man; in this sense, all men are like Jesus, both God and man. The body is the house of the *thinkthink*. In death the body is like an uninhabited house; it is left to decay, the fate of the inanimate. The house must be a suitable receptacle for the *thinkthink*; the *thinkthink* must keep the house in good condition . . . Health and life depend on the care of the body and *thinkthink*' (Schwartz 1962: 261).

Paliau developed an elaborate set of doctrines and rituals for which the Long Story of God served as a charter. He established a highly routinized cycle of daily and weekly observances, including (as in the Pomio Kivung) regular meetings at which appointed orators were required to review and reiterate the movement's doctrines and ideas. This regime, the *Niupela Pasin*, unquestionably did offer a new way of life; it encompassed economic, political, and domestic relations, reorganizing them in the light of a coherent and logically integrated morality and religious cosmology. It did so against a background of intellectual disintegration and confusion. Prior to Paliau's programme, many aspects of missionary Christianity had been perceived as contradictory or mystifying. One of the numerous examples given by Schwartz was the sectarian antagonism prevailing among Catholic and Protestant missions which (from the native point of view) awaited a plausible explanation. Paliau's Long Story of God accounted for the differences on points of doctrine among competing missions in terms of the ignoble intention of colonists to mislead and confuse the natives, thereby maintaining the latter's subjugation (Schwartz 1962: 260). This also served to explain why missionaries were prepared to forego the luxuries of their Western homes in exchange for the relative poverty and discomforts of mission outposts. Their purpose was to safeguard white supremacy, further motivated by monetary incentives (secretly paid to missionaries by the Administration) and the threat of execution (at the hands of government forces) in the face of non-compliance (Schwartz 1962: 260–1).

In both the Paliau Movement and the Pomio Kivung, the revelatory power of logically motivated cosmology and doctrine, codified in language, was brilliantly exploited. In the Pomio Kivung, the movement's founder, Koriam, won many converts through the evident force of his arguments. Like Paliau, Koriam integrated the more plausible elements of native cosmology and mission teaching, and he dismissed as obfuscation all ideas that failed to cohere with or flatly contradicted his synchretic programme.

Such forms of proselytism are particularly effective in conditions of rapid change. In the decades after the Second World War, the peoples of Papua New Guinea were continually throwing up questions for which, in some cases, answers were most earnestly desired. Here, the intellectualist perspective on religion seems to be supported by the claims of converts themselves—that what motivated their conversion was a yearning for answers to the most pressing questions of their epoch (Whitehouse 1995: 175–82).

Nevertheless, we should not overestimate people's intellectual curiosity and the extent to which Paliau or Koriam answered questions already deemed to be important. The revelatory power of doctrinal religion also lies in its capacity to *link* the specific questions it chooses to address, and thus to attach an importance to questions that they might otherwise have lacked. To take Schwartz's example of missionary sectarianism, it need not be assumed that the Manus and Usiai had been going around distractedly scratching their heads and worrying about the significance of differences between Methodist and Catholic liturgies. But when Paliau persuasively linked this question to a series of other issues that were shrouded in mystery, there was no doubt a general sense of 'ahh . . . now I get it!'. Various bits of the picture fell into place and thereby acquired a new and far greater significance: why the missions taught spiritual equality before God, yet worked in tandem with an exploitative and dominating colonial regime; why missionaries exchanged Western comfort for ill-health and poverty in the bush; why the white man had the monopoly of 'cargo' (Western technology and power); why the behaviour of Germans, Australians, and Japanese was so markedly different from that of the generous and egalitarian Americans (one million of whom passed through Manus at the end of the Second World War). All these issues and many more besides were tied together in a logically coherent and integrated fashion, proceeding from assumptions already widely accepted (based on both personal experience and prevalent stereotypes). Thus: 'Paliau's religious teachings were by no means merely a rejection of parts of the mission doctrine. He mapped out the relations between religion and all aspects of everyday life. Again, he drew upon the ideas current in the diffuse substratum of Melanesian Christianity . . . Through a development of the concept of the *thinkthink* the religious and the secular were made coextensive' (Schwartz 1962: 261).

But plausibility and logical argumentation would not have been enough to secure the endurance of Paliau's or Koriam's programmes. For, having convinced their audiences, a necessary condition for maintaining their support was to establish clear sanctions against defection. Thus the wholesale adoption or rejection of Paliau's and Koriam's teachings, by their respective followers, was presented as a matter of life and death. For followers of Koriam, rejection of his doctrines implied eternal damnation, whereas for Paliau's supporters, the price of nonconformity was illness and premature death (either of oneself or one's young children).

Without such sanctions, the power of intellectual argument must always be tenuous, not so much because one could shrug and say 'now I know that, so what?', but because another argument of equal intellectual calibre might be presented at any time, winning converts in its turn. This is one of the weak points of doctrinal transmission, but it can also be one of the sources of its political potency, as I argue in Chapter 6. For now, let us consider the contrasting nature of indigenous modalities of codification and revelation, exemplified by initiation rites among the Baktaman of inner New Guinea and the Taro Cult of Northern Papua (see above).

Imagistic Revelations

Barth (1975; 1987) has argued that Baktaman religious understandings are not produced primarily through verbal explanation or exegesis. On the contrary, in the context of male initiation rites, religious insights seem to be constructed through the *withholding* of explanation, and primarily through the cultivation of mystery. The Baktaman system of initiation into successive grades has the effect of impressing upon the novice that what he does not know is more powerful and dangerous than what he does know. Excessive secrecy and taboo surround all sacred knowledge, and at every stage the novice is given to understand that behind the veils of deceit and partial truths lie ever-deeper mysteries. Moreover, the fully initiated men, and even the masters of initiation who know more than any other men alive, are apparently humbled by the unknowable mysteries of existence and fearful of unleashing powers that they only vaguely comprehend. The mystery, secrecy, and danger surrounding Baktaman religious life is clearly associated with the absence of casual speculation and exegetical discussion.

This state of affairs is quite unlike that in the Pomio Kivung or in the Paliau Movement. It is true that there are elements of mystery in these movements as well, but they emerge out of rather different conditions. Pomio Kivung religious knowledge, for example, is distributed more or less evenly throughout the community and exhibits a high degree of logical integration. Not only is exegesis available for every detail of ritual action, but these explanations and their logical implications are discussed at great length almost every day, whether in the formal conditions of a public meeting or the more casual contexts of amicable conversation. The experience of religious understanding tends to be focused on what one explicitly knows and can articulate, rather than on what one dimly conceptualizes, profoundly fears, and cannot express verbally. A mystery in the Pomio Kivung is something which is logically implied, but not authoritatively confirmed, whereas a Baktaman mystery is something which is authoritatively confirmed, but inaccessible and indifferent to logical constructions.

Barth himself laid particular emphasis on the distinction between what he called 'analogic' and 'digital' communication (cf. Bateson 1972: 372 sqq.). Digital processing is, of course, just a computing expression for the principle of binary opposition or polarity, central to the endlessly exploited idea (in formal lingusitics, and structuralism generally) that values derive from abitrary contrasts. In the 1970s, Barth was pulling against the tide of structuralism (e.g. 1975: 212–14), and wanted to stress the limitations of an approach that, for example in relation to animal symbolism, would want to envisage 'sets' of natural species as 'recipro-cally arranged in structures which are isomorphic with social arrange-ments or other features of reality' (1975: 189). Rather, Barth wanted to demonstrate that the symbolism of animals used in rituals was to be understood in terms of an analogic code, such that natural species 'enter individually into larger ritual contexts, each of them as a separate, more or less dense symbol carrying an aura of connotations' (1975: 189). In an analogic code, Barth argued, the meanings of symbols are not arbitrary, but derive from a resemblance between the inherent characteristics of the symbols and their referents. In other words, such codification is essen-tially iconic. A familar example of the use of an analogic code is the conventional 'stick figure' by which the human being is commonly depicted in the West. Although this affords the possibility of binary contrast (as between the stick man and the stick woman in the labelling of public conveniences!), there nevertheless remains an independent rela-tionship between the stick man and the 'real' man, based upon shared, inherent charateristics of sign and referent. Barth's argument is that Baktaman religion is predominantly cast in an analogic code, and indeed he does seem able to demonstrate, for example, that there is a link between many of the religious understandings of growth, increase, removal, and loss, and the natural characteristics of ritual images such as dew, fur, running water, and so on.

It should be emphasized, of course, that Barth has never subscribed to a facile view of Baktaman religion, which would see it as something really constructed out of the local equivalents of stick figures. What Barth seems to be saying, at least in part, is that ideas of growth and increase need to be communicated effectively in a fertility cult which is concerned with the growth of humans and taro. A useful way of conceptualizing this process happens to be the 'miracle' of dew, which appears on leaves apparently out of nowhere. The link between maturing taro, and water that 'grows' on leaves, is cast in an analogic code. The relationship between the two types of 'growth' is in some sense self-contained and can occur independently of other codifications. The Baktaman, however, have many complementary ways of conceptualizing growth, for example, through the imagery of domestic pig fat, fur, and hair. Thus, Barth writes: 'The Baktaman seem to be groping for something only diffusely understood, and the metaphors used are such as can provide a minimal cognitive grasp of it: Dew accumulates on leaves. Fat grows inside the pig and makes its skin hard and tight. Hair grows out where it is cut off. Fur covers the body, like vegetation covers the ground. All these are images that can evoke the idea of increase' (1975: 200). These sacred images, however, are not really comparable to stick figures. Each metaphor seems to trigger multiple connotations which often have a strong emotional or sensual character. The terrifying experience of being forced into the nocturnal forest at the beginning of first-degree initiation will perhaps always be associated with the metaphor of dew, which is first applied on this occasion. Each image of growth and increase will carry its own peculiar associations, and each will 'harmonize' in varying degrees with related images and connotations. Thus, the image of dew is far from being merely another way of communicating the same idea as that conveyed by pig fat, namely the idea of growth.

As I understand Barth's argument, to treat each image as simply standing for an idea would be to reduce Baktaman religious experience to the comparatively sterile medium of language. For, taken on its own, there is nothing particularly persuasive about the proposition that taro growth and dew are manifestations of a single process. When this insight is cultivated in ritual, however, it is through the contrivance of ambiguity and multivocality based around emotionally charged connotations. Many anthropologists have drawn attention to the persuasive power of this process, and to the fact that verbal statements, such as those in an exegetical commentary, could never present a substitute for the communicative functions of ritual imagery. Indeed, in the Baktaman case, Barth's analysis suggests that exegesis would undermine the persuasive power of condensation and multivocality, by simplifying, trivializing, and desacralizing the act of revelation. And it could surely add little to the experience of partial comprehension, awe, fear and, above all, mystery that Baktaman religious imagery sets out to accomplish.

As in the Baktaman initiation system, the religious revelations of the Taro Cult in Northern Papua were not codified in language. F. E. Williams, the government ethnographer who wrote extensively on the cult, despaired of obtaining a coherent account of Taro ideology, or even a set of doctrines (coherent or otherwise), and reached the conclusion that, for Taro adherents, 'theory or doctrine is wholly subordinate to action or ritual . . . those who carry out all the observances of the Taro cult with precision and confidence are often ignorant of or indifferent to its theories' (1928: 83–4). It is clear that whatever religious understandings were generated by the Taro Cult, these were rarely communicated in language and certainly not in the kind of logically integrated ideology transmitted in Pomio Kivung oratory, or in the Paliau Movement.

Williams's approach, which ought not to be judged too harshly, was to account for the absence of exegetical commentary, and of doctrinal elaboration generally, in terms of a lack of intellectual curiosity or imagination among adherents to the cult. Nevertheless, thanks largely to the detail of Williams's account, it is possible to develop a more sophisticated picture of Taro Cult imagery than Williams himself put forward. Although, as Williams fully recognized, religious understandings were not codified in language to any great extent, there is good reason to suppose that the Taro Cult generated powerful revelations through the medium of its rituals.

The principal observances of the Taro Cult were: *Kasamba*, which involved harvesting, feasting, singing, and drumming; *jipari*, which involved a kind of contagious shaking fit; a number of taboos; a range of magico-medical and fertility rituals, some of which entailed collective performances.

Large-scale *Kasamba* began with the harvesting of taro for the feast. This was undertaken by the whole community. When the guests arrived, they were received with considerable excitement and hospitality. Often, a special bandstand was used to accommodate the choir, which sang to the accompaniment of a consciously slothful drum beat. The food was presented in a distinctive fashion (Williams 1928: 39–40), connoting Western domestic habits.

Jipari, which Williams described as 'uncontrollable body movements or paroxysms' (Williams 1928: 48), resulted from possession by the spirit either of the taro or of a dead person. This kind of possession could occur at any time, although it could not usually be 'brought on' at will, and when one person was afflicted there was a tendency for those around him or her to exhibit *jipari* as well. Among the most graphic accounts of this kind of contagion are those of Chinnery (Chinnery and Haddon 1917) and Williams (1928), who observed directly instances of individual possession triggering collective shaking fits. The word *jipari* referred to a whirling or swaying motion and was used, for example, to describe the swinging of branches in a wind. Prior to the Taro Cult, Baigona men were afflicted by fits known as *dutari*, of which the archetypal symptom was trembling rather than swaying. A person who experienced *jipari* was said to have 'acquired the taro' and, having achieved this sacred condition, was obliged to forego certain kinds of foods. These taboos applied as long as the spirit remained immanent in the Taro adherent, a condition which could be instantly terminated by bathing in running water (washing in still water, however, did not have a desacralizing effect).

The Taro Cult provided techniques of treating illnesses caused by invading spirits. For example, *Kasamba* songs were sometimes performed at the house of a patient; this was held to stimulate a return of vitality, and perhaps to attract the invading spirit away from the victim. Another variety of this kind of magic, involving *Kasamba* songs, was performed in gardens, to promote the growth of taro. Certain garden rituals encouraged the onset of *jipari* so that the 'energy' produced might benefit the crop.

All the practices of the cult were expected to promote the growth of taro, but Williams had great difficulty establishing the ideological bases for these expectations. In the case of *Kasamba* songs, he concluded: 'Very often it is futile to search too deeply for a meaning, because the words of the song have been learned by rote, and so confused in the course of transmission that they have become little more than gibberish. But whatever their meaning, or lack of it, the songs are understood to contribute in some way to the growth of taro' (Williams 1928: 39).

Likewise, beyond the fact that *jipari* was understood by Taro adherents to be a form of spirit possession, Williams was unable to discern any religous significance in the specific movements of afflicted persons. For Williams, the behaviour pattern described as *jipari* was modelled on the involuntary paroxysms of 'abnormal' or 'neurotic' individuals (Williams 1928: 54), whose symptoms had no symbolic value. Mimicry of this behaviour, on the part of 'normal' individuals, was in turn attributed to a 'low standard of self-control' and 'the native's craving for excitement' (Williams 1928: 92). Had Taro adherents presented Williams with an exegetical account of the movements entailed in *jipari*, his appeals to psychiatry would no doubt have remained, but since Williams could see no cultural dimension in the manifestations of possessed behaviour, he explained the form of *jipari* exclusively in terms of the arbitrary symptoms of pathology. Yet even he would have acknowledged, I should think, that this was an attempt to explain variables in terms of a constant: for if the Baigona *dutari* and the Taro *jipari* originated in similar neurotic' conditions, then why did one entail trembling, and the other swaying? Even if a psychiatric theory could account for such specific variations, the question could remain open as to whether these two kinds of behaviour might in some way have cultivated different religious understandings.

It was mainly in his discussion of taboos and garden ritual that Williams began to develop insights into the ideas of the Taro Cult:

Pauri, the cuscus, is forbidden because of the yellowish colour of its fur, dappled with brown spots. Should the Taro man eat *Pauri* it is likely that the taro leaf will develop similar properties instead of keeping the rich green colour which is indicative of health. *Auja*, the red pandanus seed, and *sasaru*, a kind of frog, are tabooed for the same reason. It was explained that the frog, when cooked, is of a yellow-brown colour which is unwholesome not so much for the Taro man as for the taro. *Ambe*, or sago was avoided in some quarters because the roots at the butt of the palm are often exposed in a way that is not desirable for the taro tuber. *Imbaga* the crocodile, *wotomo* a kind of flat fish, and *ohiti* the eel were 'too heavy'. The idea of weight seems to be associated very commonly with sickness, and it is felt that the Taro man who ate creatures in which this quality is so obviously embodied, would be endangering his powers of healing. (Williams 1928: 45–6)

Williams regarded such taboos as evidence of a particular kind of (magical) thinking in which 'the symbolic representation of a hoped-for [or feared] result . . . is felt to assist in the realization [or prevention] of that result' (Williams 1928: 195). As such, he envisaged Orokaiva conceptions of supernatural processes as being strikingly simplistic and even banal. Stated in words, the idea that consumption of a heavy animal will produce the 'heaviness' of limbs that accompanies sickness (e.g. fever) sounds rather like a childlike fantasy, and this in fact appears to be the spirit in which Williams regarded 'magical thinking'. Moreover, his low opinion of the intellectual abilities of the Orokaiva was reinforced by his view that even such very facile explanations for specific taboos eluded many of those who observed them. The exegetical passage quoted above was prefaced by these remarks: 'In a great majority of cases the man who observes the taboo is completely ignorant of any logical basis for it . . . not only has he never heard a sensible argument in its favour, but, if taxed for such an argument, can think of none save *ad verecundiam*. But sometimes one meets a native with a spark of imagination. The explanations which he may give of the taboos are not necessarily the original ones, but notwithstanding they are typical native explanations, and at least as good as the original' (Williams 1928: 45).

At least two assumptions need to be challenged here. The first is that people who did not supply verbal interpretations of taboos had no insights into their significance. An alternative hypothesis, explored below, is that the religious ideas surrounding taboos in the Taro Cult were not amenable to expression in words, and were most effectively codified non-verbally. Secondly, and related to this, the fact that some people could be persuaded to proffer tentative exegesis was not necessarily indicative of superior powers of imagination. It could imply the very opposite, namely a failure to appreciate the multivocal character of the symbolic process, and thus a willingness to render it in a simple and rather sterile form. But perhaps the main reason why some people struggled to explain Taro Cult taboos was that, for whatever motives of their own, they desired the approbation of the enthnographer.

A more fruitful way of analysing religious knowledge in the Taro Cult might be to interpret *Kasamba, jipari*, and taboos as ways of bringing into focus rather more compelling and sophisticated mysteries than Williams recognized. Among the examples mentioned, the fur of a certain marsu-pial, the skin of a certain frog, and the butt of a certain palm, exhibit qual-ities which are undesirable in taro. Dappled fur and yellow-brown skin, however, are not merely reminiscent of a dying taro plant, but are physi-cal manifestations of 'something else' which, in the case of taro (but not in marsupials or frogs) causes sickness and death. Fur, skin, and sago palms are not physically the same as a dying taro plant, but their resem-blances indicate the immanence within them of a mystical and intangible process. Indeed, what is explicitly feared is not so much the contamina-tion of one physical material (e.g. taro leaf) by another (e.g. fur) but the contamination of one 'force', dimly conceived as the taro spirit which is immanent in the *jipari* victim as well as the crops, with a hostile and deadly force immanent in certain natural species and indicated by the presence of particular physical attributes.

This interpretation accords, not only with Williams's data on Taro ritual, but with the ways in which cosmologies are constructed in certain other traditional Melanesian religions. Here we might return briefly to Barth's (1975; 1987) work on the use of 'concrete metaphors' in Baktaman initiation rituals. Like Williams, Barth was confronted with ritual acts for which exegesis was not forthcoming, and in which concrete resemblances could be discerned between the materials used in rituals and the characteristics which were desirable in taro; an object of these rituals (as in the Taro Cult) was to promote vegetable fertility and growth. But instead of attributing to practitioners the Frazerian principle that 'like produces like' (Williams 1928: 194), Barth showed that, in seizing upon certain common properties of natural phenomena, Baktaman rituals generated sophisticated and compelling conceptions of the world, which could not in any satisfactory way be shared through the medium of language.

In this light, certain attributes of fur, skin, and palm appear not merely as correlates of vegetable decay but as separate manifestations of an underlying process which is simultaneously of crucial importance to human prosperity and yet intrinsically difficult to explain.

The specific form of *jipari* becomes intelligible as a concrete manifestation of the force (the spirit of the taro) which produces vegetable growth. Having surrendered to the spirit, the victim of possession exhibited the physical attributes of the supple, healthy plant. The limbs and trunk of the *jipari* victim swayed like the leaves and stems of the taro. Like the wind animating plants, the forces causing taro to increase in size were construed as invisible (Williams 1928: 17). Thus, like the wind, the spirit of the taro was 'seen' by its effects. The interconnectedness of these images was astutely observed by Worsley: 'Others believed that the wind brought waves of *jipari* trances, and that drumming for the south-east wind would cause the taro leaves to sway and stimulate the growth of taro. Such practices as moving the head like swaying leaves, and drumming as if in "gusts" of wind, were akin to similar ideas about the south-east harvest wind in the Milne Bay movement' (1957: 62).

A similar principle was probably operative in *dutari*, the Baigona practice which preceded the invention of *jipari* by several years. *Dutari* victims trembled or shivered instead of swaying, but these paroxysms probably had similar cosmological implications.[4] Yet *dutari* and *jipari* could not have been merely alternative ways of conceptualizing the same thing, namely the forces of growth. They each cultivated different sets of connotations. For example, *dutari* (unlike *jipari*) symptoms must have resonated strongly with experiences of sickness, especially malaria, which induces shivering fits. It is too late, however, to explore the full range of associations which these Baigona and Taro rituals are likely to have triggered in the minds of participants. Such a project would have required greater methodological rigour than Williams could afford (or than his prejudices would allow).

---

[4] For further evidence of the link between wind and prosperity in the Baigona cult, see Wetherell (1977: 190–1).

A comparable problem besets analysis of the Taro injunction against bathing in running water. It is clear enough that powers of desacralization were thought by Taro adherents to be immanent in streams and rivers. Moreover, the theme is quite common elsewhere in Papua New Guinea, for example, in the Ok region described by Barth:

The power of water as an agent of removal is widely recognized in Ok imagery. Water washes away dirt, erodes the land, streams carry away flotsam and debris. Telefolmin, Faiwolmin, and others throw dead persons (hated enemies, sorcerers, etc.) into rivers to eliminate their spirits as well as their bodies; novices exposed to sacred influences but not yet assimilated to the higher sacred positions must not wash, or step into streams. Water in which you see the reflection of a bewitching spirit is thrown over the bewitched to remove the spirit. The basic cognition is thus focused on transportation and removal, rather than laundering and purity as in Eurasian consciousness. (1987: 32)

It is not clear, however, how these images of running water, in the case of the the Taro Cult, related to other desacralizing rites (if at all), nor whether water in other contexts was seen as a vehicle for other types of forces. For example, was rain or dew thought to contain taro-nurturing powers, or was the coldness of running water associated paradoxically in people's minds with the shivering of *dutari* victims (cf. Williams 1928: 48)?

Nevertheless, it is plain that the practices of the Taro Cult were more than a childlike fantasy that 'like produces like'. They provided ways of locating, guarding, and channelling mysterious forces of life and death. The persuasiveness of this kind of cosmology has to do partly with the way specific images connote and therefore shed light on others. The reve-latory character of *dutari* may have had to do with the fact that its symp-toms resembled those of a condition deadly to humans (e.g. malaria), while simultaneously bringing to mind the trembling of a thriving taro plant. If so, then *dutari* was not what it might have seemed, a threat to human life, but the very opposite, an embodiment of life-giving force, and something therefore to be welcomed. The experience of *jipari* must in turn have resonated with these understandings by evoking a slightly different image of the wind: no longer a breeze but a gust, an invisible yet palpable force activated with renewed vigour.

The two regimes of codification which I have looked at, namely the doctrine-based ideology of the Paliau Movement and the Pomio Kivung, and the ritually transmitted revelations of the Baktaman and the Taro Cult, bring us back to Barth's distinction between 'digital' and 'analogic' communication (see above). Analogic codes are constructed around concrete relations between images and their referents which are not in the least arbitrary, as are the relations between values cast in a digital code. In the Taro Cult, the skin of a frog referred to dying taro, not because of an arbitrary contrast with another species corresponding to healthy taro, but because the patterns on the skin resembled the patterns on a sickly taro leaf. The principle of polarity is of no particular relevance in an analogic code, and if reduced to such a medium, for example, through verbal commentary and exegetical discussion, this would fail to convey the real nature and power of the analogic process. As Barth put it: 'Dichotomies and duality become powerful and interesting only within the closed worlds of digital codifications; as analogic imagery [expressed in language] they remain trite compared to the complex harmonies of which such codes are capable [when transmitted non-verbally]' (1975: 229).

Closely connected with the divergent regimes of codification described above, are two very different patterns of dissemination. The Pomio Kivung was spread over great distances by a handful of proselytizing leaders, who undertook wide-ranging patrols, addressed large audiences, and trained teams of officials to sustain the Word after they had moved on. The basic models for this process were provided by missions and colonial administrations. Likewise, Paliau spread his teachings through direct proselytism, although he initially did so by attracting potential converts to his headquarters at Baluan, rather than by holding meetings in each village before moving on.

In contrast, the Taro Cult was spread by rank and file adherents, through a process of 'contagion', for example, where a mass possession in one village induced *jipari* among visitors from another village. Each group thus affected tended to elaborate its own distinctive versions of the cult rituals. Instead of being tied to a single authoritative ideology, Taro adherents were bound to localized 'sects', the autonomy, chauvinism, and solidarity of which were emphasized in collective performances. The models for this fragmentary pattern were provided in 'traditional' religion, especially the Orokaiva initiation complex. The Baktaman initiation system, also dominated by the imagistic mode of religiosity, could not be spread by proselytizing leaders, but only through contact between whole populations. Revelations were triggered by group action, and it was thus the group rather than individual leaders who carried the burden of transmission. Partly because Baktaman religion could not be spread by heroic figures, of the Paliau or Koriam mould, it had a very different political character from the large doctrinal religions.

Dissemination in the Doctrinal Mode

In the early period of the Pomio Kivung, religious conversion was inspired directly by the persuasive oratory of the movement's founder, Michael Koriam Urekit. Some of the basic ideas of the Pomio Kivung were initially formulated in the early 1960s by a Maenge prophet, Bernard Balitape (of Kraiton village in the south-west of East New Britain), who proclaimed the imminent arrival of a new leader. In 1964, Koriam (originally from Ablingi village, West New Britain), visited the Maenge region seeking support for his candidacy in the first House of Assembly elections. His arrival was greeted as a fulfilment of Bernard's prophecy, and Koriam rapidly became associated with the cargoist doctrines already in place. Koriam was duly elected to the Pomio-Kandrian seat by a handsome majority. He was consistently re-elected to office until his death in 1978, three years after Papua New Guinea's independence.

Koriam did not merely appropriate the fruits of Bernard's visionary leadership, he brilliantly modified, extended, and systematized the ideas which Bernard had begun to crystallize. Koriam had a genius for what Lawrence called 'double-talk' (1971: 212), the capacity to frame cargoist and other religious ideas in the 'politically correct' discourse of the colonial administration. Koriam was a tireless advocate of law and order, astute investment, development, and self-government for the non-Tolai peoples of East New Britain. Yet these central messages were understood by his supporters to refer to 'deeper' religious themes. Law and order was desirable, not merely in its own right, but as a means of expediting a cargoist miracle. The massive fund assembled by Koriam's followers was to be invested in manufacturing industry, but this was understood to mean the purchasing of shares in 'companies' established by the returning ancestors. Likewise, the achievement of self-government was primarily a millenarian vision. The 'government' was said to exist already on a transcendental plane, and would be established on earth once the 'fence' separating the living and the dead was broken. Thus, the ancestors as a collectivity were referred to as the 'Ancestral Council' (Trompf 1990b: 69) or, more commonly nowadays, the 'Village Government'.

Koriam's political career enabled him to undertake wide-ranging patrols, with the approval and material support of the colonial administration. Koriam carried his new and compelling ideas beyond Maenge populations to the Sulka and Baining regions, where the cargoist undertones of his orations were also readily appreciated. Wherever support was forthcoming, Koriam appointed local 'orators' (*komiti*) to keep the ideology

alive, and he instructed them extensively in the main ritual activities of
the movement (including their nature and significance). These were
mainly based around meetings, temples, monetary donations, and sacred
gardens. Pomio Kivung activities were highly routinized, being
performed according to fixed cycles of daily, twice-weekly, fortnightly,
and monthly performances. Back at his headquarters in the Maenge
region, Koriam appointed 'supervisors' (Koimanrea and Bailoenakia
1983: 175) to undertake regular patrols on his behalf, to ensure that the
ideas of the Pomio Kivung were being correctly and uniformly sustained
throughout the movement.

Over the past thirty years, the institutions of the Pomio Kivung have
undergone strikingly little change. Although particular supporters and
leaders in the movement have come and gone, the basic ideas, organization, and practices have persisted. Since Koriam's death, religious and
political leadership has been split between Kolman Kintape Molu and
Alois Koki respectively, operating from the original headquarters. The
first generation of local orators has for the most part died out, and a new
generation, including persons baptized into the Pomio Kivung in infancy,
is gradually taking over the managerial tier. This combination of
longevity, doctrinal uniformity, and centralization, which is operative
across a vast region of East New Britain, is connected to the emphasis on
oratory, and verbalized ideology generally. Pomio Kivung revelations
were seen as emanating from a single inspired leader, disseminated by
direct proselytism and through the routinized speeches of selected dele-
gates.

A strikingly similar pattern has been evident throughout the somewhat longer history of the Paliau Movement. Like Koriam, Paliau established his movement through direct proselytism. Paliau's skills as an
orator evoked the highest admiration, not only among his converts, but
among European observers who included Mead (1956), Schwartz (1962),
Otto (1992), and Wanek (1996). Early in his career, Paliau mastered the
style of oratory known in Pidgin as *tok piksa* (anglicized by Schwartz as
'*talk picture*'), in which the phrases and images evoked carry 'dual-level
meaning' (Schwartz 1976: 188; see also Wanek 1996: 284). To some
extent, Paliau used *tok piksa* as a way of maximizing ambiguities in his
vision of the future, thus enabling him to appeal both to the magically
and pragmatically inclined. For some, Paliau was a messianic figure,
preparing his followers for a massive supernatural intervention that
would provide the Manus with European life-styles as part of a millenarian utopia. For others, Paliau's vision of the future was to be realized

only through practical efforts, aimed at establishing and developing the New Way. Schwartz in particular has argued that, on this account, there was a fairly even split between the orientations of Paliau's audiences and subsequent followers. Those who wanted to 'read into' Paliau's speeches a millenarian programme found abundant succour, but so too did those who expected only to reap what had been sown by physical toil (Schwartz 1962: 265–6; 367–8).

It is also clear that Paliau's *tok piksa* was used as a mechanism of concealment from outsiders of the movement's millenarian agenda. Throughout the history of the Paliau Movement, there has been widespread government and mission opposition to 'cargo cult' ideas, and during certain periods of colonial history the deliberate promotion of such ideas was a criminal offence (Lawrence 1971: 220). Thus, like Koriam and Yali, Paliau actively disguised the activist religious elements of his teachings through the use of eliptical and ambiguous phraseology (Schwartz 1962: 251). But, as well as protecting the movement from external criticism, Paliau's layered discourse helped to stimulate curiosity among potential converts. The new *tok piksa* only partially concealed the promise of momentous revelations, and encouraged many to attend Paliau's meetings and thereby to receive his teachings directly. Paliau appears to have exploited this curiosity quite deliberately. In his initial programme of proselytism, immediately after the Second World War, Paliau put it about that something which had been kept secret, in fact deliberately concealed by the agents of colonization, would soon be revealed. Paliau, who had already received this revelation, glossed as 'the inner meaning of the work of Jesus' (Schwartz 1962: 249), would transmit it verbally once the construction of his meeting house at Baluan had been completed.

Thus Paliau's initial strategy for the dissemination of his movement was to engage people's curiosity, partly by withholding salient details of his message and partly by casting his ideas in an ambiguous discourse. Unlike Koriam, who delivered lengthy speeches to potential converts on his vast patrols of East New Britain, Paliau initially travelled only to invite those he met to attend his meetings at Baluan. Prospective followers of the movement were thus encouraged to go to Paliau, rather than he to them, in order to receive his teachings. As waves of people came to Baluan and returned home as converts to the movement, Paliau's doctrines spread far and wide, attracting tens of thousands of supporters.

Paliau appointed as local officials some of those who came to Baluan, granting them the authority (and obligation) to relay his teachings to fellow villagers and to begin the work of establishing the New Way. Like Koriam and Yali, Paliau stressed the importance of strict adherence to his doctrines and programme. The orthodoxy was fixed by Paliau and deviation from it carried terrible supernatural sanctions (Schwartz 1962: 267). In addition, following the initial phase of proselytism at Baluan, Paliau made regular patrols to supervise personally the setting up of his programme in member villages, and to ensure that his doctrines and practices were being faithfully reproduced. As Schwartz put it, henceforth Paliau was constantly 'reviewing, drilling, and censuring' in the villages of the movement, so as to maintain the newly established orthodoxy (Schwartz 1962: 288).

In practice, Paliau's uniform, centralized regime readily took root. During the initial phase of dissemination, Paliau's speeches were heard and repeated so frequently that there was little opportunity for unconscious corruption of their content. Moreover, those who were able strove to write down Paliau's doctrines in exercise books and took these back to their villages as a point of reference (and as sacred texts). Schwartz emphasized the lack of deviation in people's accounts of what Paliau had said in these early meetings (Schwartz 1962: 252, 257). All the central elements of Paliau's teachings came to be learned by rote and recited very much like prayers or sung as hymns (Wanek 1995: 209–10, 262).

Centralization in the Paliau Movement, as in the Pomio Kivung, followed directly from the existence of a single individual as the source of revelation. From the very outset of his programme, Paliau stressed that his doctrines were incontrovertible by virtue of his messianic status (Schwartz 1962: 249, 252; Wanek 1996: 209). His direct revelation from Jesus meant that 'Paliau continued to be inspired and empowered by his appointed role as the spokesman of Jesus' (Schwartz 1962: 258). Thus, Paliau's meeting house at Baluan became the centre of the movement, the origin place and ongoing source of the movement's ideas and policies. As in the Pomio Kivung, the Paliau Movement was run at the local level by officials appointed at the centre, who relayed the leader's instructions to grassroots supporters. In the late 1980s, Wanek observed that this ecclesiastical hierarchy was still in place, with local officials being personally trained, supervised, and co-ordinated by Paliau from his headquarters (1995: 191). Paliau also rapidly established a centralized fund for the movement, collected from supporters by deputized officials at the local level.

It is clear then that the large-scale, centralized structure of both the Paliau Movement and the Pomio Kivung was linked to the style of codification in these regimes. Verbalized doctrine was eminently transportable, whether by means of patrols or by attracting potential converts to a central location. Its source was readily attributable to a single messianic leader, whose claims to incontrovertibility consolidated both uniformity and centralization within the movement. And verbalized doctrine, having been fixed, could be relayed at the local level by appointed deputies, thus establishing the beginnings of an administrative hierarchy. These political features find further reinforcement from other components of the doctrinal mode of religiosity, explored in Chapter 5. But first, let us consider the relationship between codification and patterns of spread in the imagistic mode.

Dissemination in the Imagistic Mode

In a brief but suggestive article, Barth (1990) has linked language-based codification with patterns of wide dissemination of religious materials. Barth associated this combination of features with Balinese gurus, whose verbalized, decontextualized, and logically integrated materials could be readily transported over large distances by one or a few individual operators. In Barth's terms, Paliau and Koriam would be gurus *par excellence*. Barth juxtaposed this style of codification and transmission with the practices entailed in Melanesian initiation systems, exemplified by the Baktaman case. Barth, as we have seen, associated the initiation complex with non-verbal analogic codification, transmitted through infrequent collective performances. In systems of this type, revelations emanate from group action rather than from the oratory of a single, heroic individual. Consequently, the Baktaman fertility cult was inherently difficult to spread, and in practice took the form of a highly localized tradition, radically different in many specific ways from neighbouring systems in the Mountain Ok region (which in turn radically differed from each other). The overall picture with regard to religious systems in inner New Guinea was one of extreme fragmentation (Barth 1987: 5). Barth made the point that this fragmentation was, at least in part, an outcome of the style of codification and transmission in which revelations were triggered by the collectivity rather than by a comparatively mobile guru figure. As Barth put it: 'the initiator is linked to his context, and his knowledge is untransportable except to immediately neighbouring groups, or through the movements of whole populations' (1990: 647). This point can be examined in some detail in relation to the Taro Cult, thanks to the wealth of information that Williams provided on patterns of dissemination.

People were not persuaded to join the Taro Cult by the power of the

Word. There was no corpus of doctrine to inspire conversions, and nobody was ever 'talked into' joining the cult. The first man to be visited by the spirit of the taro was Buninia. When asked by Williams to relate the experience, Buninia seemed to struggle to put it into words, eventually resorting to a sort of miming of the events (1928: 13–14). The experience of possession passed by contagion from Buninia to those in his vicinity (especially those who touched his body). Back in their own villages, or during their travels, these people in turn infected others, and so on like the spread of a virus. Those who received the spirit indirectly from Buninia had no knowledge of how the cult began and certainly no special reverence for the originator (Williams 1928: 30). In many cases of contagion through contact with a *jipari* victim, transmission was unintended. Nevertheless, having been infected, the newcomer felt he had little choice but to observe Taro rituals and taboos. The rules governing these observances were probably not communicated by word of mouth. The indigenous theory was that ritual knowledge was conferred by 'strictly private inspiration' (Williams 1928: 17), during possession or sleep. But presumably these experiences were informed by a knowledge of the taboos and rituals observed by existing Taro adherents.

The Taro Cult appeared to spread widely and rapidly, and this is the main reason why it arrested the attention of Western observers. But manifestations of this religious fervour were highly fragmented and sporadic. Williams distinguished the Taro Cult from contiguous but distinct movements at the time (1928: 68–77). He mentioned the Diroga Cult (concerned with warlike imagery), the Rainbow Cult (concerned in part with auspicious conditions for hunting), the Rooster Cult (which emphasized yams as well as taro), and the Manau Cult (which was the most remote from the Taro Cult, being focused around cargoist and Christian-syncretic themes). Moreover, within the Taro cult proper (as defined by Williams), adherents were fragmented into numerous 'sects' (1928: 66–8), many of which were named after distinctive varieties of taro. Sects differentiated themselves most prominently by adopting idiosyncratic forms of *jipari*, by decorating the skin with peculiar markings, or by concentrating their rituals on the promulgation of particular species of taro.

In addition to variant cults and sects, there were other parameters of variation, many of which were established unintentionally, but subsequently became the markers of group identity. Williams commented, for example, on the fact that, in some regions, Taro adherents propitiated spirits of the dead, rather than of the taro (1928: 30). Williams related this sort of variation to the peculiar pattern of dissemination in the cult which involved strings of contagion rather than direct contact with a single centralized authority: 'Where travel is so difficult and communication so imperfect, a new idea must spread itself principally by a succession of impacts. It will radiate from the place of origin, but those who dwell on the outskirts of the circle will have received their impulse, not directly from the centre, but from some intermediate source. Not only will the idea itself be changed by the time it reaches them, but the credit for orig- inating the idea will be bestowed on the many and various who were merely agents in its transmission' (1928: 11).

Now, this 'Chinese Whispers' explanation for the fragmentary charac- ter of the Taro Cult is unsatisfactory. The 'difficulties' of travel ought not to be exaggerated for, as Williams observed a little further on, 'the Orokaiva are great walkers and much given to visiting their distant rela- tives' (1928: 17). Much more relevant are the specific channels of dissem- ination which, in the case of the Taro Cult, were primarily 'traditional'. Contagion tended to occur along the lines of kinship, and to spread between villages on occasions when dispersed relatives were brought together, for example, at feasts and burials (Williams 1928: 18). These sorts of links did not emanate from a central group but connected communities indirectly, through strings of contact transmission.

In the case of the Pomio Kivung, on the other hand, the channels of dissemination were initially provided by the state, specifically the estab- lished routes of government patrol officers and police, which were utilized in Koriam's election campaigns. With the appointment of 'super- visors' linking outlying regions to the centre, the Pomio Kivung estab- lished the beginnings of its own state-like structure which operated independently of kinship ties. Morauta highlights a similar contrast between the centralized structure of Yali's movement and the many smaller cults of the Madang area:

The smaller cults travelled along traditional kinship links or along traditional type channels involving person-to-person relationships . . . The result was that these cults tended to occur in patches which corresponded to the clusters of villages between which there were the largest number of inter-personal ties . . . However, the majority of villages came to see and hear about Yali through his work for the Administration . . . it was largely through the camp leaders and contacts he had made during this period that he established a network of communications. (1972: 434–5)

The really interesting question, as far as this discussion is concerned, is how these different channels of dissemination were related to patterns of codification. In the case of the Pomio Kivung, there was only one authoritative earthly source of religious revelations, and that was Koriam (after his death, this role was assumed by Kolman). Pomio Kivung ideology was (and still is) predicated on the assumption that Koriam's statements were divinely inspired and therefore incontrovertible (Whitehouse 1995: 181–2). Likewise, Paliau's absolute authority on matters of doctrine was incontestable (Schwartz 1962: 258). Being a member of either of these movements meant, among other things, acknowledging the infallibility of the leader's words, whether these were consumed directly or transmitted from his headquarters by teams of officials. Either way, centralized organization, transcending all other social relations (e.g. kinship ties), was logically implied.

In the Taro Cult, by contrast, revelations were not transmitted by an individual leader, but through a process of personal inspiration. Each adherent to the cult experienced conversion as a result of 'seeing' and 'feeling' for him or herself the powers of growth, decay, health, and sickness, and the appropriate procedures for controlling them. These insights were not perceived as emanating from any one, enlightened individual or group. The crucial revelations could not in fact be adequately communicated between individuals, but could only be cultivated through the personal trauma of *jipari*, dreams, and participation in ritual. The religious significance of these experiences emerged slowly and only partially into consciousness, in a way that people could not communicate to the uninitiated, or even discuss among themselves.

This chapter has examined in detail the contrasting modalities of codification entailed in doctrinal and imagistic traditions, and argued that these are connected to divergent patterns of transmission and dissemination. Religious thought in the Pomio Kivung and the Paliau Movement, both inspired by the doctrinal models of missionary Christianity (see Chapter 2), emphasized the coherence and logical integration of orally-transmitted rhetoric and narrative, facilitating the growth of ecclesiastical hierarchies and the spread of relatively stable orthodoxies across wide areas. By contrast, Baktaman initiation and the Taro Cult were modelled on indigenous religious forms, in which revelations primarily took the form of loosely connected iconic images, resulting in more fragmentary or localized patterns of dissemination. In Chapter 5, these divergent processes of codification and transmission are shown to be linked even more profoundly to patterns of political association, via the cognitive and affective processes entailed in their reproduction.

4

Order and Disorder in Melanesian Religion

The contrasting modalities of codification and dissemination in Papua New Guinea, explored in the last chapter, raise issues at the heart of a long-standing debate about religious 'order' in Melanesia. The major differences between missionary Christianity and indigenous fertility cults bring to prominence a contrast between, on the one hand, relatively coherent, integrated, widely shared, and stable doctrinal systems and, on the other, comparatively unconnected, poorly shared, and innovative local cults. Arguably, this contrast has been obscured by a tendency for at least some anthropologists to envisage all Melanesian religions as doctrinal systems.

A comparable argument was put forward some twenty years ago by Ron Brunton (1980), in an article in *Man* entitled 'Misconstrued Order in Melanesian Religion'. Although asserting a high degree of order in the religious ideologies of Melanesia, Brunton argued that anthropologists had failed to demonstrate its existence. Moreover, there was some evidence (largely ignored in the anthropological literature) of considerable *disorder* in native cosmologies (1980: 113–14). Brunton accounted for the tendency to exaggerate the orderliness of Melanesian cosmology, and to overlook evidence for disorder, in terms of professional pressures within institutional anthropology. For a fieldworker to declare that a particular indigenous cosmology lacked coherence was to invite the charge that he or she had been unable to win the confidence of native informants, had failed to ask the right questions, or had simply lacked sufficient wit or imagination to see how various parts of the jigsaw puzzle fitted together. Thus, even if cosmological coherence was lacking, ethnographers were obliged to invent it.

Brunton's principal example of a seriously disordered Melanesian cosmology was provided by ethnography on the Kunimaipa, studied by Margaret McArthur (1971). According to McArthur, Kunimaipa discourse on the subject of spiritual agency tended to be vague, unsystematized, internally contradictory, and often unintelligible. This confusion was compounded by a common failure to specify the *type* of spirit alluded to in discussions of supernatural happenings. In such circumstances, people were continually at cross-purposes, but apparently uninterested in resolving their muddles and indifferent to the validity, accuracy, and effective communication of their own and other people's views. Brunton pointed out that McArthur's work had attracted little serious attention from Melanesianists, even in the specialist edited volume in which it was published (Hiatt and Jayawardena 1971). According to Brunton, McArthur's honesty had proven to be counterproductive professionally in so far as her work had been 'generally ignored' (Brunton 1980: 114). The implication was that, had McArthur 'played the game' by exaggerating the coherence of Kunimaipa cosmology, her work would have been taken more seriously.

Brunton argued that the extent to which Melanesian cosmologies are ordered intellectually is likely to be a function of differential patterns of political organization and competition. He wrote: 'We can expect to find a high degree of order in those parts of a religious system being used to advance a group's political interests, and where individuals can somehow be precluded from using elements from these parts in ways that might cut across the interests of the group' (Brunton 1980: 125). Where individual interests do cut across those of the group, Brunton anticipated the growth of conflicting versions of authoritative cosmology, a process tending to produce incoherence and disorder in the group's representational systems. Nevertheless, for Brunton, the most disordered cosmologies arise in conditions where neither individual nor group divisions motivate the elaboration of coherent religious ideologies (1980: 126). In the absence of political pressures to organize their theories about the world in a coherent fashion, Brunton argued that people cannot be bothered to do so; indeed they display immense tolerance for cosmological confusion, inconsistency, and incoherence.

Brunton's stance was determinedly anti-intellectualist, directed explicitly against scholars such as Peter Berger (1969), who envisaged religion as an expression of some pan-human intellectual need to form an ordered understanding of the mysteries of their cosmos. According to Brunton:

This supposed universal trait gains its existence from the fact that people who study intellectual and religious activities are the product of, and work within, a very specific type of social institution. By creating a strong nexus between intellectual production and personal rewards, and by organizing forums for the dissemination and evaluation of scholarship, the academy and theological college put a great premium on intellectual order. But for people whose ideas are not employed in the same political manner, the pressures to create an ordered world-view are less intense (1980: 113).

Thus, Brunton accounted for the elaboration of intellectual order, whether in New Guinea religion or Western academic life, in terms of political pressures to produce it, and conversely accounted for a lack of order in terms of the absence of such pressures.

Ritual and Exegesis

Brunton's article serves as an important reminder that the degree of orderliness of any religious tradition ought to be a matter for empirical investigation. The scepticism aroused by McArthur's work should be extended to portrayals of Melanesian religion as highly ordered systems and, likewise, the serious attention accorded to evidence for order should be invested also in the evaluation of evidence for disorder. Nevertheless, Brunton's argument came in for unusually heavy criticism in the corre-spondence pages of *Man*.

Bernard Juillerat noted that Brunton had illustrated his argument with reference to Alfred Gell's seminal study of a fertility ritual known as *ida*, performed in Umeda village in the West Sepik region of Papua New Guinea. According to Brunton, Gell had exaggerated the neatness with which sets of binary oppositions form part of an internally coherent and consistent model of the cultural system. Juillerat had recently conducted fieldwork not far from Umeda village, among the Yafar, who performed a variant of the *ida* ritual known as *yangis*. In his published comment on Brunton's article, Juillerat claimed that the cosmological system under-pinning the *ida/yangis* ritual complex was, in fact, probably far more ordered than Gell had been able to demonstrate. According to Juillerat, however, the logical integration and coherence of Yafar religion could only be discerned with reference to local exegesis, which Gell had been unable to collect. Among the Yafar, such exegesis was a closely guarded secret and took the form of a corpus of mythology monopolized by a handful of male elders. Through close collaboration with these elders, Juillerat claimed to have discovered a 'local theology' (1980: 732) that was 'perfectly coherent' (1980: 733) and of which *ida* or *yangis* rituals were coded enactments. Juillerat derided Gell's attempt to 'reconstitute this coherent picture by his own intellectual means', relying on 'the miraculous properties of structural analysis, performed at home' (1980: 733). According to Juillerat, the full extent of the coherence and order of Melanesian cosmologies could only be discovered by consulting indigenous ritual experts.

For instance, performances of *ida* and *yangis* conclude with the shoot ing of arrows into the sky. Gell originally interpreted this act withou reference to exegetical commentaries, by focusing on the fact that the arrows landed in the surrounding forest. According to Gell, this ritual ac paralleled the penetrative act of coitus, renewing the fertility of the surrounding flora and fauna and symbolically reproducing the social order. Juillerat argued that this interpretation, along with the rest o Gell's analysis, failed to incorporate particular sectors of indigenous reli gious knowledge concerned, for instance, with celestial objects. According to Juillerat, however, the significant feature of the ritual finale o *ida/yangis* was not where the arrows happened to land, but the fact tha they were aimed at a particular celestial target: the sun. Juillerat main tained that this discovery had been facilitated by local exegesis.

More than a decade later, some of Juillerat's ethnography[1] on the *yangis* ritual complex was published in an edited collection entitled *Shooting the Sun* (1992).[2] In this volume, Juillerat argued that *yangis* may be analysed at three levels (1992: 95). At a 'public level', it is primarily a non-verbal performance that, following structuralist analysis, can be shown to focus symbolically on the promotion of natural growth. There is, secondly, an 'exegetical level', wherein symbolic meanings are codified with greater specificity in language. Finally, there is the level of 'anthro pological or psychoanalytic interpretation' which can only procee correctly with reference to the second level. For example, exegesis reveal that, in the ritual *finale*, the 'bowmen' are directed by their 'materna uncles' not to shoot at the earth (linked with the mother's womb—the piercing of which implies incest), but at the sun, which explicitly repre sents the mother's breast. Only then, according to Juillerat, does i become possible to interpret the ritual symbolism correctly in terms o such themes as the Oedipus complex and the appropriation of the mother's feeding function.

Juillerat's psychoanalytic approach was subjected to a critique in the

---

[1] This has been enriched more recently by further descriptions of Yafar ritual and cosmology (Juillerat 1996).

[2] The following summary of *Shooting the Sun* (ed. Juillerat 1992) was first published as part of a book review in the *Journal of the Anthropological Society of Oxford* (*JASO*) 25(2): 213–17 (Whitehouse 1993b).

same volume by a number of leading Melanesianists, who pointed to the lack of evidence in Juillerat's ethnography that Yafar (or more generally Melanesian) family life engenders Oedipal episodes or other classic complexes envisaged by Freud. Marilyn Strathern (1992: 191–2), for instance, emphasized the risk of ethnocentrism inherent in Juillerat's Freudian (and more generally Western) assumptions about Yafar conceptions of 'nature' and 'culture'. Gell, meanwhile, observed that 'the representation of the mother throughout Melanesia is monotonously geared to the provision of food, not so much milk as vegetable staples' (1992: 141) rather than being an object of incestuous desire.

Arguably, another form of ethnocentricism ensuing from the Freudian interpretation of Yangis is the assumption that Yafar society is authentically 'primitive' in the sense that 'its system of collective psychical representations puts us in closer contact with . . . the primordial' (A. Green 1992: 146). In much psychoanalytic theory, of course, the terms 'primitive' and 'primordial' refer to processes that are rooted in sexual drives. Thus, the imagery engendered in the act of shooting the sun at the finale of *yangis* seems more basic or 'in closer contact with the primordial' than 'the vegetal and animal symbolizations that came before' (Green 1992: 165). For the psychoanalyst, the culturally celebrated role of *yangis* as a way of understanding and promoting natural growth, especially of sago palms, is assumed to be less primary than its sexual meanings. Juillerat's analysis of *yangis* focuses most substantially on the finale, a bias Gell attributes to our (Western) 'prejudice that makes us think that the end of a ritual (for example communion) is the most significant part' (1992: 140). Nevertheless, an obvious reason for Juillerat's special interest in the last phase of the ritual is that it entails a 'frankly human characterization' (Green 1992: 165), whereby human sexuality is divested of its obfuscating 'projections' into the surrounding flora and fauna, most apparent in the preceding symbolism.

It seems to me, however, that there is no compelling reason to privilege the sexual themes of *yangis* over those of (for example) sago growth. The cosmological ideas codified in *yangis* concern the mysterious processes whereby things sprout from the earth, and gestation in humans and animals is brought into the service of this theorizing. The assumption that the process of understanding ends with the discovery of sexual content derives from the writings of Freud, but there is little evidence for this in Yafar thought.

By contrast, Juillerat's insistence on the importance of indigenous exegesis does at least seem to direct attention to evidence of what native cosmologists themselves regard as the meanings of ritual performances. Unfortunately, it is not so simple. As already noted, the exegetical tradition relating to *yangis* is a closely guarded secret among the Yafar. In so far as this tradition, taken in conjunction with the ritual actions themselves, might form an ordered intellectual system, it may do so (at best) only for a very small number of senior men. Thus, for the overwhelming majority of ritual participants, the meanings of *yangis* must be inferred in the absence of substantial exegesis, or else be lacking in meaning altogether. This point was persuasively made by Gell in his letter to *Man*, following the publication of Brunton's article, as well as in his more recent contribution to *Shooting the Sun*. Gell was unable to obtain evidence of a secret corpus of mythology relating to the *ida* ritual, and it is possible that an exegetical tradition simply did not exist in Umeda village, in contrast with the situation among the Yafar. As Donald Tuzin has observed

it is the sad lot of some ethnographers to fall among people who are apparently devoid of exegetical insight, who exhibit an exasperating lack of curiosity or stubborn ignorance about the 'meanings' of their words and deeds. Are we to say of such people that their performances are without meaning, or merely that whatever meaning they have is inaccessible by any known interpretive procedure? In rejecting both alternatives—as, I believe, we must—we are led to conclude that exegesis is essential neither to the generation of meaning nor to its scientific determination. (1992: 254)

Unless the rituals in question are entirely meaningless for most (if not all) of the participants, they must be capable of generating meaning independently of any kind of exegetical tradition. As Gell has pointed out, exegesis (where it exists) would then be an additional body of data requiring interpretation, rather than itself a solution to the problem of interpretation (1980: 736–7; 1992: 139).

This leaves only Juillerat's first level of analysis, relating to the 'public', primarily non-verbal ritual actions themselves. Here, Juillerat favours a structuralist approach to the ethnography, presumably in recognition of the considerable empirical productivity of Gell's original analysis. Despite his criticisms, even Brunton conceded that Gell had been able to demonstrate a 'considerable degree of coherence in the *ida*' (Brunton 1980: 121), using the structuralist method. Nevertheless, both Juillerat and Brunton failed to appreciate the fact that Gell never claimed to have revealed cosmological coherence as formulated in the minds of Umeda villagers. His project was to construct a set of ordered observer's models of the culture, not an Umeda person's account of it (Gell 1980: 735–7).

This is an extremely important point because, while it is one matter to criticize anthropologists for exaggerating the orderliness of people's cosmologies, it is quite another to criticize anthropologists for producing ordered analytical models of their cosmologies. For instance, an anthropological observer may discern a highly ordered system of signs on the basis of observing a Christian wedding and proceed to write this up as a structuralist thesis on the subject. The observer's system might attach great importance to the fact that a white wedding dress is not black, even though none of the participants in the ritual had ever considered 'not black' to be a property of the bride's gown. Problems arise when structuralist anthropologists assume *a priori* that their models have psychological reality for their informants. Pascal Boyer has made a similar point, in rather stronger terms: 'structuralism assumes that the most important aspect of conceptual structure is binary opposition, as well as various complex structures, like analogy, based on the combination of several binary oppositions. Psychological research, however, has never found anything of the sort in the mental representation of concepts and categories . . . In so far as it is making claims about the "human mind", structuralism seems to be pointing to realities which elude any psychological investigation' (1993: 16–17). It is not necessary to go as far as Boyer in denying the importance of binary thought in cosmological structuration and, in fact, I shall argue below that digital codification plays a greater role in some religious traditions than in others, but the point is that we should not conflate the orderliness of anthropological models of cultural phenomena with the orderliness of informants' mental representations.

In short, Juillerat's claim that the *ida/yangis* ritual sustains a far more ordered cosmological system that even Gell's work suggested has never been convincingly demonstrated. If anything, Juillerat's subsequent publications have added weight to Brunton's original argument that anthropologists tend to exaggerate the orderliness of Melanesian religions. Firstly, Juillerat's ethnography suggests that Yafar religious knowledge is not uniformly shared. Exegesis is monopolized by a small number of ritual experts rather than being generally distributed among religious adherents. Moreover, Andrew Strathern has pointed out that Juillerat collected most of his exegetical material from two men, but that he does not explain 'what overall systematic differences, if any, emerged in their viewpoints on the system' (1992: 262). Juillerat makes plain that substantial inconsistencies arose, but it is not clear how wide the range of variation might have been among all participants' understandings (nor could it be, given Juillerat's methodology). Secondly, Juillerat's reliance on both

structuralist and Freudian interpretation prevented a more direct engagement with the conscious representations of Yafar cosmologists. Thus, the
coherence, integration, and stability of these representations over time
could not be demonstrated in Juillerat's account.

Analogic Codes

As we saw in the last chapter, a rather different line of interpretation,
developed by Barth (1975; 1987) focuses on the possibility of establishing
the range of consciously entertained semantic properties of ritual action,
in conditions where most (if not all) participants abstain from substantial
exegetical discussion. In his monograph on the Baktaman of inner New
Guinea (1975), Barth showed that Baktaman male initiation rites sustain
a somewhat fluid corpus of esoteric knowledge, transmitted through
iconic properties of sacred objects and ritual choreography. At each stage
of the initiation process, Baktaman novices are presented with particular
images of *growth*, such as dew, pork fat, hair, and fur, which have in
common the property of mysteriously increasing in volume. Dew appears
and increases overnight apparently out of thin air; fat accumulates
beneath the skin of a pig; hair and fur grow back when shaved or cut. The
properties of these objects draw the attention of novices to the mystery of
growth and increase, forces which the initiation cult is concerned with
activating in the world. Conversely, running water is an image of
decrease, because rivers are used to wash away dangerous substances,
including the corpses of slain enemies. Among the Baktaman, however,
Barth claimed that it is strictly taboo to render these understandings
verbally. Any kind of exegetical discussion of the meanings of sacred
imagery carries extreme supernatural as well as natural sanctions.

Barth argued that this modality of codification has profound implications for the organization of Baktaman cosmology. In a ritual setting, dew
and running water (for instance) are never directly contrasted as images.
They are encountered at separate times in distinct ritual contexts and
evoke relatively discrete sets of connotations. The images and connotations of dew and running water may resonate in the imaginations of initiates but these two sacred substances are not directly juxtaposed. Such a
process of juxtaposition is, according to Barth, an artefact of the analytical operations of language. As soon as we *talk* about dew and running
water as images of growth and decrease respectively, they are deprived of
their multivocal and multivalent meanings and reduced to a sterile
schematization, of the sort popularized by Lévi-Strauss and his followers,

such that 'dew is to growth as running water is to decrease'. According to Barth, Baktaman cosmology is not reducible to a structuralist formulation because each iconic image evokes a relatively discrete set of mysterious, half-understood connotations, which are simultaneously affective, sensual, and conceptual.

Curiously, none of the contributors to *Shooting the Sun* referred to Barth's insights, in spite of the fact that his work is at the roots of the history that gave rise to the volume. Brunton's original article concerned itself as much with Baktaman initiation as with the Umeda *ida*. Barth's reactions, however, were noticeably absent from the ensuing correspondence, and interested parties were obliged to await the publication of his book, *Cosmologies in the Making* (1987), for a formal critique of Juillerat's, Gell's, and Brunton's positions. Passing (but not very illuminating) reference was made in *Shooting the Sun* to Barth's puritanical line on exegesis, but the most directly relevant aspects of his work were not taken up. In spite of this, André Green's observations in *Shooting the Sun* on the multivocality of ritual symbolism in *yangis* strongly recall Barth's perspective: 'what will be said by the collective psychical representations [of deflowering, conception, pregnancy, and birth] . . . will tend to refer these various figures back to one another perpetually, stressing their analogical resonances in the imaginary' (A. Green 1992: 149).

If the multivocality of ritual symbolism is accepted, then, as Roy Wagner has observed, this presents a possible problem: 'The range of potential analogies or glosses evoked by a verbal image or trope, or by a tactile, kinetic, or visual one is indefinite, possibly infinite' (1992: 207). Wagner went on to propose ways in which the field of potential interpretations might be constrained, disallowing the extravagances of structuralist analysis. Barth's earlier solution to this problem was that the images cultivated in ritual may be cast in 'analogic codes', that is to say, in the form of clusters of concrete metaphors for focal mysteries such as natural growth, the semantic properties of which are in a state of flux, though broadly patterned across time and space. This certainly seems to be true of the way performances of *yangis* cultivate images of reproductive energy that builds up beneath earth, bark, skin, etc., to burst explosively forth as vegetation, sago, new-born infant, and so on. This does not imply such a schematization as 'ground is to bark is to skin as underworld is to sago is to foetus/womb'. Still less does it imply the priority of human gestation in these symbolic processes, as Freudians would have us believe (see above). It is mainly in the context of exegesis that such digital codes are likely to be formulated. For the general group of ritual participants, who do not verbalize their experience of *ida* and *yangis*, each sacred image of natural growth may be cognitively generated independently, creating a 'harmony of connotations' (as Barth put it) rather than a table of polarities.

Barth's concept of analogic codes constituted a valuable attempt to get to grips with the meanings of ritual imagery in Melanesia. Nevertheless, Barth's work was hampered by a very limited knowledge of the local language and by the relative brevity of his fieldwork among the Baktaman. Moreover, impressed by the similarities between his notion of analogic imagery and psychoanalytic models of condensation, displacement, primary association, and symbolization, Barth betrayed his own empiricist inclinations by speculating (like Juillerat) about various forms of unconscious processing (see Chapter 3). In many ways, this is unfortunate, because processes such as primary association might equally be understood as conscious cognitive functions, entailed for instance in diverse forms of aesthetic perception (see Crozier and Chapman 1976; Goodman 1976; Freeman and Cox 1985).

Finally, in stressing the absence of an exegetical tradition in relation to Baktaman initiation rites, Barth overstates his case. More recent studies in inner New Guinea, for instance, the doctoral research carried out by Tony Crook (1997), suggest that Barth may simply have been unaware of local exegesis. Moreover, there are other societies in Papua New Guinea with systems of initiation that certainly do sustain exegetical traditions (e.g. Poole 1982; Young 1983; Harrison 1990). This does not in any way seem to corrupt or undermine the salience of revelations triggered in ritual. In other words, the two principles of cosmological codification, the ritual and the exegetical, seem able to coexist. The explanation for this, it seems to me, is that they tend to operationalize quite distinct systems of memory.

The revelatory images constructed in Baktaman initiation rites are remembered as part of a distinctive set of actual experiences in the life history of the initiate. The image of dew, for instance, is encountered in the first stage of initiation when novices are hauled from their beds in the middle of the night in a manner that must be experienced as a violent and terrifying abduction. The first experience of being rubbed with dew is part of a traumatic experience, punctuated by unexpected physical and psychological tortures. Such experiences, which are both surprising and emotionally intense, tend to produce enduring memories, as has been documented in a large number of studies of the memories of survivors of other traumatic episodes, such as natural disasters, invasions, and holocausts (e.g. Wagenaar and Groeneweg 1990; Heuer and Reisberg 1990; Bohannon 1992). In the psychological literature, memories of this type are described as 'episodic' or 'autobiographical' (Cohen 1989: ch. 5). One remembers actual events, with varying degrees of accuracy, as opposed to general schemas of how events of a certain type usually unfold. Baktaman initiation rites are very different from highly repetitive rituals in which one encodes an abstract schema or script of how the liturgy proceeds. Baktaman rites are remembered as distinctive one-off episodes in which figure a very particular and non-repeatable set of occurrences, objects, persons, and inner states. It is this that makes the image of dew not comparable to other metaphors of growth, and impossible to reduce to a binary code in which dew is opposed to running water. Dew is understood as part of a singular experience, a desperate quest for meaning in a world dramatically and unexpectedly disrupted. Having been abducted and forcibly sequestered in the eerie nocturnal forest, novices inevitably and anxiously seek to make sense of their extraordinary experience, and the significance of being rubbed with dew thereafter will always be linked to that original episode of confusion and the emotional struggle to come to terms with it.

Melanesian fertility cults and a number of other indigenous ritual complexes appear to sustain revelatory understandings embedded in ritual episodes. Religious experience and knowledge are generated by autobiographical memories for ritual performances, pregnant with powerful feelings, sensations, and unusual images and events. What is encoded in these distinct and separate memories cannot be reduced to general abstract schemas, whether in the structuralist paradigm, from which Barth struggled to distance himself, or in the esoteric narratives which Juillerat regarded as so important for the interpretation of ritual action.

These points encourage a re-evaluation of the relationship between ritual, exegesis, and secrecy. Regardless of how elaborated and wide-spread exegesis may be in relation to a particular set of imagistic practices, the episodic memories triggered by such practices constitute somewhat immutable reference points for each religious participant, in terms of religious experience and understanding. The nature of these experiential dynamics should be accorded at least as much attention as the presence or absence of exegesis, or the varying degrees by which access to such exegesis may be socially restricted.

In practice, of course, these two dimensions are interconnected. Exegesis may enrich, guide, and in some sense 'complete' revelations triggered by experientially intense ritual episodes. But, at the same time, there is a danger that continual discussion of revelatory episodes may corrupt the multivocality of ritual imagery, as personal memories are brought into conformity with standard narrative schemas. Restricting access to exegetical discussion has the effect of insulating the intense, autobiographical quality of imagistic revelations from the 'noise' or 'interference' of everyday discourse. Viewed in this light, however, prohibitions on idle chatter about sacred cult activities amount to something rather different from what is usually meant by the term 'secrecy'.

Tony Crook (1997; n.d.) has shown that in Bolivip village (not far from Baktaman settlements), the acts and metaphoric properties of initiations are occasionally alluded to in conversations, not only among initiated men but, under certain circumstances, between respectful women and close relatives. On the face of it, such discourse appears to violate the ideal, prevalent in Bolivip, that knowledge of the details and significance of male cult activity should be concealed from the uninitiated. In an illuminating discussion of this problem, Crook (n.d) suggests that male initiation should be understood as a means of reproducing certain social and material relations rather than as an intellectual exercise for its own sake. Thus, it is not the preservation of secret information (e.g. taboos, formulae, ritual sequences) but the restriction of efficacy (in relation to social and material processes) though ritual performances that is of central importance. Expressed slightly differently, what is restricted through initiation is not information as such, but distinctive forms of experience that have relational implications. Crook's discussion of the diverse ways in which these relational implications are construed locally in Bolivip is highly instructive and persuasive. A more general point, however, may be made about the relational implications of imagistic practices.

In so far as they produce episodic memories for revelatory experiences, encoding particular co-participants, imagistic practices establish distinctively particularistic social relations. Ritual experience itself is restricted to a particular group of participants, specified in episodic memory. From one point of view, the restriction of this form of religious experience, for instance to a cohort of novices, does not require secrecy, because no matter how much a non-initiate is told about what goes on in ritual and what it 'means', this is not the same as having experienced the episode, or being part of people's memories of it. But, from another point of view, the sacredness and gravity[3] of the initiate's experiences may be threatened by

---

[3]   A common Melanesian idiom, expressing this quality, is 'weight' or 'heaviness'.

frequent, careless talk about the content and meaning of male cult activities. Although stereotypically formulated as a taboo on all flows of information about male cult activity between initiates and non-initiates, in practice what is really important is that the intensity and salience of imagistic revelations are safeguarded by restrictions on the frequency, content, affective quality, and context of socially acceptable talk.

Cosmology that is ritually transmitted in the way I have described is not highly ordered, at least by Brunton's criteria. The episodic memories of ritual participants and the associations they evoke are convergent in certain respects, but by no means necessarily uniform or stable over time. Since religious experience is shaped by the specificity of ritual episodes, each major transmissive event is enhanced rather than undermined by subtle innovations. Since the revelations generated in this way are conceptualized as separate events, they do not substantially cohere, and they are not subject to extensive logical integration.

Brunton's criteria for order seem to describe a rather different modality of codification, in which religious representations are reified and juxtaposed in narrative discourse. This modality is much more apparent within missionary Christianity and new religious movements modelled upon it than within the more ancient religious traditions of Melanesia.

Doctrinal Codification

In the last chapter, we examined some of the prominent features of codification and transmission in the Pomio Kivung and the Paliau Movement. Among these features were a high degree of ideological integration, coherence, uniformity, and stability. Thus, in terms of Brunton's criteria, these are clearly very 'ordered' religious traditions. This orderliness derives substantially from the models of missionary Christianity.

In the first place, the coherence of Koriam's and Paliau's teachings arose out of extensive use of the structuring devices of doctrinal exposition, as exemplified in Christian teaching and sermonizing. Perhaps the most frequently and widely used of these devices are rhetoric, narrative, and binary opposition.

In Christianity, religious ideation archetypally unfolds through a series of questions and answers, drawing the listener (or reader) in to the inexorable implicational logic of the teacher. This is the method of instruction demonstrated by Christ in the Gospels, and most highly developed in evangelical (including missionary) versions of Christianity. A particularly rich ethnographic account of this is presented in Susan Harding's work on American fundamental Baptists. In the following passage, Harding describes how, after lengthy interviews with a proselytizing pastor, she began to assess quite everyday situations through the lens of the Church's teachings and discursive styles:

I had been invaded by the fundamental Baptist tongue I was investigating . . . The Christian tongue locks into some kind of central, controlling, dominant place; it has gone beyond the point of invading the listener's mind to occupy the listener's identity. The Holy Spirit, the very Word of God, has come, as fundamental Baptists say, to 'indwell the heart of the believer,' who may now publicly display in speech and action a personal, which is to say, conversational, relationship with God. (Harding 1987: 169–70)

In addition to its rhetorical or dialogical character, much Christian discourse relies heavily on chronological and binary schemas. Chronology provides a fundamental organizing principle of narrated mytho-historical events and processes, such as the formation of the world and the lives of inspired or divine leaders. Binary oppositions (e.g. Heaven/Hell, Good/Evil, God/Devil, life/death, etc.) meanwhile provide conceptual frames for the interpretation of narrative discourse, sacred texts, ritual actions, and cycles. All these structuring principles are activated in the same breath, so to speak, as rhetorical arguments are illustrated by narrative examples, and successive pairs of binary oppositions conjoined in the exposition of both.

The last chapter set out in detail how these devices were employed in the establishment of the Pomio Kivung and the Paliau Movement. Although substantially reinterpreting Christianity, Koriam and Paliau stressed the implicational logic that justified each departure from missionary teaching, and that served to integrate the resulting assemblage of doctrines into a coherent theology. In both movements, local orators were trained in the arts of dialogical sermonizing and rhetoric, so that they were able to draw others into their 'conversational' relationship (see above) with God and the ancestors.

As in missionary Christianity, rhetorical discourse in the Paliau Movement and Pomio Kivung was extensively illustrated by chronological narratives. Paliau's 'Long Story of God' detailed the history of humanity while in the Pomio Kivung the very recent past figured much more prominently in stories about Koriam's life and the development of his movement. Also as in Christianity, binary logic was heavily exploited in both rhetoric and narrative with the result that, in the Paliau Movement, such diverse concepts as communism, the English language, and Lucifer formed a common family of negative values in opposition to 'custom', Pidgin, and God.

Meanwhile, we saw in the last chapter how ideological uniformity and stability in the Paliau Movement and the Pomio Kivung were secured through the borrowing of transmissive and organizational features from Christianity.[4] On the one hand, routinization, and in particular repetitive sermonizing, had the effect of minimizing the risks of unintended innovation, as religious adherents came to rote-learn the entire corpus of authoritative doctrine. And, on the other hand, the establishment of ecclesiastical hierarchies responsible for policing the orthodoxy established mechanisms for detecting and punishing non-conformity.

Thus, in terms of Brunton's criteria, the Pomio Kivung and the Paliau Movement established well ordered religious traditions. Their ideologies were, and remain highly integrated by the implicational, narrative, and digital schemas delivered through the dialogical/rhetorical discourse of the leaders and their delegated officials. The uniformity and stability of doctrine in both movements has meanwhile been safeguarded through the organizational and transmissive features of both movements. It is clear that all these features of the Paliau Movement have their origins not in any tradition indigenous to Melanesia but in the models of missionary Christianity.

There appears to be some truth in Brunton's claim that anthropologists have tended to exaggerate the orderliness of traditional Melanesian religions (see above). Expressed in this way, however, Brunton's argument might be felt to trespass on the liberal and relativistic sensibilities of most anthropologists. To maintain, for instance, that certain Melanesian religions are incoherent, inconsistent, poorly articulated, and so on, seems to amount to a denigration of indigenous intellectual activity.

Rather than pointing out that anthropologists have tended to exaggerate the orderliness of Melanesian religions, it might be more instructive to say that what anthropologists have exaggerated is the extent to which Melanesian fertility cults possess certain transmissive features found in Christianity. To write, as Juillerat does, about Yafar 'theology' and Yafar 'priests' is to present a somewhat distorted picture of the modality of transmission entailed in the *yangis* ritual complex. Alternatively expressed, the salient criticism of anthropologists is not that they tend to disguise the intellectual defects of Melanesian religions but that they tend

---

[4] This is not to say that Paliau's doctrinal system has remained unchanged throughout the history of the movement, for there have, in fact, been several major upheavals in ideology (Worsley 1996). Nevertheless, these have always been instigated from the centre, apparently on the initiative of Paliau himself. In the interstices of these upheavals, there has been remarkable uniformity and stability of dogma and practice.

implicitly to assume the superiority of Western transmissive forms. Clearly, however, it should not be necessary to dress Melanesian traditions in the clothes of doctrinal traditions in order to demonstrate their intellectual respectability.

Such a recasting of Brunton's argument does not run the risk of denigrating the intellectual output of Melanesian religions. The real challenge is to establish more precisely the transmissive processes activated in Melanesian rituals. Thus, in contrasting Melanesian and Christian traditions, my argument focuses on a positive characterization of both rather than on how the former lacks properties of intellectual order prevalent in the latter. An important starting point, I have suggested, should be the cognitive underpinnings of various forms of cosmological transmission.

The teachings of mainstream Christianity, for instance, are by and large part of the general semantic knowledge of the worshipper, established through highly repetitive transmission. What Christians know about their religion is mostly conceptualized as an abstract theology which is communicated to each new generation through a process of gradual socialization at home, at school, in Bible-reading classes, in church, and so on. As such, Christian representations can be treated as essences to be juxtaposed and revisited in myriad different discursive events. Although the absolute presuppositions of Christianity are relatively fixed in more or less similar ways across a range of churches, they are constantly and creatively revisited through the implicational logic of sermons and of Christian discourse more generally. The dynamic of doctrinal religions is thus directed towards cosmological integration through the logic of question and answer. In contrast, the dynamic of many Melanesian religious traditions is towards the production of relatively atomized but highly condensed ritual images, encoded in episodic memory, capable of moving and multivocal resonances but not of logical integration. These issues are examined in greater detail in the next chapter.

Brunton's anti-intellectualist stance, which assumes that cosmological production and elaboration are invariably driven by political forces, is also problematic. It is not clear why 'degree of elaboration' should be an index of intellectual order at all. It is, of course, perfectly possible to envisage a highly coherent, stable, and uniform religious ideology which addresses a somewhat narrow range of topics. Conversely, a relatively disconnected, unstable, and poorly shared religious tradition might be very highly elaborated.

Brunton's rejection of the intellectualist perspective was founded on dubious psychology. Cognitive activity does not come to a halt, or even necessarily slow down, in the absence of political pressures to think. Although humans may be capable of tolerating considerable vagueness and muddled thinking, and perhaps require incentives to clarify and systematize their thoughts, they are nevertheless remarkably active animals in cognitive terms. We automatically produce and update schemas for our experiences of the world as part of continuous processes of acting and remembering and for this reason, rather than because of any particular set of political conditions, we are immensely susceptible to cosmological theorizing. In other words, the effect of political processes is not to make people think, but to channel their thoughts along certain lines. Melanesian cosmologists are not less intellectually productive than anthropologists have made out. It is more accurate to say that the intellectual tools of indigenous fertility cults are very different from those of doctrinal traditions.

Nevertheless, the contrasting modalities of cosmological codification we have examined are indeed shaped by political as well as cognitive processes. It is clear that in Melanesian fertility cults, public discussion of ritual symbolism is heavily sanctioned. Anybody attempting to generate such discourse would be silenced and (in pre-colonial times, at least) most probably killed. Even in those societies where exegetical traditions are elaborated, they are passed on within tiny élites in conditions of intense secrecy. I know of no cases where they are publicly transmitted in the form of explicitly connected bodies of teachings, as in the dialogical sermonizing of missionary Christianity and the new religious movements it has inspired. Among Yafar ritual experts, for instance, even Juillerat acknowledged that 'the local theology must belong to the realm of the unspoken; to expect a full and clear description of it from the people is *fundamentally incompatible with the actual nature of this type of religion'* (1980: 732–3, Juillerat's emphasis). Conversely, what causes a genuinely *doctrinal* tradition to appear more ordered is its reliance on precisely those structuring principles that we applaud in essayist literature. The 'well argued' essay, like the persuasive sermon, is one that organizes narrative and digital schemas through a chain of transparent logical connections. Nevertheless, Brunton's point about the 'high premium' placed on intellectual order in academia needs to be refined.

Political pressures within the social sciences, far from fostering intellectual stability and coherence, encourage critical originality which in turn tends to produce intellectual fragmentation. It is hard to see in the relatively recent proliferation of postmodernist perspectives, for instance, the consolidation of intellectual coherence, consensus, or stability in social and cultural anthropology, and rather easy to identify a *penchant* for stylish obscurity resisting reasonably consistent and uniform interpretation. In short, certain schools of thought in academia may place a high premium on intellectual *disorder*, at least as Brunton used this term.

Thus, if anthropologists exaggerate the orderliness of Melanesian religions, it is neither because academics place a high premium on order, nor because certain traditional Melanesian cosmologists lack intellectual vitality. It has much more to do with the fact that Western models of religion, informed (however implicitly) by centuries of Christian transmission, are extremely hard to relinquish in the face of ritually transmitted cosmologies, reluctant to part with their secrets.

5

Cognition, Emotion, and Politics

This chapter examines in more detail the cognitive dimensions of alternative styles of codification and transmission, relating these to the social structure, cohesiveness, and the moral character of religious traditions. If a corpus of doctrine is to be sustained intact as a coherent, uniform, and stable ideological system, then there must be mechanisms for monitoring, remembering, and enforcing the orthodoxy. Paliau and Koriam introduced a variety of sanctions against non-conformity. As well as proclaiming supernatural sanctions, both Koriam and Paliau used the threat of excommunication to discourage would-be innovators (Whitehouse 1995: 89–90; Schwartz 1962: 348). Moreover, on various occasions these leaders were obliged to intervene personally to block splinter organizations within their movements (see, for instance, Schwartz 1962: 342–53). But, in addition to the threat of rival visionaries, the leaders of doctrinally based religions face the perpetual threat of unintended deviation from the orthodoxy on the part of relatively isolated populations of adherents.

Unintended deviation is largely a problem of memory failure. With all the best intentions, loyal followers are prone to misremember, forget, or unconsciously reconstruct the intricate logic of any substantial corpus of doctrine. This problem is only partially obviated by mass literacy and the dissemination of sacred texts, since even then there are abundant opportunities for unintended reinterpretation. In the largely non-literate regions of rural New Britain and partially literate Manus, constant repetition of conventional religious ideology was the principal solution to the problems of memory loss and distortion. The resulting routinization of religious life in the Paliau Movement and the Pomio Kivung in turn led to forms of cognitive processing that facilitated the emergence of universalistic

This chapter reproduces extracts with only slight modification, from pp. 53–5 of the article, 'Strong Words and Forceful Winds: Religious Experience and Political Process in Melanesia', published in *Oceania*, 65(1): 40–58 (Whitehouse 1994), and likewise from the article, 'Memorable Religions: Transmission, Codification, and Change in Divergent Melanesian Contexts', published in *Man* (NS), 27(4): 777–97 (Whitehouse 1992b).

orientations (see Chapter 2). Highly schematized forms of liturgical ritual produced, for the first time in certain regions of New Guinea, the possibility of cognizing large anonymous communities—proto-nations, if you will—in which group identity assumed a new and politically portentous form.

In contrast, the iconic imagery of the Baktaman initiation system and of the Taro Cult was not threatened by memory failure. The episodic memories engendered in sporadic ritual performances had an altogether different character in both cognitive and affective terms. These memories of religious experience and insight were not subject to decay or garbling in the same way as a body of doctrine might be. Moreover, the memories evoked by imagistic practices bound participants together in tightly cohesive groups, greatly reinforcing the particularism of local communities.

Frequency of Transmission and Memory

Pomio Kivung practices are extensively routinized (Whitehouse 1995: ch. 3). Highly schematized rituals involving the laying out of offerings in temples, the pursuit of catharsis and absolution, the release of souls from purgatory, and so forth, are continually repeated according to a fixed timetable. The most elaborate of these rituals, for example, those performed in temples, are repeated daily, while the most simple rituals tend to be less frequent (e.g. fortnightly in the case of the sacred garden ritual and monthly in the case of the collective absolution ritual). Moreover, it is not merely the technical side of Pomio Kivung ritual which is rigorously standardized through continual repetition. The exegeses of ritual, and indeed all the cosmological intricacies of Pomio Kivung religion, are likewise fixed by convention as a result of frequent repetition. Two afternoons of every week are set aside in all Pomio Kivung communities for the purpose of public meetings, which all members of the cult are expected to attend (except for sick or menstruating persons). At these meetings, three orators along with their assistants are charged with reiterating the details of Pomio Kivung religious ideology. Admittedly, they cannot cover all the ideas at every meeting or, indeed, in the course of one week, but they do cover considerable ground and probably set out almost all the religious ideas in any given five-week period. It happens to take exactly five weeks to repeat all the doctrines surrounding the ten central tenets of the movement before the cycle begins again and the tenets or 'laws' are repeated from the beginning. Since attendance at these meetings is compulsory for everyone, regardless of age, the effect is to 'drum home' every detail of the religion to the community at large. The explicit goal is to create a single, unified system of ideas within each individual mind.

Regular public meetings stand out among Pomio Kivung rituals as a principal forum for transmission; but temple rituals also provide a daily forum for public speech-making. On these occasions, group ideology is persuasively conveyed on the model of the sermon, and transmission takes place through a combination of collective rote-learning, and schema-based memorization. But whereas a church sermon is not supposed to repeat substantially another recent sermon, but rather to reinforce or illuminate in 'new' ways principles enshrined in a written text (and is not, in consequence, particularly memorable), Pomio Kivung speeches *are* the 'text', in the sense that they are constitutive of authoritative religious ideology and are required to sustain it accurately through regular repetition.

An equally high degree of routinization was apparent in the Paliau Movement. During the intitial phase of proselytism (1946–7), Paliau's teachings were endlessly reiterated and his new rituals established as part of an unremitting programme of daily repetitions. Mead has described how, in the early 1950s, the activities of every weekday were determined by a detailed and invariable timetable (1956: ch. 10). Each day began with the 'rising bell' (also known as 'the gong for washing and dressing') which acted as a cue for collective bathing sessions at the beach. About an hour later there was a 'gong for church', where Paliau's standardized liturgy would be conducted. After church, villagers formed a line and listened to an oration by one of four official orators (who took turns on a rota to address the gathering). The orations tended to focus on breaches of morality in the community, taking the form of a public harangue (Mead 1956: 221). As in the regular public meetings of the Pomio Kivung, these line-ups involved the continual reiteration of moral and other doctrinal principles. They also provided a forum for the allocation of communal tasks. After the line-up and until 4 p.m., people were permitted to go about their normal workaday business (with a break, demarcated by bell rings, between noon and 1 p.m.). Between 4 p.m. and 6 p.m., the community was at leisure, performing no productive tasks and commonly engaging in Western sports such as ball games and darts. At 6 p.m. another church service was held, repeating the standardized liturgy of morning worship. After church, there would be an 'evening council meeting' at which, once again, the moralistic discourse of the 'New Way' was reiterated by the official orators, supported by other pious souls who were moved to speak.

This emphasis on the rote-learning of doctrine through continual repetition was part of a conscious desire (also articulated in the Pomio Kivung) to establish uniform orthodoxy throughout the movement. Moreover, Wanek (1996) has described how, in recent years, many of Paliau's doctrines have been made into songs and disseminated on cassette as part of a deliberate tactic to foster rote-learning of the movement's ideology.

Schwartz summed up the general ethos of Paliau's routinized regime as follows (1962: 285):

Under the leadership of their *teachers*, they were taught to march and drill. They were taught to order their lives according to a routine that coordinated the activities of the whole village. This routine was derived from such models as the plantation, the *kiap*'s patrol, and the army camp. To the signal of the village gong . . . they all left their houses together in the morning, bathed together, and went to church together and to the line-up to be assigned their part in village work. Noon and afternoon bells signaled the end of work, the time to bathe again, to eat, and to attend church. Finally, after a curfew at about nine o'clock, they remained in their houses. Daily meetings preceded by singing and marching were filled with endless reiterations of the new 'laws', the vices of the past, and the virtues of the *Newfela Fashion*. The emphasis was on virtual simultaneity. There was an attempt to perform each activity in unison.

Wanek, describing routinized practices in the Paliau Movement as recently as the late 1980s, painted a strikingly similar picture. In the village of Chipeul, on the remote island of Nauna, people rose to the clanging of a gong at 6 a.m. and were then instructed by further strikes at 6.15 a.m. to bathe in the reef, and at 6.30 a.m. to eat breakfast (Wanek 1996: 257–8). Wanek went on to describe in some detail the unremitting round of line-ups and church services at which Paliau's doctrines were still broadcast, endlessly reiterating what all members of these congregations had known for years, and possibly from early childhood (Wanek 1996: 261). Just as Mead described for Manus some thirty years before, communal tasks in 1980s Chipeul were still allocated at the daily line-ups and Wanek estimated that young people devoted about twenty per cent of their working time to the performance of these communal tasks (1996: 258). Moreover, leisure time (as in the past) was still given over to 'social activities such as soccer, picnics, feasts, dancing, and sports' (Wanek 1996: 259). Thus, the continuity of these highly routinized practices has been striking.

Religious transmission in the context of Baktaman initiation and the Taro Cult, occurred through very much longer cycles. In contrast with the daily liturgies of Paliau's and Koriam's followers, Baktaman initiation rites were performed only about once every eight to ten years.

Opportunities for witnessing the rites of neighbouring communities during the long periods separating one's own performances were somewhat limited. Moreover, the crucial revelatory experiences engendered in each of the seven successive degrees of intiation were encountered once only in the role of novice. The details of religious imagery and practice had to be remembered in the absence of frequent ritual episodes. Since this sort of knowledge was considered dangerous to discuss to any great extent,[1] the system imposed considerable burdens on memory. We shall see, however, that Baktaman initiation was the outcome of an evolved structure of ritual communication that was peculiarly adapted to infrequent transmission, in which memory failure was minimal and innovation did not necessarily present a threat to the reproduction of the religious tradition as a whole.

A similar pattern of periodic transmission was evident in the Taro Cult. Communities that underwent collective possession (*jipari*) tended to do so as a one-off experience (albeit extended in many cases over days or weeks). There was a deliberate avoidance of repetition of the *jipari* experience on the part of adherents, in spite of the fact that the experience was welcomed and highly valued as a source of revelation. Chinnery, for example, in commenting on the sporadic pattern of *jipari* outbursts, observed that cultists were reluctant to perform the *Kava Keva*[2] too frequently, and refused all requests to repeat the experience while it was less than a month since the last attack of *jipari* (Chinnery and Haddon 1917: 451; see also Williams 1928: 33; 55–6).

The Taro Cult is probably best understood as part of a historically entrenched mode of religiosity, that finds overt expression only every few years or so—roughly the same frequency that we find in Baktaman initiation rites or, for that matter, in the initiation rites of the Orokaiva themselves (see Chapter 1). Thus, the Baigona Cult, which preceded the Taro Cult by just a few years (and which, as indicated in the last chapter, evoked related imagery), would be seen as part of the same religious tradition. Unfortunately, this is a tradition that has only been documented over a relatively short time period. Nevertheless, it is possible to put together a clear and plausible picture of the cognitive dynamics of sporadic transmission in this mode of religiosity, and likewise of routinized transmission in the doctrinal regimes of Paliau and Koriam.

---

[1] See, however, my discussion of Crook's (1997; n.d.) work (Chapter 4).

[2] *Kava Keva* was the original name for the Taro Cult, but rapidly fell out of use (Williams 1928: 4).

The extreme routinization of Pomio Kivung practices and those of the Paliau Movement was clearly related to the demands placed on memory by a doctrinal mode of operation. A high degree of standardization of elaborate and logically integrated ideology was only possible, in largely non-literate conditions, because of the frequency of repetition. It would be quite impossible to maintain an oral tradition of this kind according to the schedule of Baktaman initiation rites. If, for example, a significant proportion of Pomio Kivung rituals and ideas were communicated only once every decade or so, then each performance would require elaborate preparation with reference to recorded materials. Even an undergraduate student, who may be under considerable pressure to memorize the contents of lectures and who revises over an extended period, employing written records and a battery of mnemonic devices to maximize recall, is nevertheless liable to forget a very considerable proportion of this material over a subsequent ten-year period of non-academic employment. To ask somebody to reconstruct even the most basic elements of Pomio Kivung religion after a single experience of exposure a decade ago would be equivalent to asking an ex-student to repeat a lecture from memory ten years after graduating.

But my argument goes further than this. I would anticipate strong correlations between analogic communication and irregular reproduction, and between exegetical codification and frequent repetition. A plausible mechanism for the production of these correlations is at hand, and at the heart of this mechanism are the differential demands placed on memory in doctrinal and imagistic modes of religiosity.

At first glance, it may seem that the issue of memory is only relevant if one presupposes a uniform ideological emphasis on continuity in religious transmission. In the absence of this apparently ideological requirement, memory would seem to have little bearing on the matter. I do of course recognize the ideological importance that both Pomio Kivung and Baktaman traditions, for instance, attach to the accurate reproduction of religious institutions at each performance. This does indeed seem to introduce an element of inflexibility, opposing innovation and making legitimate religious expression contingent upon accurate recollection. But this is really only part of the story. One cannot say that ideological complexity, for example, is ruled out in Baktaman religion, merely because of the emphasis on continuity based on faithful recall—the argument being that too much ideology is too hard to remember accurately over a ten-year period. In many ways, a much more important factor relates to the subjective experience of the validity of religious understandings.

Although complex ideology could not be accurately reproduced once every decade in an oral tradition, it could conceivably be invented or recreated in a profoundly modified form at each, rare performance. But in a hypothetical system of this type, which does not emphasize continuity, it is hard to imagine how the authority of religious ideas could be generated or upheld. This is not a question about ideology itself—it is obvious that a spontaneously invented system of religious thought is no less capable than any other of invoking transcendental legitimation. Nor is it a question of what drives the innovator to make pronouncements, although it may indeed be unrealistic to hope that every decade some charismatic prophet will step forth to achieve feats of intellectual creativity sufficient to compare with the ideological intricacies of Paliau's 'New Way'. Even that, however, is not beyond the bounds of possibility. What is really hard to envisage is how such experiences of ideological transmission might sustain any sort of religious life through the long years that separate performances. In a pattern of very infrequent reproduction, systems of logical relations will fade into virtual meaninglessness before some replacement is constructed. This would imply an oscillation between intense intellectual religiosity and a sort of expanding secular void, or at least a predominant experience of religion as a set of vague and rather dull ideas—much as an ageing alumnus remembers his university courses. Such a system could scarcely be called a religion at all, and certainly it is hard to think of an ethnographic case which comes close to it.

The reason why analogic communication is so well adapted to Baktaman conditions of infrequent reproduction is that the messages which are transmitted are not concerned with something so dull and forgettable as the logical implications of ideas, but with the intense experience of mortal danger, mystery, pain, and other extreme or abnormal sensory stimuli. All these elements are agonizingly cultivated in Baktaman initiation, and they haunt the initiate through life by forming a complex harmony of associations with the objects and processes of everyday experience. Barth vividly describes, for example, how the otherwise 'dull business' of taro cultivation is transformed into 'something of meaning and value' through the remembrance of initiations and the powerful images, emotions, sensations, and other associations that they evoke (1975: 236).

If it is accepted, therefore, that analogic communication is an adaptation to the excessive demands placed on memory in an oral tradition which is very infrequently reproduced, then I suggest that the converse is also true: that the systematic, logically integrated character of Paliau's and Koriam's institutions is an adaptation to conditions of frequent reproduction. A religion which transmits its messages through continual repetition is unlikely to rely primarily on analogic communication. In order to understand why this is so, it is first necessary to appreciate that the emotive quality of imagistic practices, and what makes each concrete metaphor different from another, is the uniqueness of the original set of associations between signs and their referents.

In Baktaman religion, hair is not different from fur as a symbol of growth simply because hair is hair, and fur is fur. Nor, to refer to an old joke, is the difference between hair and fur the fact that they are spelt differently. Barth is emphatic that hair and fur are not alternative metaphors for the same thing, namely growth. In fact, the first set of ritual associations with hair, as these are cultivated among novices during fourth-degree initiation, relate to male sexuality and potency. In the course of fourth-degree rituals, shredded pandanus leaves are tightly bound to the hair of novices to create pigtails arranged to suggest strongly the act of coitus. Besides the phallic symbolism of pandanus and hornbill, which are both used in the head decorations, other images of male potency are employed. The faces of the novices are extensively stung with nettles and they are forced to dance for several days and nights before the women, during which time they are deprived of sufficient sleep, food, and water. The extreme sensations evoked by these rituals provide unique and powerful associations with hair and sexuality. The heat and swelling of the face, the exertion and intense craving for physical satisfactions—all these unique experiences come together in the original appreciation of hair as a sacred image. In subsequent initiations, a deeper understanding of hair is provided and the significance of fur is introduced as a complementary but different way of conceptualizing the process of increase and growth. But hair could never be the same thing as fur after the experience of fourth-degree initiation, and fur could never adequately replace it as a sacred iconic image.

Barth has long taken the view that culture change among the Baktaman is 'largely unacknowledged' (1975: 240). According to this view, initiation rituals are unconsciously changed at each performance as a result of memory failure and the fact that only a very small number of experts are responsible for remembering the details of rituals. The minds of Baktaman cosmologists are thus likened to 'melting pots' (e.g. Barth 1987: 29), in which cultural materials are unwittingly remoulded. The title of Barth's book, *Cosmologies in the Making*, echoes the point.

So far as I am aware, Barth has never published any direct evidence of unconscious memory failure among the Baktaman, and there is perhaps a risk of exaggerating the extent of unacknowledged innovation. Studies by psychologists of long-term memory retention suggest that memories tend to evaporate rather than melt (see Cohen 1989: 156–9), and that such innovation as occurs may be primarily a function of the procedures of recall. Neisser (1988) has described the optimal conditions for accurate remembering, and these happen to correspond quite closely to the procedures used in the planning of Baktaman initiations (Barth 1987: 26), where ritual experts adopt the technique of 'free recall' at leisure and are explicitly guided by a concern with 'verity', apparently in the absence of motives which might produce distortions (cf. Neisser 1988). It should also be reiterated that the materials concerned are, by their very nature, memorable. Ritual experts are not required to recollect a great volume of verbal exegesis or mythology, but rather a limited number of graphic actions, rendered all the more vivid by their association with powerful emotions and sensations.

Thus, unacknowledged innovation may well be the exception rather than the rule and, in the absence of empirical evidence, certainly cannot be invoked to explain the gradual and piecemeal character of culture change among the Baktaman. Barth, however, also advances a theory of incremental change in relation to documented instances of deliberate or conscious innovation in Baktaman rituals. In this context, the argument turns on a concept of 'blocking' rather than 'melting', as I shall explain.

Of the nine cases of *conscious* innovation in Baktaman ritual which Barth collected (1975: 239–40), three concerned the symbolism of wild pig. Traditionally, it would seem that the Baktaman have been reluctant to make use of the image of wild pig in fertility ritual, because the boars in particular are notorious for ravaging crops and are thus, as Barth puts it, construed 'as primarily an anti-taro and anti-gardening force, an enemy and rival to Baktaman male success' (1975: 241). For this reason, it had long been expressly forbidden to bring the meat or bones of wild boars into the *Yolam* temple. Nevertheless, Barth cites an occasion in the 1950s (already mentioned in Chapter 1) when a group of warriors, initiated merely to third degree, undertook a successful raid while carrying with them the mandible of a wild boar which had recently been killed in the act of copulation. Following this incident, the mandible was incorporated into the *Yolam* sacra, where it was still to be found some fifteen years later, at the time of Barth's fieldwork.

It would no doubt be interesting to discover why this instance of innovation was successful, and why a comparatively large proportion of innovations generally seemed to focus on wild pig. Barth's explanation begins with the fact that the attitude towards wild boar in everyday life is somewhat ambivalent. Whilst this beast is undoubtedly a villain, its meat has a high value, and domestic sows depend upon the wild boar for impregnation (1975: 201). Thus, the wild boar could quite convincingly serve as a vehicle for ideas about male virility and aggressiveness (1975: 241). In this light, the introduction of the mandible to *Yolam* sacra becomes intelligible. Barth, however, seems to regard the ambiguity of wild pig as something approaching an explanation for the tendency to focus on the symbolic potential of the animal in ritual innovation. Thus, Barth formulates the general rule that 'elaborations . . . occur where problems and discrepancies are felt and *require* a resolution' (1975: 244). This argument raises problems in view of Barth's foregoing demonstration that the Baktaman go out of their way to cultivate discrepancies and ambiguities in many areas of their ritual life. A good example would be the failure to use the most symbolically 'fitting' marsupial for the sixth-degree initation in place of the much less suitable species of marsupial which is actually used (1975: 185–6). As Barth subsequently puts it: 'messages are often made increasingly cryptic in the service of mystery by the veiling of insight behind layers of symbol substitition' (1975: 189). It would be facile, however, to see this as a straightforward contradiction. Barth clearly envisages Baktaman religious experts as being pulled in opposing directions. On the one hand, they are concerned with clarifying cosmological themes, and on the other hand, their task is to cultivate a mystery. Thus, the temptation to innovate in pursuit of clarity may be counterbalanced by the need to confuse, a need which Barth associates generally with the 'blocking . . . [of] interpretive elaboration' (1975: 244).

In my view, the tension between clarification and mystification, which expresses itself in 'blocking', cannot be used to explain the gradual or incremental character of culture change among the Baktaman, because 'blocking' and gradual change constitute two aspects of the same 'thing' for which a suitable explanation is required. I have shown that the problem is not resolved or clarified by the idea of unintended memory failure. Rather, the impact of memory on culture change is, I believe, largely indirect. I have attempted to demonstrate that it is due to a combination of the strengths and weaknesses of human memory that a religious tradition so infrequently transmitted as that of the Baktaman is cast in an analogic code. Now, where this principle of codification is used, culture change is likely to be piecemeal, as Barth has intuited. But I would argue that this pattern of gradual or incremental change is not to be readily explained in terms of ideas about melting pots, clarification, mystification, or blocking. What it comes down to is the fact that all the kinds of innovation that Barth has documented tend to have very limited ideological ramifications. Since the relationship between image and referent is somewhat self-contained in an analogic code, interference in any particular metaphoric process has only minimal consequences for the religious tradition as a whole (cf. Barth 1975: 210–12). In particular, the lack of logical integration serves to isolate innovations and protect the continuity of the religion as a whole. Consider, once again, the introduction of a wild boar mandible to the *Yolam* sacra. Barth categorically states that this instance of creative elaboration occurred: 'without changing the basic rule banning all other . . . boar meat or bones from the temple. The various codifications of . . . boar have still not been brought into harmony, nor its connotations as a concrete symbol clarified' (1975: 241).

Likewise, the experience of revelation among Taro adherents was intrinsically very memorable, because the analogic links between *jipari* and vegetable growth, or between taboo species and taro diseases, were startling and simple. The complex harmonies between metaphors in this religious system may not all have been reproduced in subsequent cults, but this does not detract from the potency of individual revelations, nor change the underlying experience of gaining control over life and death, however these mysterious forces were conceived by different individuals at different times, or patterned among variant cults and sects. In these general circumstances, there was no necessity for continuous, routinized transmission and, on the contrary, some pressure to adopt a regime of infrequent transmission.

This pressure had to do with the fact that analogic insights are most compelling and memorable if they are cultivated in conditions of extreme emotional and sensual stimulation. Whether this stimulation is ecstatic or traumatic, its long-term capacity to haunt people's minds is related to the uniqueness of the experience. If people strive to recapture that intensity by reconstructing the conditions of its original occurrence time and again, the power of the experience is rapidly diminished.

The experience of *jipari* was emotionally very intense and left participants feeling 'strained and drowsy for hours afterwards' (Chinnery and Haddon 1917: 450). In some areas, *jipari* entailed a degree of violence, ranging from 'vigorous rubbing and slapping' (Chinnery and Haddon 1917: 450) to the self-infliction of injuries by 'rushing aimlessly through the bush, careless of roots and trailers' (Williams 1928: 67). The general feeling among Taro adherents appears to have been that the sufferings entailed in *jipari* could not be endured very often. In order to protect themselves from further attacks (until the state was induced again through contagion), many *jipari* victims washed in running water. Intense psychological stimulation in the Taro Cult was not confined to the traumatic experience of possession. Williams laid great stress on the emotion and general 'high excitement' (1928: 43–5) which accompanied *Kasamba*.

The transmission of imagistic practices depends upon the unique and intense quality of ritual experience. It is not conducive to the cultivation of such messages to repeat them very often. Repetition deprives the experience of its uniqueness. Meanwhile, the intensity is largely generated by suffering which nobody would be anxious to repeat and which, if it were repeated, would not yield up its original fruits of revelation. In conditions of regular reproduction, the essence of religious understanding—the experience of revelation—has to be cultivated by some other means. The obvious and most accessible means is logical persuasion, the construction of an intellectual system of absolute presuppositions that are interwoven by the logic of question and answer. Such is the essential character of the doctrinal mode of religiosity.

In an oral tradition, persuasion by the logic and coherence of cosmology and ritual at the same time necessitates frequent repetition. That is to say, the two features are mutually reinforcing. As I have pointed out, logical structures become disconnected if they are not regularly contemplated, and their persuasive capacities are in no small degree a function of the extent to which they can be preserved as an entirety through frequent transmission. Thus, all areas of the institutional system must be continually reproduced, in order to preserve the logical integrity and comprehensiveness of the religion, through which its potential to reveal and persuade is realized.

These issues are raised by the different mixtures of statement and action in doctrinal and imagistic modes of religiosity. Clearly, although Pomio Kivung religious knowledge is for the most part capable of being transmitted verbally, as logically connected doctrines, this does not imply that exegesis could be substituted for ritual performance. The Pomio Kivung is not just about knowing, but also *doing*. The standard exegetical commentary on the presentation of offerings in Pomio Kivung temples has to do with bringing about the miracle of returning ancestors, but simply 'knowing' this meaning is no substitute for going through the actions. In this respect, Pomio Kivung rituals are like productive technical procedures, and explicitly likened to them by participants. It goes without saying that the statement 'I am felling a tree' is no substitute for the act itself. But whereas the felling of a tree does not require any verbal commentary in order to communicate the meaning of the act, Pomio Kivung ritual undoubtedly does. The attempt to expedite a miracle could not possibly be inferred from observing non-verbal behaviour. Thus, so far as the native appreciation of religious insights is concerned, the most important communicative capacities of Pomio Kivung ritual action largely result from, and correspond to the standard verbal commentaries available.

To varying degrees, Pomio Kivung members undoubtedly engage in some intellectual speculation, and experience certain emotions and sensations in relation to rituals, so there is bound to be some variation in the subjective appreciation of the meanings of rituals. But my impression is that these variable responses are of much less importance in the construction of Pomio Kivung religious knowledge than they are in the context of Baktaman initiations. A range of associations are probably evoked by the images of Western culture in Pomio Kivung ritual, but these sorts of connotations are under-exploited due to the continual repetition of rituals. For example, placing flowers on tables in the temples may originally have connoted Australian domestic habits, but when these flowers are daily arranged in the temples, year in and year out, they come to be taken for granted. Thus, potentially diverse metaphors and connotations are not in fact exploited, and the individual's appreciation of religious knowledge tends to converge on the standardized interpretations, that are endlessly articulated at Pomio Kivung meetings.

This suggests another way of expressing the contrast between doctrinal and imagistic modes of religiosity. Just as Pomio Kivung rituals ought to produce a miracle, so Baktaman rituals are supposed to 'do' something of material and practical value: above all, to promote the growth of humans and taro. But in one respect, Baktaman rituals are slightly more like the productive, technical act of felling a tree, because novices receive messages about growth and increase, for example, without extensive verbal guidance. Thus, ritual symbolism conveys religious understandings in the way that felling trees, under certain conditions, communicates the intention of clearing a garden. Whereas, in the Pomio Kivung the most important things which rituals 'say' cannot be successfully communicated without words, in Baktaman rituals the most persuasive aspects of religious statements can only be conveyed by the actions themselves. The result, for the Baktaman, is a low level of uniformity in individual interpretations of symbols. In such conditions, exegetical commentary becomes more or less redundant and, even if it were elaborated, it would fail to represent the variety of religious understandings which the imagery is able to evoke in different individuals. The infrequency of ritual performances, and the cultivation of emotions and sensations at the moment of first exposure to sacred images, produces an ongoing sense of revelation as connotations with sacred images are evoked in the everyday experiences of life. 'Doing' and 'saying' in such rituals are so deeply interconnected that one can never definitively say what one has done, or express the resulting knowledge as a body of doctrines.

Memory and Political Association

In the doctrinal mode of religiosity, routinization is associated with a distinctive style of cognition, specifically, schema-based memory for repetitive observances. Here, I shall focus on the relationship between this sort of remembering and the universalistic orientation of Paliau's and Koriam's movements. At the same time, however, routinization may be associated with a low level of excitement in religious activity, celebrated in the virtues of parsimony, endurance, and strict discipline. Such movements, although large-scale and universalistic, generate somewhat diffuse cohesion centred on the sharing of relatively humdrum, repetitive practices. They do not tend to sustain the sort of high excitement and religious fervour that underpins the intense solidarity of local congregations engaged in imagistic practices.

The experiential quality of imagistic rites is founded on extreme sensual and emotional stimulation, or what are sometimes called 'ecstatic' states (e.g. Lewis 1971). This may be achieved in pleasurable ways, through feasting, erotic excitation, singing, dancing, and so on, or in terrifying, horrifying, or agonizing experiences, for example, though ritualized murder, mutilation, physical deprivation, and the like (see Chapter 1). Most commonly, imagistic practices utilize a combination of these elements, juxtaposing and sometimes combining experiences of intense pleasure and pain. These sorts of activities are cognized very differently from routinized practices. In contrast with the schema-based representations of the doctrinal mode, imagistic practices generate enduring autobiographical (or 'episodic') memories of unique episodes. These haunting memories serve to bind together members of local religious communities, whose common revelatory experience evokes intense and lasting solidarity of a sort that cannot be verbally articulated.

The cognitive dimensions of routinized religion can be grasped to some extent in terms of the notion of 'semantic memory'. Tulving (1972) argued that there are two relatively distinct memory systems: the one ('semantic memory') concerned with abstract knowledge of the world, encoded in generalized schemas; the other ('episodic memory') concerned with actual occurrences in a person's experience, in which the time and place of encoding form part of the representation in memory.

Thus, for example, if you ask an anthropologist to compare and contrast Malinowski's and Radcliffe-Brown's brands of 'functionalism', you are attempting to elicit semantic knowledge. The anthropologist will probably not recall where or when various bits of this knowledge were acquired, and will be assembling elements of related schemas that have become familiar through a cumulative process of transmission and contemplation. The same is true of the sermonizing that took place in the endless rounds of village meetings within the Paliau Movement and the Pomio Kivung. Official orators in both movements constantly reiterated schematized 'chunks' of doctrine, weaving them together by means of a fixed network of logical connections, accessed in different sectors according to the demands of any given situation. Thus, for instance, a brawl in any Pomio Kivung village would trigger extensive sermonizing on Koriam's Fifth Law (a variant of the Commandment 'Thou Shalt not Kill'), on the impossibility of collective salvation while the living remain sinful, on the horrors of damnation, and so on. In the Paliau Movement, the same crime would give rise to pious speeches about the necessity to 'straighten' one's *tingting*, the importance of 'hearing the talk', and the 'laws' against provocation and quarrelling (e.g. Schwartz 1962: 264).

Likewise, followers of Paliau and Koriam did not, on the whole, recall their ritual activities as singular events, located in time and space, but as general schemas for 'how to do' such-and-such a ritual. Consider, for example, the daily presentation of offerings in the Cemetery Temple of any Pomio Kivung village (Whitehouse 1995: 66–74). Anyone could tell you the sequence of actions that together constitute a correct performance. Food has to be collected and prepared by a female task force (operating on a rota system). At 2.30 p.m., the village gong must be struck, in response to which a male task force must carry food offerings to the Cemetery Temple and present them, along with monetary offerings, in carefully specified ways. The ancestors must be addressed by a particular male official, who then leaves the temple. A male 'witness' must then enter the Temple and take up a vigil until the gong is sounded again. The community then gathers outside the Temple and any sounds heard by the witness are described to the assembled throng by a male 'orator', who offers standard interpretations as part of a familiar moral discourse. After reciting a version of the Lord's Prayer, the congregation eats the food in a stipulated fashion. These are the bare outlines of the ritual and, in practice, it involves many more detailed schemas. But because the ritual is repeated day in and day out, month after month, and year after year, it is rarely possible to remember any but the most recent performances as concrete episodes located at a particular place and time.

In practice, then, the followers of highly routinized movements tend to encode their ritual activities as general schemas ('we do this, and then we do that') as opposed to actually remembered episodes. It is not merely the units of action that become abstracted in this way but also the *actors* themselves. This is a crucial point, if we are to grasp the relationship between cognition and political ethos in the doctrinal mode of religiosity.

When members of the Pomio Kivung describe the scripted actions that together constitute the 'Cemetery Temple ritual', they do not conjure up images of particular actors ('Tom the orator', 'Harry the witness', etc.) but of shadowy, anonymous figures, like faces in a crowd. In fact, if you ask people 'who were you thinking of when you described what an orator does in such-and-such a ritual?', a common answer is 'nobody' (followed, on reflection, by names of people who could fulfil such a role on any given occasion). It would be the same if somebody asked us to describe some element of British parliamentary procedure. We might describe, for instance, how the Speaker's attention is attracted but without having a specific MP in mind (when pressed, of course, we could then furnish names of possible specific antagonists in the scenario we have described).

This point might seem trivial to us in a world where anonymous faces constantly impinge on our experience. But in a New Guinea village, where the sight of an unfamiliar face is a rare event indeed, the establishment of ritual forms in which social actors are cast as anonymous, non-specific beings involves a radical shift in identity-formation. And this shift lies at the roots of the universalistic orientations that crystallized for the first time in Paliau's and Koriam's movements.

The anonymous communities associated with doctrinal practices are in large part an outcome of routinization. It is not merely the knowledge that in other villages people are performing the same rituals as you, and reiterating the same doctrines. The simultaneity of action in separate communities provides, in itself, only a fragile basis for common identity. If one's own rituals were cognized as the uniquely authored actions of particular members of one's own village, the institutional uniformity of

Paliau's or Koriam's movements would have meant comparatively little. But since all these rituals were encoded as generalized schemas, they took on a special identity as forms of action—they were not the actions of particular persons but of 'everyman', of an abstract and anonymous portion of humanity. This radically new conception found extensive reinforcement in the ideologies of both the Pomio Kivung (Whitehouse 1995: 85–6) and of the Paliau Movement:

Paliau sought to build new, larger units. He tried to reverse the process of schism . . . He attacked all the dividing lines of native society as inimical to the desire to have a life similar to that of Europeans. 'Although the bodies of men have many parents,' he said, 'the *thinkthinks* of all men have only one source in God.' The meeting house symbolized the new unity . . . He preached that all natives were alike in their condition and in the broad outlines of Melanesian culture. Cultural differences were to be of no importance to those who would follow him. These differences derived from the past and would be abandoned with it. (Schwartz 1962: 262)

Nevertheless, one of the implications of routinization in the doctrinal mode, is that daily repetitions of doctrine and of liturgical ritual may become dull and humdrum, a state of affairs which I have labelled the 'tedium effect' (see Chapter 2). In the Pomio Kivung (Whitehouse 1995: 86–7) and in the Paliau Movement (Schwartz 1962: 286–7), there is abundant evidence that repetitive rituals and other observances were, for long periods of time, undertaken in a mechanical and even despondent fashion, suggesting a considerable degree of boredom. Members of both movements stood in line or sat in their meeting houses with glazed eyes, scarcely participating or else speaking somewhat automatically, reiterating formulaic phrases and parables. The more complex ritual procedures (Pomio Kivung temple offerings or Paliau's conventionalized church liturgy) were undertaken much of the time without conscious thought, as thoroughly embodied habits like sailing a Manus outrigger (Mead 1956: 52) or clearing a garden. In such activities one's mind could be elsewhere, disengaged from the religious context that had once been a source of excitement and revelation (at least at the time of conversion, if not during other periods).

By their very nature, routinized religions engender a highly disciplined form of social life. Repetition is itself a discipline, especially so as it becomes more onerous with the passing of time. But this discipline is inevitably converted into a virtue by the religious ideology. The diligence with which one participates in the daily round of speech-making and mechanical observances becomes a measure of piety. A particularly valued aspiration of worshippers in both the Pomio Kivung and in the

Paliau Movement was to 'hear the talk' (*harim tok*). Hearing, however, was not necessarily the same as listening. What was required was the dutiful and timely observance of all the routines of life in the movement (see Schwartz 1962: 263). 'Hearing the talk' was primarily to conform to the unremitting demands of routinized existence.

The strict discipline entailed in the Pomio Kivung and in the Paliau Movement applied to the performance of painstakingly repetitive observances, but it did not necessarily preclude high excitement in secular contexts. Throughout the history of the Pomio Kivung, a censorious line was taken against immoderate consumption and hedonism, and there was also an implacable intolerance of certain forms of sexual expression (primarily adultery, or the entertaining of adulterous fantasies). Nevertheless, excessive drunkenness, if not habitual, was considered acceptable, and high-spirited parties often startlingly broke the otherwise quiet and sombre tonus of village life. In the Paliau Movement, not only were wild parties tolerated but considerable licence was given with respect to sexual exploits. In the 'New Way', adultery was positively condoned, as long as adequate compensation was paid and any ill-feeling placated.

Nevertheless, the crucial point to make about these forms of sensual indulgence is that they were not put directly to the service of religious experience. Drunken parties and sexual conquests were not forms of religious expression. Church services, temple rituals, line-ups, sermons, and other collective observances—these were the ingredients of routinized religious life, and the moral ambiance of all these activities was one of strict discipline. In the Paliau Movement, the constant injunction to 'hear the talk' was also a demand for unity, based on the uniformity of routinized practices throughout the movement (Schwartz 1962: 263). Moreover, great stress has always been placed in the Paliau Movement on the notion that *not* 'hearing the talk' would endanger collective unity (Schwartz 1962: 264).

What we have then, in the doctrinal mode of religiosity, is typically a combination of large anonymous communities coupled with relatively low levels of religious excitement. This is not to say that people's investment in religious ideology is 'weak' or 'shallow'. On the contrary, the knowledge that one has endured for years the burden of routinized activity and strict discipline elicits a marked reluctance to 'give up' lightly or to tolerate the waywardness of others (see Schwartz 1962: 289).[3]

---

[3] Such an attitude may be readily comprehended in the framework of 'cognitive dissonance theory' (Festinger 1957).

Moreover, the ideology itself retains a certain intellectual persuasiveness that can be re-evoked in moments of doubt or serious contemplation (for all that it is lost much of the time in the automatic habits of day-to-day worship). But what needs to be emphasized is that routinized practices do not stimulate intense religious fervour and, therefore, the cohesion of these large-scale movements is comparatively diffuse. The Paliau Movement and the Pomio Kivung were expansionary, inclusive, and in a real sense 'united', but this tended to be a conceptual unity rather than an intense 'collective effervescence' (see Schwartz 1962: 285–91).

In contrast with the doctrinal mode of religiosity, imagistic practices evoke very intense feelings and sensations. In the case of Baktaman initiation rites, the predominant emotion triggered in novices is terror. The treatment of novices is deliberately calculated to maximize fear and apprehension. Examples of this include the violent abduction of first-degree novices by painted warriors in the middle of the night (Barth 1975: 51), the endless threats (somewhat capriciously carried out) that precede major revelations (Barth 1975: 60), the beating with stones and whipping with nettles of the novices' defenceless bodies (Barth 1975: 65), the ordeal of burning and protracted dehydration before the flames (Barth 1975: 65–6), and the offering of comforts that were then sadistically denied (Barth 1975: 65–6). At other times, the purpose of rites seemed to be to excite feelings of horror and disgust rather than simply mortal terror, as for instance in the enforced licking and sucking of a dead dog's penis in third-degree initiation (Barth 1975: 65).

As we saw in Chapter 1, terrorization of novices is common to many intiation systems in Papua New Guinea. But intense emotional states are also evoked in many 'cargo cults' and other new religious movements operating in the imagistic mode. We have already observed, for example, how traumatic the experience of *jipari* was in the Taro Cult, but it is well known that climactic millenarian ritual the world over tends to take on an 'ecstatic' character through such common activities as the destruction of property, excessive consumption, sexual licence, mass suicide or self-mutilation, and so on.

Nevertheless, there is a great deal more to 'ecstatic religion' than simply the evocation of intense emotions and sensations. Barth hints at this when he observes: 'From that first, frightening early morning when initiations started, and through a series of subsequent stages, the novice develops a fearful awareness of vital, unknowable, and forbidden power behind the secret and cryptic symbols. He realizes the existence of veil behind veil, and how modest and largely incorrect his own understandings have been'

(Barth 1975: 219). Barth here is drawing attention to the fact that Baktaman religious experience, at least for novices undergoing initiation, is not simply a very emotional (predominantly terrifying) process, but *also* a process discovery or revelation in which everyday assumptions are over- turned. The cumulative effect of bombardment by the iconic imagery of Baktaman initiation is conceptual as much as it is affective. Everyday objects (such as dew, fur, fat, and hair—see above) come to be seen in a radically new light as vehicles for a sacred process of growth that is being channelled within the bodies of novices. The increasing conceptual grasp of Baktaman analogic codes on the part of novices is managed in the rites through carefully orchestrated deception, and concealment, as well as revelation. Barth describes this delicate process as follows

deceit is not just an expression of opportunistic self-interest, or the supremacy and whim of senior men. It is shown to be a means to generate deeper truth. And some time, the question seems inevitably to arise: where does this end? Are there not secrets withheld in the 5th degree revelations, that create deeper knowledge for others by virtue of being withheld from me? And what about 6th, and 7th degree? Pursuit of true knowledge becomes like peeling the layers of an onion, or exploring a set of Chinese boxes: information on one level may be the deceitful cover that creates another kind of truth at a deeper level. (1975: 82)

The persuasiveness of imagistic practices hinges on the cultivation of surpise as well as the evocation of emotion. These two elements might be described as the building blocks of enduring, episodic memory. Christiansen (1992) has shown that much recent psychological research points to a causal link between affective stimulation and the longevity of episodic recall (see also McCauley 1999). This is little more than common sense, of course. We all know that experiences of frightening, euphoric, hilarious, enraging, or horrifying episodes tend to 'stick' in our memories. Where these sort of emotions are also hitched to an experience of sudden conceptual breakdown and reorganization (i.e. a significant experience of surprise and revelation) memories often acquire a peculiar vividness. Thus, highly formulaic scenes of violence in a 'cops and robbers' film may be exciting but not exactly surprising or particularly memorable. More sophisticated films in this genre, however, very obviously go to great lengths to surprise audiences with unexpected acts of violence that conform rather less easily to established schemas. It is the cultivation of surprise as much as the 'thrill' that makes such scenes memorable and worth talking about. It has been found that these tricks of the trade make good box office. Classic examples include scenes in which a creature bursts out of an astronaut's belly (in *Alien*) or in which a little girl speaks with a hideous adult male voice (in *The Exorcist*).

In real life situations, where it is more than a matter of 'suspending disbelief', such experiences affect people rather more profoundly. Some episodic memories of surprising and emotive events are so vivid in fact that psychologists have postulated a special type of neural process known as flashbulb memory (Brown and Kulik 1982, and see above). The term 'flashbulb memory' is used to describe exceptionally vivid and detailed memories of specific episodes which appear to have a canonical structure (Cohen 1989: 128–31, but see also Neisser 1982). People often claim to have particularly rich and detailed representations of the episodic moment of learning about John F. Kennedy's assassination, and this has long been one of the classic examples of the flashbulb phenomenon. An outstanding feature of this even for most Americans was that it was extremely upsetting as well as surprising. Precisely the same state of affairs is contrived in Baktaman initiation. Novices are both traumatized and 'surprised' by their experiences, as they advance through the ritual grades, and it seems most likely that their memories of these episodes have a 'flashbulb' clarity. I have elsewhere discussed this possibility in relation to imagistic practices among the Baining (1995: 195), as has Herdt in relation to similar practices among the Sambia (1989: 115).

The concept of flashbulb memory has produced considerable debate and experimental research in recent years. One of the most vocal critics of Brown's and Kulik's (1982) original formulation of the mechanism has come from Neisser, who initially suggested that the canonical structure of flashbulb memories might be an artefact of repeated rehearsal and narration of the unusual experience (Neisser 1982). In response to this suggestion, Winograd and Killinger (1983) designed an experiment to test recall of Kennedy's assasination among subjects who had been aged between one and seven at the time of the tragedy. Subjects in this study were found to have increasingly detailed recall of the assassination the older they had been at the time, suggesting that narrative conventions did not greatly affect the structure and content of their recollections.

More recently, however, Neisser and Harsch (1992) reported on an experiment which suggested that people's recollections of the explosion of the Challenger space shuttle were greatly affected by subsequent reporting of their experiences, and that the accuracy of subjects' recall was not related to their degree of emotional arousal at the time of the disaster. More recently still, Neisser *et al.* (1996) conducted a study of subjects' recall of an earthquake in Loma Prieta in 1989. This study revealed that the memories of residents in Georgia, who had received news of the earthquake indirectly (e.g. by word of mouth or via the mass media), were subject to distortion over time, apparently linked to subsequent rehearsal of their experiences (as in the Challenger study). Nevertheless, Neisser *et al.* found ceiling levels of accuracy in the recollections of Californians who directly experienced the effects of the earthquake, and these recollections were not subject to modification as a result of subsequent rehearsal. This suggests that a necessary condition for the production of genuine flashbulb memories is firsthand experience of the surprising event, as is clearly the case with regard to Baktaman novices and followers of the Taro Cult in the performance of their rituals.

Despite these impressive findings, Neisser *et al.* (1996) remain sceptical about the importance of affective stimulation in flashbulb memory. McCauley (1999) suggests that emotional arousal may be only one of a number of ways of triggering flashbulb memories, by flagging particular events as ones that are personally or socially salient. According to this view, affective stimulation may set off flashbulb memories of surprising occurrences but other triggers are possible too (such as an awareness that an experienced event is regarded by others as highly significant).

Wright and Gaskell (1992) have put forward a model of flashbulb memory which accords in some respects with McCauley's more recent suggestion, and which also helps us to envisage both semantic and episodic memory as part of a unified cognitive process. Brown's and Kulik's original theory of flashbulb memory (1982) proposed that it is a special mechanism which comes into play when an event violates normal expectations. Wright and Gaskell, by contrast, argue that all events are processed in the same way but that what gives certain memories 'flashbulb' clarity is the processing of indiscriminate details as a result of the failure to attach unfamiliar events to existing schemas. Wright and Gaskell (1992: fig. 5.1) envisage a cognitive processing loop, a simplified version of which is presented below.

Routine and familiar episodes do not go around the loop, or not for any significant duration, whereas abnormal events result in a process of 'going round in circles', searching feverishly for some aspect of the event that will at last trigger a suitable schema, and render the experience intelligible. This would explain why people remember so many apparently irrelevant details about abnormal episodes, which they describe as having a peculiar 'vividness'.

Wright and Gaskell add that 'abnormality' is not enough to produce the longevity associated with flashbulb memory. Something could be

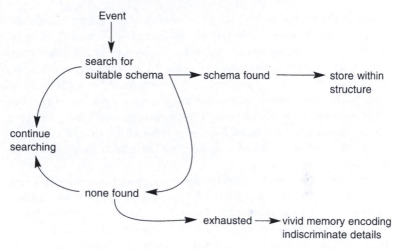

Wright's and Gaskell's (1992) cognitive processing loop

surprising but trivial and, therefore, eminently forgettable. Moreover, if all events that violate our existing schemas produced long-lasting and vivid memories, then clearly we would remember large portions of early childhood with flashbulb clarity. In fact, the opposite seems to occur. Since very young children lack appropriate semantic knowledge with which to make sense of many experiences, retrieval cues used in later life do not correspond to early encoding and recall becomes difficult or impossible. Thus, most people have great difficulty remembering very much at all from early years of childhood (see Schachtel 1947 and Winograd and Killinger 1983).

The solution proposed by Wright and Gaskell is that enduring and vivid episodic memories result in part from the fact that they have emotional value. They focus in particular on the role of such memories in conferring identity (1992: 286–8). In the case of very young children, many of the episodes they experience that fail to conform to existing schemas have little emotional value either for the children themselves or for the adults around them. This is consistent with varying degrees of childhood amnesia.

From the viewpoint of a theory of modes of religiosity, these arguments are of the greatest interest. In the case of routinized ritual in the doctrinal mode, we should expect each repetition to be fed directly into the storage structure, composed of schemas to which elements of the ritual correspond (see the figure above). Over time, the episodic nature of each ritual performance 'fades' irretrievably into general schemas. Thus, whereas most elements of today's performance might be possible to recall, yesterday's performance is easily conflated with that of the day before and performances of last week or last month become indistinguishable.

Imagistic practices, by contrast, are remembered as unique and vivid episodes over very long periods of time. Indeed, like other flashbulb memories, they are presumably carried to the grave. In the case of Baktaman initiation rites, novices are truly changed for life by their traumatic ordeals. These rites violate their normal expectations, and cannot be assimilated into existing schemas. But they also have profound emotional value and, indeed, are subjectively perceived as identity-forming experiences in Wright's and Gaskell's terms. Once the unique schemas are in place, no repetition of the episodes they encode would ever evoke the same vividness and salience. This is why it makes no sense to repeat imagistic practices, and certainly not to organize them in a routinized form. Initiation rites are undergone (in the role of novice) once in a lifetime, but a similar pattern of transmission is evident in 'cargo cults' operating in the imagistic mode. The Taro Cult, for instance, did not simply repeat the rituals of the Baigona Cult—it transformed both the practices and the iconic imagery they engendered in the course of stimulating vivid and memorable revelations (see Chapter 3).

The political ramifications of enduring episodic memory contrast starkly with the universalistic orientations engendered in semantic memory for ritual performances. Imagistic practices generate vivid memories of particular climactic experiences in which the actual participants are vividly specified. Such memories strongly reinforce particularistic biases, because they underline the sharing of momentous episodes by a specifiable group of flesh-and-blood people. The sharing of such memories generates the most profound solidarity and cohesion. Those who have endured together the ordeals of war or natural disaster, like those who have undergone together the traumas of initiation, are bound together in a uniquely intense and enduring way.

Among Melanesianists, it is almost a truism to say that initiation rites promote a solidarity among men that is put into the service of male domination and group defence. Perhaps because most anthropological research in Melanesia has been conducted in communities 'pacified' by colonial government, the principal focus of attention has been the implications of male initiation for gender relations.[4] Nevertheless, in the context of new religious movements, such as the Taro Cult, imagistic practices have comparatively little to do with the construction of gender relations. Solidarity and cohesion is generated among localized groups of men *and* women. For instance, *jipari* and *kasamba* (the focal practices of the Taro Cult), generated a fragmentary political landscape, founded upon the cohesiveness and chauvinism of local communities, and expressed in the rivalrous relations between them.

Some commentators mistakenly interpreted the Taro Cult as an attempt to unify native peoples in opposition to colonial authorities. Worsley, for instance, claimed that 'doctrines of unity, co-operation, comradeship, etc. [were] central to the cult' (1957: 66), and that this entailed some kind of unified opposition to colonial oppression. In this, Worsley was echoing Haddon's views, which he cited approvingly. Likewise, Lanternari (1963: 165) and Wetherell (1977: 189) conflated the wide dissemination of the Taro Cult with the idea of political unification. Such interpretations are fundamentally at odds with Williams's original account. In talking about the 'doctrines' of the Taro Cult, Worsley missed the point that Taro ideology for the most part emerged out of localized ritual performances. That is why many Taro adherents neither knew nor cared whether their ideas were similar to those of the founder. Distant or unrelated practitioners could do and think what they liked; what mattered was that a local community, physically gathered in one place, shared an intense experience of revelation and solidarity. This experience was unique to the group and could not provide a basis for wider unity founded on doctrinal similarities. The use of terms like 'prophet' (Wetherell 1977: 190) and 'messianic' (Lanternari 1963: 165) to describe Taro cultists likewise gave a false impression of the way ideas were codified and transmitted. Meanwhile, Worsley's claims about 'unity' and 'comradeship' derived from a questionable interpretation of the significance of hand-shaking in the Taro Cult (Worsley 1957: 65–6), which the Orokaiva associated with *insecurity* rather than unity, specifically the fear of sorcery (Williams 1928: 66). To envisage the Taro Cult as a failed or unsophisti-cated experiment in unification would be to miss the point that it success-

---

[4] For further discussion of these topics see, for instance, Barth (1975); Modjeska (1982); Lindenbaum (1984); Feil 1987, Godelier (1991); Whitehouse (1992a).

fully produced a fragmentary politico-religious regime based on intense solidarity within small groups or 'sects'. Non-verbal codification was conducive to the cultivation of traumatic and memorable revelations which were unmediated by prophets, messiahs, or other leaders, and productive of numerous, competing, localized, communities.

The Taro Cult took its inspiration from the Orokaiva system of initiation that likewise operated in the imagistic mode. Among the Orokaiva, both boys and girls were initiated, and experienced some of the more terrifying ordeals, such as the *embahi* ceremony, together (see above, Chapter 1). A major political goal of Orokaiva initiation was to create ferocious warriors, a point underlined by the culminating rites in which initiates danced aggressively in full military regalia and received the emblems of homicide. The Taro Cult, however, was not put into the service of any very obvious wider political purpose. In the absence of tribal warfare, part of the *raison d'être* of imagistic practices had been removed without, of course, detracting from the importance of the revelatory power of these experiences. Nevertheless, a new and extremely important role for imagistic practices began to crystallize with the establishment of large-scale associations, such as the Paliau Movement and the Pomio Kivung, operating in the doctrinal mode. This is the topic of Chapter 6.

6

Interacting Modes of Religiosity

The foregoing arguments may have created the impression that religions gravitate towards either the doctrinal mode (e.g. the Pomio Kivung, the Paliau Movement) or the imagistic mode (e.g. the Baktaman initiation complex, the Taro Cult). If this were so, however, it would make little sense to speak of *modes* of religiosity. Rather, we would be dealing simply with a typology by means of which different *religions* may be classified.

It is true that, prior to colonization, the communities of the Ok Mountain region, who included the Baktaman, had an abundance of imagistic religious practices, whereas the doctrinal mode was unelaborated. This state of affairs helps to account for the radical differences of ritual and cosmology between proximate and contiguous tribes. In attempting to convey a sense of this fragmentation, Barth wrote: 'If one were to imagine a Christian from one English village who entered the church of a community some miles away and found an image of the devil on the crucifix, and the altar wine being used for baptism, this seems the closest analogy I can construct. But by no means do all the contrasts have this stark character of inversion. In other cases, sacred symbols explicitly elaborated by some Mountain Ok communities are left entirely tacit or unelaborated by others' (1987: 5). The Baktaman and their neighbours sustained religious traditions, founded around initiation, that produced highly cohesive and localized military units. It is hardly surprising that each community had its own distinctive fund of sacred imagery. Barth's comparison with Christian England is startling, not simply because it evokes a sensation of sacrilege, but because it envisages an unheard-of form of Christianity that is stripped of its doctrinal mode of operation. Christianity has always used argument-based rhetoric as a medium of transmission; it has always sought to spread the Word to potential converts; it has always achieved homogeneity on a greater scale than the cults of the Ok region (which is not in any way to deny that many permutations of Christianity may be found around the world). In the religious systems of the Ok Mountain region of inner New Guinea, there was no place for an encompassing, universalistic ideology. Religious ideation was wedded inextricably to traumatic episodic memories, binding together small ritual groups.

Nevertheless, there are many religions that incorporate both imagistic and doctrinal modes of operation. The Pomio Kivung and the Paliau Movement provide examples of how the two modes of religiosity may be combined within particular regional traditions. Although my description of both movements has so far focused exclusively on their doctrinal aspects, this chapter will be concerned with the complex interplay of both doctrinal and imagistic practices in relatively discrete fields and phases of operation. But an exploration of these dynamics requires that we first clarify both the potentialities and limitations of these two modes, in sociological terms.

Potentialities and Limitations of the Two Modes of Religiosity

Doctrinal practices bring together under a common banner large numbers of people who could not possibly all know each other personally. By contrast, religions operating more or less exclusively in the imagistic mode do not produce this sort of unification. Nevertheless, imagistic practices are eminently capable of uniting very small communities and a great many of the sub-state political systems of Melanesia cannot be adequately understood in isolation from this mode of religiosity.

The unification achieved in the doctrinal mode, by spreading the Word over ever-greater territories, is often somewhat diffuse. Conversion itself may evoke temporary cohesion but, as a set of doctrinal practices becomes established and routinized, the humdrum repetitions of both dogma and ritual can rob the original revelatory experience of its intensity. In such conditions, the stirring up of religious fervour and political activism requires forms of stimulation outside the doctrinal complex. In some cases, this stimulation is supplied by imagistic practices, occasionally leading to intense sectarian conflict within and between established churches.

The political implications of imagistic practices, where they occur in isolation from the doctrinal mode, are not always clear-cut. For instance, although I have argued against the common assumption that the Taro Cult was an unsuccessful attempt to unify indigenous peoples in the face of colonial oppression, I am nevertheless hard pressed to say *what* the Taro Cult achieved in political terms. The cult provided an enduring stock of religious revelations but these were not then put to the service of successful raiding and warfare, as in traditional Orokaiva society. It is as if the Taro Cult was out of tune with the colonial political climate, in which peace between traditional tribal enemies was systematically enforced. Yet the fact that so many people were involved in the various sects of the Taro Cult suggests that some distillation and re-working of its themes, *codified as doctrine* by a messianic leader, might have caught on (just as it did on Manus and New Britain). In that case, the Taro Cult would have developed into a very different sort of tradition and the old cult's most poignant and memorable revelations would have enhanced and animated the new dogma.

In this preamble about the 'potentialities' and 'limitations' of the two modes of religiosity, it may seem that I am talking about 'strengths' and 'weaknesses'. For instance, a strength of the doctrinal mode is its capacity to unite large populations, and its principal weakness that this unity tends to be based on comparatively diffuse cohesion, at least in the long run. Or, again, a strength of the imagistic mode is its capacity to bind together small but extremely cohesive groups, and a weakness that such groups may have limited political leverage in the modern state. But there are problems associated with couching the argument in these terms. To suggest, for instance, that the cohesion produced by Baktaman initiation was a 'strength' because it enhanced the defensive capabilities of the group implies a functionalist stance. It makes no sense to argue, however, that the 'function' of Baktaman rites was to reinforce a political system based on inter-group warfare and male domination; imagistic practices, warfare, and male solidarity are interrelated features but their covariance is neither stable nor the product of some grand design, as classic functionalist accounts of such arrangements imply.

The pacified Orokaiva of the 1920s no longer possessed a political system based on local group autonomy and inter-group warfare. This does not mean, however, that the imagistic practices of the Taro Cult were somehow anachronistic or 'dysfunctional'. The Orokaiva knew how to organize their religious rituals in a manner that created intense local cohesion; they also traditionally put this to the service of tribal warfare (see Chapter 1). But it is mistaken to think of the latter as a 'function' of the former, as if group preservation were somehow the *raison d'être* of Orokaiva initiation. Traditional initiatory practices were most explicitly 'about' religious revelation, empowerment, and natural fertility. This is as close as one may get to their *raison d'être*. And it is hardly surprising that the imagistic practices of the Taro Cult were oriented to a similar set of goals. As such, the cult rituals were a somewhat predictable, or at least intelligible adaptation to circumstances in 1920s New Guinea. New opportunities for religious experimentation had been opened up by the colonial system of administration, and many of these were not explored in the Taro Cult. But this did not make it a failure on its own terms, nor can it be viewed as such in the context of my theoretical model.

More radical forms of experimentation in Melanesia began largely after the Second World War, with the rise of leaders such as Yali, Paliau, and Koriam. These new leaders and their supporters, drawing on their experience of missionization and other imported colonial forms, developed the first Melanesian religions operating in the doctrinal mode. Such adaptations made possible new kinds of political formation, including micronationalist groupings. But after these new patterns of political association became established, people did not forget their more ancient imagistic practices. During the repetitive and mechanical rituals and orations of the great messianic movements of Melanesia, people learned to 'switch off' and carry out their routinized duties with a kind of automaticity. But they strayed in fantasy to the mysterious and compelling revelations of traditional rituals, engraved in autobiographical memory. Against this background, followers of the new messianic movements would periodically break away in small groups to explore the possibilities of the imagistic mode, before returning to the fold. Sometimes, of course, splinter-group rituals were proposed locally and rejected, their exponents possibly even excommunicated (Whitehouse 1995: 89–90). But sporadic recurrence of such programmes has been both widespread and well documented (Whitehouse 1995: 172–3).

By and large, leaders of large-scale, routinized movements publicly condemn splinter-group activity. This is logical because such splinter groups, by definition, fail to conform to the religious orthodoxy, and such deviation normally carries heavy sanctions (from expulsion to supernatural punishment). Nevertheless, it is very probable that mainstream movements could not survive without these sporadic outbursts of splinter-group activity, at different times and places, at a local level. Within doctrinal regimes, whenever enthusiasm for orthodox practices begins to wane in response to the strenuous round of routinized activity, there is a risk that local communities (or large portions of them) will abandon the religion altogether. Such trends have been observed on numerous occasions within Paliau's, Koriam's, and Yali's movements, and in other comparable organizations. Sometimes the defecting community is never won back. Communities that remain loyal to mainstream orthodoxy in the long run are, paradoxically, often the ones that break away temporarily during periods of low morale.

The terms 'break away' and 'splinter group' suggest a radical division between mainstream and local religious ideology but this is seldom the case. What crucially takes place in these splinter groups is not so much a reformulation of orthodox dogma but a *re-codification* of it. The central principles of mainstream ideology are recast in iconic imagery. Thus, a splinter group in the Pomio Kivung recently took up ideas about Koriam's Ten Laws, collective salvation, and divine leadership, and condensed these in a series of images relating to 'posts' and 'rings' (Whitehouse 1995: chs. 4 and 5). Posts represented the Ten Laws (inscribed on actual wooden posts at the entrances to all Kivung villages). But they also brought to mind the central posts in traditional temples that supported the rafters—a trope that related to the role of the divine leader, 'supporting' his community on the path to salvation. The ring of house posts corresponded to a ring of people (the splinter-group community) who formed the 'elect'. Such images were cultivated in a series of highly evocative and climactic rituals that had an enduring impact on memory. These haunting and revelatory experiences were not forgotten when people returned to the routinized practices of the mainstream movement, but rather added greater depth and meaning to them and thus renewed commitment to these institutions (see Whitehouse 1995: 149–54).

To some extent, the above process is facilitated by astute management on the part of mainstream leaders. That is, figures such as Paliau, Koriam, and Kolman did not apply the usual sanctions against non-conformity to splinter-group members, but allowed these sporadic local cults to run their course. In some cases, when splinter-group rituals collapsed (usually due to the depletion of resources needed to sustain them), mainstream leaders castigated the splinter group quite strenu-ously. In general, however, this had the effect, not of preventing a similar outburst of such activities several years down the line, but of consolidat-ing a sense of fear and awe towards the great leader himself. Paliau was particularly adept at humiliating and dominating wayward followers in this way (Schwartz 1962: 342–53). But whether or not splinter-group activities were strategically condoned by mainstream leaders, the effect of this process has sometimes been to maintain commitment in the long run to routinized institutions. Inevitably, however, the effects of interacting modes of religiosity are more complex (and much more interesting) than this brief introduction to the topic has been able to convey, as ethnogra-phy on the early Paliau Movement clearly demonstrates.

The Imagistic Domain of the Early Paliau Movement

The history of the Paliau Movement has been a history of routinized orthodoxy, operating in the doctrinal mode, punctuated by sporadic and temporary outbursts of climactic, imagistic practices. These two aspects of the movement tend to be manifested in discrete fields of operation. Whenever Paliau's followers have been engaged in imagistic cult activity, they have substantially (albeit temporarily) abandoned orthodox ritual practices. Moreover, as we shall see, these climactic outbursts have invariably been described in the literature as discrete cults. Nevertheless, the followers of Paliau and of these periodic splinter cults were one and the same people. Moreover, they did not periodically abandon the basic moral and cosmological assumptions of Paliau's mainstream movement and 'invent' an entirely new set. There has always been striking continuity between the ideas of these temporary cults and those of Paliau's orthodox regime, even on matters that might seem to be quite trivial theologically (e.g. Schwartz 1962: 272). The crucial differences between these two domains of operation concern not what people 'believed' but how these 'beliefs' were codified and transmitted. These domains must, therefore, be understood as aspects of a single, coherent religious tradition.

In order to demonstrate that cult outbursts within the Paliau Movement genuinely conform to what I have dubbed the 'imagistic mode of religiosity', we must first examine instances of these cults in some detail, focusing on the same repertoire of interconnected features that were revealed in the Taro Cult and in the Baktaman system of initiation. Undoubtedly the richest published source of ethnographic data is Schwartz's excellent monograph on the Paliau Movement (1962) which covers two brief phases of cult outbursts, the first being dubbed the 'Noise' or 'First Cult' and the second, occurring about six years later, described as the 'Ghost Cult' or 'Second Cult'.

The 'Noise' began in February 1947, shortly after Paliau's initial programme of proselytism, when Wapei, a young man from the village of Nriol, experienced a fit of violent trembling. Nriol had only just received Paliau's teachings via a local man, Lungat, who had heard Paliau's speeches at the early meetings in Baluan (Schwartz 1962: 267). Wapei, responding to these new teachings, said that he had encountered Jesus in a dream and that Jesus would return with the ancestors of Nriol who would have white skins and bring with them Western cargo. The persuasiveness of Wapei's claims resided, not so much in his statements, but in the violent paroxysms that accompanied them. These paroxysms were described in Pidgin as *guria*, a term applied to trembling of any order of magnitude, from malarial shivering to seismic activity and volcanic eruptions. It was Wapei's *guria* that made his claims credible and indicated to the villagers of Nriol the presence of genuine supernatural intervention (Schwartz 1962: 369). This *guria* proved to be contagious, rapidly seizing those in contact with Wapei either directly or indirectly. The phenomenon, and all the activities ensuing from it, became known as the 'Noise': 'This was the *guria*, the trembling of the body which in some individuals became at times fully uncontrolled convulsions . . . This was the *Noise*, as they say in Neo-Melanesian, *"skin belong me i noise too much"* (my body shook violently)' (Schwartz 1962: 268).

Along with this *guria*, which became somewhat ritualized (Schwartz 1962: 277), the most prominent feature of the 'Noise' was the destruction of highly valued possessions, which were gathered up and thrown into the sea. The Noise involved quite elaborately constructed rituals, emphasizing precise synchrony of movement and militaristic marching. On Mouk, two flags were erected and drilling was focused on the flagpoles (Schwartz 1962: 272); rings of human bodies were also formed around the graves at Mouk's cemetery (Schwartz 1962). Many people affected by the *guria* reported experiences of strange visions—the lights of approaching aeroplanes, ships, or cars (Schwartz 1962: 269–71) or ghostly footprints and money that appeared out of thin air (Schwartz 1962: 275). Visions of Jesus and of more bizarre apparitions, including a 'glowing horse' (Schwartz 1962: 279) were also reported.

In attempting to understand the meaning of these extraordinary practices and experiences, Schwartz was confronted with the same problem that confounded Williams in his study of the Taro Cult (1928). In the Noise, as in the Taro Cult, very little verbal exegesis was forthcoming in relation to cult practices, even the most dramatic forms of behaviour, such as mass convulsions and destruction of property. Not only were people reluctant or unable to articulate in words the meaning of their behaviour, but the Noise involved very little verbalized ideology *per se*. There were, in contrast with the Taro Cult, some explicit millenarian expectations described as a 'new way of life', but expressions of these were limited and seemed to have been based on truncated versions of Paliau's 'New Way': 'The constructs of the Cult . . . contained many . . . contradictions in the conception of this new way of life . . . In general, there was little elaboration on the features of the new life to be arrived at on the Day Behind' (Schwartz 1962: 370).

In attempting to interpret the practices of the Noise, Schwartz focused on the range of associations that these practices were likely to have evoked in the minds of participants, even though these associations were not formulated explicitly. A useful point of entry was provided by the Pidgin term for mass convulsions (*guria*): 'The word "*guria*" was used in the Neo-Melanesian versions of the Bible of all mission sects, referring to the *guria* that occurred at the death of Christ, the Noise, the *guria*, and the speaking in tongues that came to the followers of Jesus in Jerusalem at the first Pentecost which impressed and converted many Jews, and finally the Noise and *guria* predicted for the Day Behind' (Schwartz 1962: 390). *Guria* in the body thus signified the immanence of supernatural power, a holy state of spirit possession. This seems to have been portentous, a sign that the power immanent in the body might spread and increase. The shaking was contagious, spreading from one body to the next, threatening to spill out into the physical environment itself, in the form of earthquakes. The image here was one of escalation from small beginnings to ever-greater levels of magnitude. This may have been a way of conceptualizing the enormity of the desired transformation, the vastness of the changes entailed in establishing a new way of life. Individuals had to change and thus whole communities and, with them, the physical architecture of the world itself in stepwise progression. In the Noise, the body of each participant became the site of a miniature earthquake, prefiguring a far greater one that would change the entire environment. It was an image not simply of change but of change on a cosmic scale.

But the *guria* was also an apocalyptic image. Earthquakes do not simply change the environment: in a very real sense, they destroy it. Moreover, the *guria* of the body implied its debilitation by fever. Thus, the *guria* was seen as destructive of bodies as well as of the environment; as Schwartz noted, the *guria* occasioned by cerebral malaria implied a bleak prognosis and 'most Manus have witnessed death in convulsions of some kind' (1962: 391). The *guria*, therefore, connoted not only the establishment of a new way of life, but the apocalyptic destruction of the old one. 'This world' and 'these bodies' were felt to be no good. The environment had to be laid waste before it could be reconstructed, and the body killed before it could be reborn. Against this background, the systematic destruction of property in the cult becomes intelligible: everybody threw their most valuable possessions into the sea because these possessions had become rubbish, part of the old world that would be destroyed.

Taro cultists, like followers of the Noise, experienced bodily convulsions but the evidence suggests that these apparently similar behaviours triggered rather different sets of connotations (see above, Chapter 3). For the Orokaiva, the shaking of the body was linked to the trembling of plants whereas, for the Manus, it was linked to the trembling of the earth itself. This subtle divergence in iconic processing had significant ideological implications. The Taro Cult was not concerned with millenarian and apocalyptic revelations: all that was being sought was a rather limited set of material and physical improvements. In consequence, the old world did not have to be broken up and destroyed, merely rendered more fertile and abundant, as the trembling of the thriving taro plant, occasioned by the rising trade winds, suggested. These were the focal images evoked by the convulsing bodies of Taro adherents. The Noise, however, wanted to shake up and rebuild the earth itself and thus the convulsing body was an image of death and destruction as well as of rebirth and reconstruction.

The Noise, as is characteristic of cults operating in the imagistic mode, did not last very long—a matter of two or three months at most in any given locale. Afterwards, its followers settled down to the routinized practices of the Paliau Movement, a state of affairs that lasted for approximately six years. By the end of this period, however, morale in the mainstream movement had begun to flag.[1] It was against this background that the Second Cult (or 'Ghost Cult') fleetingly appeared.

Unlike the Noise, the Second Cult did not entail mass convulsions, although followers did occasionally experience the *guria*, with varying degrees of severity. The focal imagery of the Second Cult was evoked by rituals with comparatively complex structure and choreography. The most prominent of these rituals were of three types: ring ceremonies, militaristic marching, and seances.

As with the practices of the Noise, the rituals of the Second Cult were not accorded substantial exegesis. In fact, during the ten-month duration of the Second Cult in Bunai village, where Schwartz was living, he never heard anybody speak of its rituals or their meanings (1962: 292). When Schwartz attended a ring ceremony, he was struck by the absence of verbal allusions to the meanings and images elicited by the ritual (1962: 293). The same was true of marching: Schwartz was unable to collect any verbal commentaries on, or interpretations of the drills and marching songs or even of the general nature of the ritual, and concluded that 'marching was purely religious . . . No one was certain about its meaning or who the objects of the manifest hostility were'(1962: 315).

While it is clear that the rituals of the Second Cult transmitted

---

[1] Schwartz described this process in considerable detail and I take up the theme below.

revelations as iconic imagery, the precise nature and range of this imagery is difficult to piece together from the limited information available. The nearest thing to an exegetical commentary on the Second Cult that Schwartz was able to obtain was the miming of an old man in Bunai, called Ponram. Having fallen into a coma and been partially revived, Ponram found himself temporarily unable to speak and was obliged to communicate in gestures. Schwartz described how, in his dazed condition, Ponram was surrounded by a throng of people who watched his gesticulations intently, interpreting them as they became more animated and vigorous. Although Ponram never actually spoke, his communicative gestures were readily translated by others into speech, by virtue of invoking more or less standardized or transparent sign language:

Everyone seemed to know just what was happening, what to do, how to translate, as if they had experienced it all before. Sometimes Ponram would repeat a gesture until someone in the audience caught on and interpreted it aloud. Then Ponram would turn toward that person and smile . . . Stretching his arms over his head he indicated that he had been to Heaven. He had died as a punishment for his wrong-doing and had been brought to God. Now he had been sent back to tell of many things that had been revealed to him. He began to recite, with gestures, all the sins that he had ever committed for which he had been punished . . . Then Ponram spoke in gestures against divorce. He continued to pronounce against all the things so often condemned in the *Newfela Fashion*. Although all this had been heard by everyone almost daily since the start of the movement, it was now given again as direct revelation and listened to with the utmost intensity (Schwartz 1962: 296).

Ponram indicated his repudiation of 'this world' by seizing local arte-facts, such as an old wooden bowl, and throwing it to the ground in disgust. He indicated, by taking up an enamel bowl in theatrical admira-tion, that manufactured Western cargo was to be desired in place of this 'rubbish'. Finally, Ponram arranged pieces of firewood to form a cross, and this stellar imagery was immediately understood to refer to Heaven. Ponram indicated that Heaven would be a place of harmony and great abundance, a period of supernatural bliss. In many ways, this episode recalls the discourse of the founder of the Taro Cult (Buninia) who, in response to the probing questions of an anthropologist, was unable to find appropriate words and resorted instead to mime (Williams 1928: 13–14; see above, Chapter 3). Although Ponram's gestures were explicitly trig-gered by a supernaturally induced dumbness, they had a similar effect of forcing the audience to participate in the telling of his story, thereby drawing people into his sense of revelation.

In the collective rituals of the Second Cult (the ring ceremonies, seances, and militaristic marching) a similar principle was undoubtedly operative. For instance, at ring ceremonies, people had to complete a clockwise circuit of the 'ring' (really a square) before seating themselves on a specially constructed bench surrounded by a railing (Schwartz 1962: 313). The meanings of this imagery can only be guessed at. Did this ring demarcate the elect, God's chosen few, as in the ring ceremonies of a recent splinter group within the Pomio Kivung (Whitehouse 1995: ch. 4)? Did the ring have some celestial referent, such as the four-cornered star depicted by Ponram using firewood? Participants must have been making salient inferences, of the sort verbalized in response to Ponram's gesticulations. But in solemn collective rituals these inferences did not reduce to a story, or to any kind of verbal narrative; they had the revelatory character of imagistic practices codified in portentous iconic imagery.

Nevertheless, the concept of an 'imagistic mode of religiosity' is not simply a matter of peculiar styles of codification, but is linked to a constellation of features, including sporadic transmission, intense localized cohesion, emotionality, and a characteristic structuring of the group and its ideology. In fact, both the Noise and the Second Cult possessed all the predictable features of the imagistic mode.

To begin with the issue of frequency of transmission, the point about imagistic practices is that they are brief in duration and occur only sporadically. In the case of Baktaman initiation rites, these may be witnessed quite rarely (and only experienced once in a lifetime in the role of novice at any given grade). 'Cargo cults' operating in the imagistic mode may be rather more frequent, for instance occurring every five years or so in any given locale (Whitehouse 1995: 172). The Noise and the Second Cult were separated by a space of six or seven years and the outbursts themselves were brief, typically lasting no more than a few weeks in the case of the Noise and never more than three months (Schwartz 1962: 371). These outbursts, albeit brief and periodic, are nevertheless part of an ongoing tradition sustained in memory during the long gaps when they are not being transmitted. Schwartz in fact explicitly noted this continuity, as part of an attempt to comprehend the scarcity of exegesis with regard to the Noise, several years after its occurrence: 'Part of the difficulty in eliciting accounts of the First Cult arose because much that we sought was not actually dead in the past . . . but was part of a still-thriving ideology concealed from Europeans who had denounced it in its earlier appearance as madness and subversion' (Schwartz 1962: 292). Moreover, like Schwartz, Paliau regarded the Second Cult and the Noise as manifestations of the same tradition

(Schwartz 1962: 345) and it is revealing that the former re-evoked the same communities as those established in the Noise, even though these groupings had fallen into abeyance during the intervening period (Schwartz 1962: 309).

Like the Taro Cult, both the Noise and the Second Cult drew adherents over a wide area but, as is characteristic of such movements operating in the imagistic mode, the principal pattern of spread was contiguous contagion rather than proselytism. Moreover, the groups of people drawn into the cult were not united but, on the contrary, pitted one against the other in a state of rivalry and mutual suspicion.

In the imagistic mode, revelations are triggered by the actions of the group, specifically, through the imagery of collective ritual. Consequently, if these revelations are to travel then it must be either through contact with peoples who live close by or who are migrating. Thus Wapei, founder of the Noise, could not spread the cult to visiting Mouks simply by telling them about it. Conversion could only occur when members of the village congregated and underwent mass convulsions as a group, thereby transmitting the *guria* by contagion to groups of visitors (Schwartz 1962: 270). After the Mouks had 'caught' the *guria*, they took it to Pusu and thence back to Mouk itself (Schwartz 1962: 271), but the cult was never disseminated by a leader or set of proselytizing disciples. As in the Taro Cult, the spread of the Noise occurred through consecutive waves of contagion; indeed, the cultists at Nriol themselves used the metaphor of a wave to describe the pattern of dissemination (Schwartz 1962: 270).[2] The 'wave' metaphor was particularly apposite in capturing the rapidity with which the Noise was transmitted:

The spread of the First Cult happened within a few months . . . During the first week, its reception by any particular village was almost instantaneous. Either the first contact with carriers already caught up in the *Noise* sufficed to involve the village, or two or three successive contacts with individuals who were increasingly more intensely affected by the *Noise* had the same effect. The apex of intensity of the *Noise* was reached within a few days of this initial contact. (Schwartz 1962: 371)

In contrast, the Second Cult spread rather more slowly and this must be related to the fact that it relied on carefully organized and choreographed rituals rather than instantaneous convulsions. Like the Noise, the Second Cult could not be spread by individual leaders and their representatives and each village or ritual community had to be inspired by

---

[2] See Schwartz's map showing routes of transmission of the First Cult (1962: 372).

its own revelations, thus arriving at similar ritual forms by (theoretically) independent means. Although in reality the cult must have been transmitted through group contact, especially participation in the rituals of neighbouring groups (as Schwartz's diagram of routes of transmission in the cult suggests [Schwartz 1962: 384]), human agents were theoretically excluded from these chains of transmission, the source of inspiration supposedly coming from above. It is hardly surprising, therefore, that the spread of the Second Cult occurred over many months, rather than during a matter of days or weeks.

To some extent these differences in the rate of transmission affected the relative emotional intensity of the cults. The practices of the Second Cult were markedly less ecstatic and traumatic than those of the First, as Schwartz observed: 'In spite of an attempt to maintain the expectation of imminent climax of the Cult, it could not be maintained over a year and a half at the level of intensity that was possible to a cult with a span of a few months (weeks in most villages) as the *Noise* had been' (1962: 385). The Second Cult did not endure for long periods of time in any village, but it was slow to assemble and reliant on the innovativeness and imagination of local villagers rather than on immediately 'catching' and overwhelming convulsions. Among the more climactic and arousing activities generated by the Second Cult were impassioned collective confessions (Schwartz 1962: 313–14) and erotic bathing (Schwartz 1962: 313 and 340), but there was not the 'intensity of emotional excitement' that accompanied the Noise (Schwartz 1962: 385). Apart from the traumatic nature of the *guria*, climactic practices in the First Cult included the whipping of adherents with rattan switches (in some cases in a state of nudity [Schwartz 1962: 269]), widespread destruction of property (see above), lengthy periods of fasting that appeared to result in hallucination (Schwartz 1962: 274), threatening with spears (Schwartz 1962: 269), and, most horrifically, the public murder of Wapei (Schwartz 1962: 270). For participants, 'the *Noise* had been a profoundly important experience in their lives. Only a few were not convinced that they had been brought close to God, to the *cargo*, and to the dead' (Schwartz 1962: 283).

The intense and enduring memories of the Noise, and to a lesser extent of the Second Cult, bound together small communities (typically no larger than individual villages) into tightly cohesive units. The emphasis in both cults was on local particularism, as is always the case with regard to imagistic practices. A couple of instances may be cited to illustrate the strength of this local cohesion, which totally excluded any possibility of unification within the cult as a whole:

It was decided that no non-Mouks . . . were to be permitted to approach Mouk. At night, two canoes approached from the direction of Rambutjon. These were probably the canoes of Kosa, a native of Tawi village . . . Before he came ashore he shouted that he had seen ships approaching Mouk. Tajan sent Lukas with a group of men to repel these intruders. As they ran toward the canoe, Tajan went ahead shouting 'kill them, kill them.' Kosa and his canoes left in haste. (Schwartz 1962: 272)

Or, again, Schwartz described how some sailors, on their way home from an island where the *guria* had seized them 'stopped *en route* and gave the news to unaffected villagers but were forcibly repelled by those villagers already involved. In the first episode of the *Noise*, people did not dare to leave their villages to seek information, for fear of losing their share of the *cargo* if it arrived in their absence' (Schwartz 1962: 372).

The Second Cult, as I have mentioned, re-evoked the cohesive local communities of the Noise and therefore exhibited the same particularistic ethos: 'In each village there was . . . an insistence that the cult was something that had been revealed to it independently. Even in the composite village of New Bunai, the two Usiai hamlets that joined the cult claimed independence and even ignorance of the early cult developments in each other's hamlets' (Schwartz 1962: 387).

In consequence, as in the Taro Cult, the Noise and the Second Cult generated a great proliferation of different 'sects' or highly localized ritual practices. In the case of the Noise, Schwartz related this fragmentary pattern to 'the rapid rate of transmission and the incompleteness of the versions received by different villages' (Schwartz 1962: 388), but even in the Second Cult, which spread rather more slowly, the same pattern of local distinctiveness was apparent. Indeed Schwartz provided a detailed description of the factionalism of the Second Cult (1962: 319–30). No doubt this sectarian picture was exacerbated by the requirement of independent inspiration on the part of separate communities. But the reason for this dogma, and its corollary that 'each village would receive its cargo directly from the ghosts of its own dead' (Schwartz 1962: 387), was that the ritual communities formed through imagistic practices were inherently bounded and even pitted against each other. In this mode of religiosity, there is never any prospect of close co-operation across a wide area.[3]

---

[3]   Attempts in the Second Cult to import elements of the universalistic ideology of the Paliau Movement, and some principles of centralization, markedly failed. As Schwartz pointed out, these aspects of the Paliau Movement contradicted the inherently particularistic character of both the First and Second Cults (1962: 387).

The imagistic mode also differs from the doctrinal mode in the type of leadership (if any) that it generates. In the Noise and the Second Cult, leadership rested to a considerable degree on exhibiting acute forms of the cult symptomology (*guria*, visions, coma, etc.), whereas in Paliau's routinized movement, persuasive oratorical skills were a much more important qualification for leadership. In general, the divine leaders of religions operating in the doctrinal mode must be dynamic and inventive as well as persuasive because their words are the principal source of inspiration and revelation. In the imagistic mode, by contrast, revelations ensue from the enactment of forms of collective behaviour and this is a process that can only be individually 'led' by example, or by behind the scenes influence over ritual innovation. A detailed illustration of this is furnished by the splinter group of the Pomio Kivung described in my recent monograph (Whitehouse 1995: chs. 4–5). Similar patterns may be discerned in the Noise and the Second Cult. The Noise undoubtedly produced a leader in the form of Wapei, but 'the degree of command assumed by Wapei in Nriol was not duplicated elsewhere. In most other villages, a large number of individuals contributed their own roles, ideas, and minor prophecies to the Cult' (Schwartz 1962: 373). Moreover, even on Nriol, Wapei was not divinized or upheld as the only, or even primary source of inspiration; it was the *guria* and other collective experiences that generated the most valued revelations.

In the Second Cult, there was no leading instigator comparable to Wapei. An ancestor known as 'Thomas' was generally regarded as the principal source of revelation, and access to Thomas's instructions was only possible through the collaboration of a medium and an interrogator. Nevertheless, those who assumed these roles in each village were not regarded as leaders and often the considerable influence they exerted over local innovation in the cult was unrecognized. For instance:

The *council* [interrogator] of Johnston island, Kisakiu, who did most of the talking for Thomas, remained inconspicuous as the human organizer of the cult and as the person who made the heaviest contribution to the cult belief and programme. It seemed to occur to no one . . . that Kisakiu of Johnston Island was responsible for the ideas he contributed on behalf of Thomas, nor did Kisakiu or any of the others who played similar though less important roles elsewhere believe that they had made more than a limited personal contribution to the cult (Schwartz 1962: 386).

This concludes my summary of the key features of the Noise and of the Second Cult, which has been concerned with highlighting an imagistic

domain of operation within the early phases of the Paliau Movement
This imagistic domain has continued to be active up to the present time
periodically resurfacing according to a sporadic pattern of transmission
The crucial question is how the two domains of operation, doctrinal and
imagistic, affect each other. A start can be made by examining the rela
tionship between Paliau's mainstream movement and the two cult
discussed above.

Modes of Religiosity in the Early Paliau Movement

The Paliau Movement, in its doctrinal mode of operation, excited intens
and moving revelations when its ideology was first encountered. During
Paliau's initial phase of proselytism, which began in December 1946, hi
new and radical message stirred up considerable excitement. It was thi
excitement that triggered the Noise: a set of imagistic practices tha
'carried to an extreme' Paliau's doctrinal pronouncements (Schwartz
1962: 272). We have seen, for instance, that Paliau's followers, from the
very outset, entertained a set of millenarian expectations. In the
routinized orthodoxy of the mainstream movement, nobody ever
expected immediate fulfilment of these expectations; they assumed
merely that the millennium would arrive soon, within one's own lifetime
but not just yet. Millenarian cults operating in the imagistic mode, by
contrast, are always more climactic, building expectations of supernatura
transformation in the here and now. Thus, the imagery evoked by the
guria was of a sudden and dramatic escalation from bodily quaking to
apocalyptic earthquakes. The transition from the old world to the 'new
way' was expected to start at once and proceed with awesome rapidity
Paliau's ideas were central both to the Noise and to the Second Cult but
as well as being codified differently in the imagistic mode, Paliau's
doctrines were given a more Dionysian form.[4]

Another example would be the way Paliau's concept of the *thinkthink*
was translated, in the Noise, into an extreme form of behavioural
prescription:

They [followers of the *Noise*] started from Paliau's statements that God was the
thinkthink in each man, that God knew each man's thoughts, and that these
thoughts had to be both morally good and 'straight', in the sense of being well

---

[4] Benedict (1935: 56–7), borrowing her terminology from Nietzsche's studies of
Greek tragedy, described 'Dionysian' practices as those that evoke religious revelations
through extreme psychological states. Her illustrations of such practices included ritualized
fasting, torture, tests of endurance, and drug use.

arranged and free of disturbance. In the logic of the *Noise* it followed that, once a person had a thought to do something, it was as if he had announced his intentions to God. If he did not carry out that intention, but permitted himself to become distracted into doing something else, then he had lied to God. If he thought of going to a certain person's house, he must go straight to it. He must control his eyes and ears so that he was not deflected from his course by distracting stimuli. If someone called to him on the road he must ignore him. When he arrived at his destination he could think another thought, then act on it. As my informants described their adherence to the way of the *thinkthink*, I could visualize their moving in straight lines from point to point, setting aside their usual amiable receptivity to the social interceptions of others, fearful lest they spoil their chances of realizing that idyllic state which they thought of as the First Order of God. (Schwartz 1962: 272)

It may be argued that the Noise was a way of trying to get to grips with an unfamiliar mode of religiosity. The doctrinal mode requires the effort of worship to be spread evenly and continuously in repetitive practices and sober contemplation, but this was quite alien to new converts whose experience of missionary Christianity was very limited. Paliau's message initially evoked the intense, revelatory experiences of more traditional religious practices and it is hardly surprising that people reacted by trying to translate the dogma into the medium of these traditional practices. This process can be seen almost as a 'dialogue' carried on in two radically different religious 'languages'. Paliau, in his initial programme of proselytism, tried to speak to the population in the doctrinal mode, but people replied in the imagistic mode. A sense of this was captured by Schwartz as follows: 'Paliau's message—in part intact, in part transformed or reinterpreted—was carried out from this center [Baluan] by the initial adherents to their own villages and beyond their villages, where it thinned out into rumor. From the periphery, the backlash of these ideas came in the form of the Noise' (1962: 266). Thus, a mere three months after Paliau began to spread the new doctrines from his headquarters in Baluan, the Noise broke out among practically the entire population that had by then received at least parts of Paliau's teachings.

The Second Cult occurred against a rather different, and in many ways a much more typical, background. The Second Cult was not a response to the intense excitement generated by the initial exposure to new and radical doctrines. Nor was it a result of unfamiliarity with the doctrinal mode of religiosity *per se*. If anything, it was a response to *over-familiarity* with the doctrinal mode. After the practices of the Noise had ceased, there followed a six-year period of sober orations and highly repetitive ritual. As Paliau's routinized orthodoxy became established and entrenched, people came to understand the nature of the doctrinal mode. For a while, morale remained high. The impact of initial conversion, and of the ecstatic revelations of the Noise, were still fresh and compelling. But, eventually, the limitations of the doctrinal mode could not be ignored. Familiarity with the new doctrines and the automaticity of ritual performance gradually impoverished religious life, and created indifference to those very dogmas that had once appeared exciting and radical. Schwartz referred to this as the 'Plateau Phase':

Aside from the physical deterioration of the new villages, there were obvious signs that the *Newfela Fashion* was not being supported with anything approaching unanimity. Unless some extraordinary event was the occasion, attendance at meetings was poor. People who did attend straggled in more than an hour late. The leaders spent much of their time scolding those who attended and shouting their reproaches in the direction of the houses where those who had become bored with the repetitious speeches of the meetings had stayed. Church attendance was poor; only a handful attended most of the weekday morning and afternoon services. There were complaints that the sermons were too long . . . Through most of the Plateau Phase, there was a state of relaxed indifference in the religion of the *Newfela Fashion* (1962: 287).

The Second Cult was a reaction to this 'tedium effect' and the low morale that it engendered. Through a 'rediscovery' of the imagistic mode, Paliau's followers hoped to reconstitute and build upon their earlier sense of revelation. This was an attempt to supply more compelling and precious meanings to what had threatened to become a merely humdrum existence. But it was not an active quest. People did not go out 'looking for meaning'—it is truer to say that they were especially susceptible to it. The Plateau Phase was one in which any intrinsically compelling recodification of the prevailing orthodoxy was going to 'catch on'. It was not that people doubted the authority of Paliau's doctrines but simply that they had become platitudinous, and could only be rescued from this condition by being recast in a more revelatory form.

This was precisely the state of affairs that I encountered in a Pomio Kivung village in 1987. The villagers met every day to hear the speeches of local officials in the movement but their eyes were glazed and their minds wandered. With the formation of a splinter group, the whole village appeared to 'wake up' (a metaphor followers used themselves, to describe what had happened). The ideas of the splinter group were not new, but they expressed orthodox doctrines through novel and exciting iconic imagery, triggered in collective ritual performances that were both emotionally and sensually arousing. The switch was made from a doctrinal to an imagistic mode of religiosity with considerable ease, because people were susceptible to such a transformation. Imagistic outbursts cannot occur at just any time in the process of routinization; when advocates of splintering choose their moment prematurely they are usually denounced and possibly excommunicated, such is the importance of adhering to the orthodoxy at least for extended periods of time (Whitehouse 1995: 89–90). Thus, in the period following the Noise, Paliau's supporters became 'energized' and absorbed in the routinized practices of the mainstream movement, and at that time any aberrant behaviour (such as *guria* or coma) would not have triggered great interest and may even have been condemned (and thus dismissed) as the influence of Satan. Susceptibility to imagistic practices in such movements is necessarily periodic, corresponding to the gradual development of the 'tedium effect' associated with long-term routinization.

It might also be argued that the pattern of oscillation between relatively long periods of routinization and sporadic outbursts of climactic cultism is caused by impatience. In other words, the fulfilment of millenarian expectations can only be postponed temporarily in doctrinal regimes, the proliferation of imagistic practices being a sign that people's patience has run out. Nevertheless, impatience is not a feature of routinized activity during periods when revelations are still novel and compelling. It is only when routines have become humdrum and automatic that people appear 'impatient' or, more accurately, susceptible to fresh revelations.

A major effect of intermittent outbursts of imagistic practices within routinized regimes is to renew commitment to the latter. This might seem odd, given that the imagistic mode promotes very localized cohesion and thus pits communities against each other. But this is only true during periods when imagistic practices are being *enacted*. Afterwards, in the context of a large-scale movement, the solidarity binding together splinter groups and sects can be transferred on to the movement as a whole. Schwartz observed: 'The *Noise* left the group of villages that had become involved in it united in an unprecedented solidarity, but this solidarity developed after and not during the active cult phase' (1962: 227).

Here, we come to one of the most important features of interacting modes of religiosity in the Paliau movement. The imagistic practices of the Noise and the Second Cult took from the mainstream movement basic ideas and themes but they gave back a renewed sense of the revelatory power of these ideas and of the solidarity uniting those who upheld and obeyed them. In order to grasp this situation, we must go back to the ethnography.

Somewhere in the region of 33 villages were involved in the Noise. During the period of the *guria* itself, the relations of these villages were profoundly fragmented, even openly hostile (see above). But when the imagistic practices had run their course, Paliau declared the Noise to be at an end. He urged people to 'return to the original programme' (Schwartz 1962: 273) and to begin to stabilize and routinize the movement along the lines he had originally laid out:

Paliau quickly became aware that the Cult [i.e. the *Noise*] had contributed to the spread of the [mainstream] Movement. He worked to organize the expanded membership. Confusion and disorganization lasted several weeks in the villages that had experienced the Cult. They sought to learn now the content of the pre-*Noise* meetings as well as the Cult experiences of other villages. All the villages that had become involved in the *Noise* were left as members of the Movement. All looked toward Paliau to tell them what to do next. (Schwartz 1962: 284)

In the process of reuniting under the universalistic umbrella of the Paliau Movement, those people who had participated in the Noise came to realize that their experiences had been duplicated in many other villages as well. The Noise appeared to have been a common experience, but only retrospectively. In fact, the notion of a 'common experience' is misleading. When people thought of the Noise, they conjured up autobiographical memories of actual local people and events. These memories did not relate directly to the thirty-three other villages. It was only by imaginatively projecting feelings of cohesion, engendered in these memories, on to a wider (and fundamentally abstract) 'brotherhood' that the early Paliau Movement was drawn together. Schwartz observed: 'All those who had experienced the *Noise* felt bound to one another by it. They said that the *Noise* had changed them, that it had shaken them loose from their past' (1962: 284). It is crucial to bear in mind, however, that the revelations which 'changed' people and 'shook them up' united them in a specific local context, and these local contexts were later re-evoked by the Second Cult (see above). In the meantime, these memories were transferred on to the anonymous mass of Paliau's followers. This process was an outcome of the interaction of both modes of religiosity.

In the case of the Taro Cult, the Orokaiva of the 1920s emerged from the cult with a renewed sense of fragmentation into small ritual communities. The cohesion within these communities could not be transferred on to some larger grouping because there was no developed conception of such a grouping. The effects of the Noise were quite another matter: 'the Cult as a whole . . . had the effect of being an act of commitment to the Movement. This commitment is, perhaps, the most important factor by which the First Cult, though similar in form to other cargo cults, differed from all others in its continuous relationship to the Movement that had been its precipitating context' (Schwartz 1962: 376). To some extent before the Noise, and to a greater extent immediately afterwards, Paliau's routinized programme introduced an entirely novel set of mental representations, through which a large, anonymous community of followers could be envisaged. The forms of cognition triggered by the simultaneity of ritual repetition across a wide area, and specifically the development of schema-based memories for ritual procedures, made it possible to identify with anonymous 'others' who are 'like oneself' (see above, Chapter 2). This new kind of identity evoked minimal cohesion in itself. But imagistic practices, such as those of the Noise and the Second Cult, evoked very intense feelings of cohesion and these feelings were then *subsequently* projected on to the wider movement. Schwartz reached a remarkably similar conclusion: 'The effect of the Cult on the organization of the area affected was largely negative during the First Cult phase itself. However, while an extreme village particularism prevailed during the *Noise*, the common experience of the Cult . . . contributed to the subsequent unification of the villages concerned' (1962: 373).

Without this process of projection, it is unlikely that Paliau's routinized movement would have spread as widely as it did: 'At the end of the Cult phase, all villages recruited by the Cult remained within the Movement. The Movement area, as a new political unit, had been defined primarily by the spread of the Cult' (Schwartz 1962: 375). Likewise, it is probable that the Paliau Movement could not have survived as long as it has done without intermittent outbursts of imagistic practices that rejuvenated religious commitment and overall cohesion in the manner I have described. Indeed, the movement would probably not have survived more than five years, when the first 'Plateau Phase' occurred, had it not been for the imagistic mode of religiosity operationalized, as it happened, in the Second Cult.

In the Pomio Kivung, as in the Paliau Movement, the doctrinal field of operation drew cohesion from intermittent cult outbursts dominated by the imagistic mode (Whitehouse 1995: 172–3). The capacity of both movements to unite large populations in an unprecedented solidarity provided unique opportunities for nationalist struggle and to a considerable extent these opportunities were exploited. The Paliau Movement defined its membership as a proto-nation that would emerge triumphantly when the millennium arrived, but would meanwhile establish its separateness from the colonial order and subsequently the independent state of Papua New Guinea. Precisely the same approach was taken up in the Pomio Kivung. Both Koriam and Paliau pursued careers as elected state officials but used their leverage in the corridors of colonial power to protect the organizational independence of their respective movements.

With the arrival of national independence in 1975, both movements became markedly more hostile towards the state, Pomio Kivung supporters regarding the system of provincial and community government with particular distrust (Whitehouse 1995: 61–2), and Paliau's followers equating the state as a whole with the dark powers of 'Lucifer' (Wanek 1996: 202–3). Nevertheless, these policies and ideological orientations were neither caused nor even precipitated by the manner in which the two modes of religiosity were combined in the Paliau Movement and the Pomio Kivung. The large unified populations that were formed through the interaction of doctrinal and imagistic domains of operation could have been mobilized behind a variety of different ideologies. Moreover, it would have been perfectly possible (albeit unlikely) for Koriam and Paliau to have eschewed political struggle and to have proffered no doctrines or views on the morality of government and missionary activity.

It should be underlined that I am not concerned here primarily with the complex political, ideological, and historical specificities of particular religious movements. The focus is on generalizable features and potentialities of divergent modes of religiosity. The doctrinal mode can be put into the service of many kinds of political struggle at the level of the state, in so far as this mode of religiosity unites large populations. Likewise, we can say that no purely imagistic set of religious practices could unify large political groupings or sustain forms of ideology and organization that would contribute to the achievement of nationalist and secessionist goals. This leaves considerable scope, however, for a diversity of political trajectories in those large-scale, unifying movements in which the two modes of religiosity interact.

7

Entangled Histories

We have seen that, in Papua New Guinea, modes of religiosity tend to coalesce as constellations of mutually reinforcing features, including contrasting styles of codification, transmission, cognitive processing, and political organization. In the cases we have examined, the elaboration of a body of doctrine, organized in dialogical, narrative, and digital schemas, tends to be associated with routinization or short cycles of transmission, the cognitive processing of general schemas for ritual performances and religious discourse, the conceptualization of large, anonymous communities, and relatively wide dissemination. Conversely, we have observed a tendency for ritually transmitted ecstatic revelatory imagery to be associated with much longer cycles of transmission, the formation of enduring autobiographical memories for ritual episodes, the establishment of cohesive religious communities, and regional fragmentation. The aim has been to explain, by means of these cognitive and sociological features, some of the major dynamics of Melanesian religious life and patterns of political association both prior to contact and through processes of missionization and colonization.

It has been instructive to focus on detailed case studies in which these clusters of features or 'modes of religiosity' have been relatively easy to isolate. Indigenous initiation and fertility cults, and certain new religions modelled on them, tend to exhibit, in a highly developed form, all the features of the imagistic mode of religiosity, whereas the component features of the doctrinal mode are relatively undeveloped or entirely lacking. By contrast, certain new religious movements inspired by missionary Christianity exemplify the characteristics of the doctrinal mode, although this has not been to the exclusion of imagistic practices. Nevertheless, even here we have found it possible to discuss imagistic and doctrinal modes as somewhat discrete domains of operation. In the examples we have examined, the domains interact, rather than collapsing into each other.

I do not wish to suggest, in generalizing from these case studies, that all pre-contact Melanesian religions sustained full-blown imagistic traditions, only that there was a tendency for the various features of the imagistic mode to coalesce, and that this tendency became pronounced in many ritual complexes, concerning which we have reasonably reliable information. By the same token, it is not suggested that none of the features of the doctrinal mode of religiosity was elaborated in pre-contact Melanesia. Some more or less esoteric mythological traditions had great potential for being strung together by indigenous cosmologists in a way that could easily have led to the reproduction of a body of integrated, argument-based doctrine. In many parts of pre-contact Melanesia, the arts of rhetoric and public speaking were highly developed and could, in' principle, have been put into the service of doctrinal transmission. Moreover, there is some evidence, for instance from the New Guinea highlands, of tendencies towards the homogenization of regional religions (Biersack 1996). Nowhere in pre-contact Melanesia, however, has evidence been found of a thoroughgoing doctrine-based, proselytizing, routinized, centralized, hierarchical tradition. Where imagistic practices were highly developed, chronic warfare and extreme localism no doubt inhibited the emergence of the doctrinal mode and, in any case, the models for such innovation in that direction were lacking (a topic taken up, at a more general level, in the next chapter).

It should also be emphasized that, where missionary Christianity has contributed to the establishment of truly doctrinal traditions, this has not always led to the interaction of relatively discrete imagistic and doctrinal domains of operation. As indicated in Chapter 2, other forms of accommodation between the two modes of religiosity have also been arrived at, including ones that effectively inhibit the reproduction of full-blown imagistic practices. This often has to do with the fact that the doctrinal mode of religiosity is extremely powerful in political terms. The establishment of mechanisms for the central regulation and policing of orthodoxy means that élite groups can directly shape the form of worship across a wide area. Patterns of localized imagistic splintering can, at least in principle, be eradicated through close monitoring and the application of sanctions. A potential problem, however, is that purely doctrinal practices are susceptible to the tedium effect which, in the absence of a countervailing dynamic, could result in demoralization and defection to other churches or movements. It is against this backdrop that some Melanesian Christianities have tended to incorporate, if not an imagistic domain of operation, more sensually and emotionally evocative forms of routinized worship (for instance, as in Pentecostalism).

It should again be underlined, of course, that none of the features of our respective modes of religiosity is mutually exclusive. Doctrinal systems tend to be replete with ritual imagery, and all ritual imagery is susceptible to interpretation in ways that are doctrine like. Moreover, the encoding of religious and ritual representations in semantic memory always presupposes the prior formation of episodic memories (see Introduction and Chapter 5), and adherents to even the most routinized churches often base their religious identities partly around personal, autobiographical memories for epiphanic or revelatory episodes. Conversely, certain aspects of all imagistic traditions must be cognized in semantic memory. It should be acknowledged too, that sermonizing can induce religious fervour and excitement, as well as boredom. And, of course, as with the imagistic practices of the Noise and the Taro Cult, doctrines can spread rapidly but give rise to local innovation and regional fragmentation, rather than stable orthodoxy.

These qualifications notwithstanding, the tendency in Melanesia is for doctrinal and imagistic modes of religiosity to coalesce and, where they co-vary, to operate as relatively discrete fields of activity, distinguished in the conceptual frames of both observers and participants. This is the case even where, as in the Paliau Movement, expressions of the imagistic mode of religiosity are manifestly part of a broader doctrinal tradition. Thus, for instance, the 'Noise' and the 'Ghost Cult' were readily distinguishable from the Paliau Movement proper. This is all the more extraordinary when we consider how closely intertwined our two modes of religiosity appear to be in certain other regions of the world. These modalities may at times be so enmeshed that the analytical distinction seems to break down. What are we to make, for instance, of ecstatic practices in Hinduism, Buddhism, and Taoism that have become highly routinized or, in Sufism in Islam, ecstasy that leads to highly literary forms of religious expression? And yet, in Melanesia, doctrinal and imagistic modes of religiosity tend to retain a certain discreteness. When both are present, there is a definite tendency for them to interact rather than to become enmeshed. The key to explaining this lies partly in the origins of missionary Christianity.

Missionary Christianity is the outcome of a particular historical trajectory favouring the suppression of imagistic practices and the celebration of a purely doctrinal mode of religiosity. On the face of it, such a trajectory might be expected to have little potential for long-term survival. A major limitation of the doctrinal mode is its vulnerability to the tedium effect, which may be offset by more intense (if not always imagistic) forms of religious experience. At any rate, this appears to be a general tendency in the cases considered in this volume. Nevertheless, there may be some respects in which purely doctrinal practices, denuded as far as possible of any imagistic characteristics, enjoy a special transmissive advantage over other religious forms. This appears to have been the case with regard to Reformed Christianity in sixteenth-century Europe.

The Reformation, in all its myriad forms, attempted to marginalize the imagistic domain of operation within Christianity. This may help to account for the extraordinarily rapid and extensive spread of early Protestantism in Europe, as I explain below. Interestingly, the goals of Western missionaries in nineteenth- and twentieth-century Melanesia, and of many Polynesian and Melanesian missionaries, have certain affinities with those of sixteenth-century reformers in Europe. They too were concerned to spread a doctrinal mode of religiosity, as far as possible to the exclusion of a full-blown imagistic mode of operation. It is suggested in what follows, that the European Reformation indirectly provided the models for many subsequent varieties of missionary Christianity, and thus may help to explain the peculiar patterns of interaction between doctrinal and imagistic modes of religiosity in certain regions of Melanesia.

Modes of Religiosity in the European Reformation

Late Medieval Christianity, like the Paliau Movement of twentieth-century Melanesia, incorporated both doctrinal and imagistic practices. The latter took a wide variety of forms, including pilgrimages, carnivals, witch-hunts, folk religions, and agricultural festivals. Recurrent themes, more or less prominent in different localities around fifteenth-century Europe, included the renewal of natural and human fertility, the prevention and treatment of illness, xenophobic persecution (especially of Jews and witches), the propitiation of saints, and the celebration of miracles. Such processes archetypally inhered in fleeting collective dramas and the evocation of extreme emotions (often described in the writings of historians, with varying degrees of ethnocentricism, as 'hysteria', 'trauma', 'psychosis', 'ecstasy', etc.). Something of this is captured, for instance, in Berndt Moeller's[1] observations on late medieval piety in Germany:

Mass pilgrimages would catch fire like psychoses, from one day to the next, and just as suddenly they might collapse. Often some marvellous occurrence was the cause . . . In some cases, as at Sternberg in Mecklenburg in 1492, where a priest

---

[1] Moeller's article, cited here, played an important role in correcting the tendency among historians to view the later Middle Ages as a period of religious decline (see McGrath 1993: 27).

was burned to death because he had sold a consecrated host to a Jew, the cause appears completely inappropriate and unreasonable. In others, as for instance in the strange children's pilgrimage to Mont St. Michel in Normandy in the year 1457 . . . no concrete cause is even discernible. (Moeller 1971: 54)

Alongside these medieval imagistic traditions flourished a doctrinal mode of religiosity, manifested in its most comprehensive form only within the ecclesiastical community. The monasteries and universities of the Middle Ages had produced a highly elaborated body of doctrine, founded upon the most rigorous attention to theological detail and logical argumentation (a tradition known, with all its pejorative connotations, as 'scholasticism'). In principle, if not always in practice, the parameters within which scholastic debates (e.g. between realists and nominalists or Pelagianists and Augustinians) were carried on, were firmly fixed by church authorities, and doctrinal orthodoxy upheld with reference to sacred texts and Christian tradition. Monastic religion in the Middle Ages bore all the hallmarks of the doctrinal mode of religiosity: extensively verbalized (and inscribed) doctrine and exegesis encoded in semantic memory, highly disciplined and routinized rituals and observances, the 'intellectualization' of religious ideation (as a logically coherent and integrated corpus of teachings), a striving for doctrinal stability and uniformity, a large-scale and anonymous community of worshippers, and a hierarchical and centralized church structure.

Nevertheless, the mechanisms for maintaining doctrinal orthodoxy in the late-medieval church were weakening. Provincial synods repeatedly failed to exercise their powers to suppress heresy, partly because of a growth in the influence of secular rulers and nationalisms in certain parts of late medieval Europe (McGrath 1993: 35–6). This created a vacuum with respect to the establishment of authoritative doctrine, which was eventually filled by Reformed Christianity.

One of the most outstanding features of the Reformation in all its forms was its principled determination to transmit ordered bodies of doctrine as widely as possible—that is, to 'spread the Word'. A central concern of reformers was to educate, and one of the prime movers in educational reform was Martin Luther. As Kittelson observes

it was Luther, above all, who brought education to the public. It was he who argued that the average person could in some sense know what he believed, and who acted upon this conviction. Without this work, contemporary Christians would be facing very different difficulties from those confronting them now. The need to make religion make sense, and to do so for the average person, would not exist. (1985: 111–12)

Luther's educational programme was heavily influenced by humanist methods, emanating from the Florentine Renaissance and in particular the *loci* (or *topoi*) method borrowed from classical rhetoric, which emphasized the orderly presentation of topics essential to a given subject. Thus, in an attempt to communicate Luther's Christianity as a systematized body of doctrine, Philipp Melanchthon published in 1521 his *Loci Communes* (or 'Common Places of Evangelical Theology'). Meanwhile, Luther's catechisms became the basis for the curriculum at primary schools, detailing Christian doctrines in the most accessible form that Luther's stringent criteria for accuracy and comprehensiveness would allow.

Formal education was not, of course, sufficient for the rapid spread of Reformation ideas. A greater challenge was presented by the fact that German and Swiss reformers needed to reach out to audiences across Europe. It has often been suggested that this process was largely facilitated by the advent of printing technologies. Nevertheless, the establishment and spread of any doctrinal orthodoxy depends upon frequent reviewing of cardinal principles, such as the *loci communes* of Luther's evangelical religion. The reason for this is that a complex body of doctrine cannot 'live' in people's minds, in the absence of regular reiteration, or at least private recollection (see Chapter 5). Such a process may entail regular rereading of textual material but this is not essential. Far more important in practice, whether in conditions of mass literacy or total non-literacy, is a pattern of routinized oral transmission. It so happens that approximately nine-tenths of the population were *not* literate in sixteenth-century Germany, a proportion typical of other parts of Europe during that period, so that printing simply cannot be upheld as the key factor in the spread of Reformation ideas. Granted that the circulation of documents helped to carry the Word to distant locations, local dissemination of Reformation ideas was primarily by word of mouth (see McGrath 1993: 15). Thus, according to Bob Scribner

pride of place as the major formal means of communication must not go to printing, but to the pulpit, from which most public announcements were proclaimed. Indeed, the religious reform was first and foremost a powerful preaching revival, and the first act of any community which developed an interest in these ideas was to request a preacher to proclaim the 'pure Word of God'. It was not believed to be sufficient just to read printed tracts, or even the Bible: the great desire was to *hear* the Word. Indeed, for Protestants 'hearing the Word' became virtually a Sacrament alongside Baptism and the Lord's Supper. (1989: 84)

This emphasis on oral transmission led to the extensive codification of dogma as rhetorical strings of question-and-answer, which is so characteristic of the doctrinal mode of religiosity. Scribner describes how Reformation preachers actively encouraged dialogues with their audiences, following a spontaneous pattern of interrogation and response. Whereas sixteenth-century illustrations depicted Catholic congregations as immobile and silent, Reformation audiences were shown debating heatedly with their preachers (Scribner 1989: 85). Luther's catechisms and Melanchthon's *Loci Communes* organized Christian theology into a finite set of parts, interwoven by clearly enunciated threads of argumentation, while preachers elaborated a rhetorical style of transmission by means of which the new ideas could be continually revisited in a routinized programme of dialogue and sermonizing. Moreover, as we shall see, the next generation of reformers went further still in systematizing doctrine according to these principles of codification and transmission.

Thus, notwithstanding those historians who emphasize the importance of printing in the Reformation, it must be appreciated that ideas contained in print were only able to exercise a sustained and uniform influence on those they reached in so far as the written words were continually reviewed in memory and, in practice, rehearsed in countless speech events. Those preoccupied with the impact of literacy and printing ought not to forget that ideas are never contained in patterns of ink but only in the minds of those who read them. The information thus processed was largely organized by reformed Christians according to conventions of oral transmission, which entail patterns of cognition and codification characteristic of the doctrinal mode of religiosity all over the world. At no stage of this process could literate transmission be regarded as indispensable in principle, although it was clearly relevant in practice. Moreover, alongside the spread of documents it must also be recognized that Reformation ideas were carried by highly mobile proselytizing individuals who included 'at transregional level, carriers, merchants, colporteurs, wandering artisans or journeymen (especially weavers), travellers and wandering preachers. The last are of considerable importance for the wider diffusion of Reformation ideas' (Scribner 1989: 96).

In order to complete itself as a religion operating in the doctrinal mode, Protestantism required mechanisms for the entrenchment of orthodoxy. Church authorities would not throw their weight behind Reformation theology and practice; on the contrary, the Counter-Reformation belatedly clarified the existing doctrinal commitments of the Roman Catholic Church and tightened up its mechanisms for the prevention of further innovation, via the wide-ranging dictates of the Fourth Session of the Council of Trent in 1546. Therefore, the route to orthodoxy within the various branches of the Reformation clearly lay in the establishment of new churches, a development that many early reformers had wanted to avoid. It fell to ensuing generations to complete the tasks that Luther and his contemporaries had begun.

One of the most visionary figures of the second generation of reformers was John Calvin. Calvin realized that a doctrinal programme could not survive simply by virtue of its intellectual persuasiveness. In order to hold its ground, he argued, a theology must place the stamp of authority upon its cardinal principles. This required the establishment of an independent church in which doctrine could be regulated at the centre, and disseminated via an ecclesiastical hierarchy well schooled in the limits of doctrinal orthodoxy. It was perhaps Calvin's greatest contribution to the Reformation to set up just such an apparatus, the apex of which he called the 'Consistory'. According to McGrath:

Calvin conceived of the Consistory primarily as an instrument for the 'policing' of religious orthodoxy. It was the guarantor of the discipline which Calvin's experience at Strasbourg had led him to recognize as essential to the survival of reformed Christendom. Its primary function was to deal with those whose religious views were sufficiently deviant to pose a threat to the established religious order at Geneva. (1993: 197)

Calvin's churchly apparatus, which became a model also for subsequent varieties of Protestantism, provided the final component for a thoroughgoing doctrinal mode of religiosity. The styles of codification and transmission pioneered by the first wave of reformers were taken up by Calvin, not merely as a means of persuasion and conversion, but as a weapon with which to defend a new orthodoxy from competing ones. And within Calvin's church itself, innovation was blocked by an ecclesiastical hierarchy of ministers, elders, and deacons, regulated from the centre by the new Consistory. Routinization meanwhile ensured that both doctrine and worshipful practice were rigidly formed in the minds and actions of an expanding membership, and immune to unintended local deviation.

Collective identity among Calvin's followers was construed in terms of conformity, not only to an abstract corpus of doctrine, but also conformity to a set of routinized ritual acts encoded in semantic memory. Calvin, like other reformers, rated the Word above all else, including Christian ritual. Nevertheless, 'for Calvin, as for all the magisterial reformers, the sacraments were seen as identity-giving; without sacraments, there could be no Christian church' (McGrath 1993: 181). If Calvin recognized the central importance of the liturgy as a source of Christian identity, it was not (of course) because he apprehended the doctrinal mode of religiosity in an analytically explicit fashion. The designation of routinized behaviour as a basis for common identity produces large, anonymous communities and Calvin seems to have recognized these effects, if not the process. What Reformation thinkers crucially did not appreciate, however, was the vital long-term importance of an imagistic domain of operation (see Cameron 1991: 408–16). Amid the initial enthusiasm of the Reformation, the 'tedium effect' was not always a problem, but the determined repudiation of imagistic practices within early Protestant churches had serious long-term consequences.

In a fascinating recent publication, Patrick Collinson (1997) has argued that the earliest reformers were merely iconoclastic, whereas the secondary Reformation was characterized by 'iconophobia'. Luther and his contemporaries were opposed to certain images, and perhaps all imagistic practices, but they did not go to the extremes of repudiating images *per se*. The iconophobia that seized certain Protestants from about 1580, however, reviled virtually all representational art forms, especially when oriented to religious themes. For instance, according to one sixteenth-century writer, Philip Stubbes, 'the opening words of St John's Gospel were a proof against the religious drama: "the word is God, and God is the word". To *represent* the Word was to "make a mocking stock of him" and to prepare a counterfeit' (Collinson 1997: 288). Needless to say, Stubbes and his like were utterly opposed to any religious practices that might be described as 'imagistic'.

Not surprisingly, the most virulently anti-imagistic Protestant traditions have always been vulnerable to the 'tedium effect'. Even amid the enthusiasm and commitment that accompanied initial conversion to Protestantism, there is evidence that boredom was a potential obstacle to the iconophobic aspirations of reformed preachers. Cameron, for instance, cites the case of a newly converted Piemontese Waldenensian congregation, whose commitment to Protestantism can hardly be in doubt (expressed as it was in a willingness to face execution for their heretical beliefs), but who were nevertheless sorely tried by the tedium of routinized, logocentric religion: 'That they would *be* Protestants—that was their identity—but that did not extend to being bored stiff or humiliated by an alien preacher wished upon them by the Company of Pastors at Geneva' (Cameron 1991: 412).

In practice, the suppression of medieval imagistic practices within early Protestant churches was only partially successful. In some areas, such as Lutheran Nuremberg in 1539, popular rituals were reinstated in protest against iconoclastic preachers (Cameron 1991: 409). In England, the later part of the sixteenth century saw an intensified concern with witch-hunting which might be understood, in part, as a reaction against the suppression of imagistic forms. The war against diabolical cults was thus expressed in ecstatic and extremely violent ritual, albeit suitably informed by the intellectual climate of the Reformation (cf. Macfarlane 1970: 201–2).

In general, the spread of Reformation ideas seems to have conformed to a pattern in which newly established doctrinal orthodoxies came to be sporadically disrupted by the innovation of localized imagistic cults. As Cameron observes: '[The following] experience was repeated wherever the Reformation spread: initial feverish enthusiasm . . . then a cooling-off period in which interest might be directed to more exotic creeds' (1991: 397). There is evidence of extremely widespread disappointment among Protestant clergy at the apparent reluctance of lay converts to abandon entirely those popular religious practices, of medieval origin, that now appeared (in the words of Lutheran Caspar Huberinus) to be 'unchristian, pagan, idolatrous, frivolous . . ., seductive, ungodly, devilish' (cited by Cameron 1991: 408). Such excessively negative evaluations of religious life among the laity seem to reflect the unrealistically high standards of many sixteenth-century pastors. A largely successful transition to doctrinal practices on the part of ordinary folk was not enough; some Protestant clergy required nothing short of a total eradication of imagistic practices—an expectation which, according to Cameron, amounted to 'a piece of intellectual imperialism of colossal proportions' (1991: 416). Nevertheless, the arrogance of sixteenth-century reformers is dwarfed by the 'intellectual imperialism' of their missionary successors in nineteenth- and twentieth-century Melanesia, the topic to which we now turn.

From Reformation to Missionization

A striking continuity between sixteenth- and seventeenth-century Protestantism and all varieties of missionary Christianity is a profound preoccupation with the maintenance of a thoroughgoing doctrinal mode of religiosity, available to all. In addition, although the 'logocentric iconophobia' of early Protestantism, at least in its more puritanical manifestations, was not taken to such extremes in Melanesian missions, both reformers and missionaries seem to have shared a basically negative orientation towards imagistic practices. Notwithstanding the effects of the Counter Reformation, one might have expected Catholic missionaries in Melanesia to have been rather more tolerant of local imagistic forms than their Protestant counterparts, at least where these activities did not entail violations of the Decalogue. One might also have anticipated the importation of cults of saints and of the Virgin Mary, of Irish wakes, penitential rites, and other popular expressions of Catholic piety. In fact, however, neither of these processes has occurred to any great extent. The tendency within all Christian missions based in Melanesia has been towards the transmission of the Word, and the most basic of the sacraments (as variously construed in different churches), and the general discouragement of most other forms of religious expression.[2] In these respects, there are affinities between many nineteenth- and twentieth-century missionaries in Melanesia and sixteenth-century reformers in Europe.

It would be highly implausible to regard these affinities as simple coincidences. In the first place, the European Reformation has fundamentally influenced the history of Christianity everywhere, albeit by complex and circuitous routes. Contemporary Catholics and Protestants alike, in many parts of the world, tend to possess a much more extensive grasp of Christian doctrine than the laity of Medieval Europe, and this is attributable at least as much to the pioneering intellectual and pedagogic achievements of reformers as it is to the spread of mass literacy. Thus, the aim of missionaries, of whatever denomination, to instil the teachings of Christianity into the hearts and minds of non-literate Melanesians has its historical origins not in the medieval church (which had no such lofty ambitions) but in the aspiration of leaders such as Luther and Calvin, and members of the Council of Trent, to create a doctrinal system accessible to all. A second reason why missionary Christianity is similar in so many ways to early Protestantism, has to do with the transmissive dimensions of doctrinal and imagistic modes of religiosity, and this is a rather more complicated story to tell.

At the root of the issue is the fact that the doctrinal mode of religiosity is supremely adapted to evangelical or expansionary projects, spreading both efficiently and rapidly. Even in a region such as Melanesia, with

---

[2] The reality is more complicated, since different missions exhibited varying degrees of tolerance at different times and there was a general tendency towards liberalism and cultural relativism in all Pacific missions from about the 1930s (Forman 1978: 44).

no experience of the doctrinal mode and about as far removed culturally from a Christian world-view as it is possible to be, missionaries were remarkably successful in spreading the Word. It is hard to imagine any religion of comparable elaborateness spreading to Papua New Guinea faster or more extensively than have the many varieties of Christianity. A major factor in the success of doctrinal regimes is their style of codification.

As discussed at length in previous chapters, missionary Christianity is codified more or less exclusively in dialogical and rhetorical schemas (expressed primarily through sermonizing and proselytism), narratives (e.g. parables and mytho-historical sequences), and linked sets of binary oppositions. The emphasis is on oral transmission (albeit referenced to textual materials) and it follows that just one or a handful of proselytizing individuals (whether messiahs, disciples, and prophets, or reformers and missionaries) are capable of carrying the Word to large populations, either by addressing congregations at consecutive locations before moving on, or by establishing themselves at fixed locations and urging potential converts to attend their routinized services and orations. As long as congregations can be secured, the force of argument of Christianity is often sufficiently compelling for most listeners that it is eventually internalized.

In stark contrast, the spread of imagistic practices as part of a missionary project, or indeed as part of the establishment of Protestantism in sixteenth-century Europe, would have been extremely inefficient and impossible to monitor and police. In the first place, imagistic practices, being codified in ritual choreography rather than as a body of teachings, are transmitted by groups of ritual participants rather than proselytizing individuals. They spread, if at all, through strings of contiguous contagion among neighbouring communities or through the migration of ritual sects, not through the oratorical skills of one or a few individuals. Moreover, since the religious ideology is primarily inferred from the multivocal imagery of ritual choreography and sacred objects, and experienced as direct revelation, the history of dissemination tends to pass unnoticed, and each ritual community experiences its ceremonial practices as unique. In practice, manifestations of the imagistic mode do tend to produce locally distinctive variants, with no overarching superstructure capable of dissembling these diverse ritual activities into a homogeneous cultural tradition. Since processes such as the European Reformation and the missionization of Melanesia were premised upon the establishment of stable orthodoxies, it is obvious why they did not emphasize an imagistic mode of operation, and tended to oppose existing local ritual traditions and the sectarianism and social fragmentation these practices typically engendered.

We are now in a better position to understand why, when doctrinal and imagistic practices come together in Melanesia, they tend to retain a certain discreteness with regard to the domains in which they operate, *interacting* rather than becoming thoroughly enmeshed. The colonization of Melanesia entailed a series of confrontations between, on the one hand, populations familiar with the imagistic mode but with no experience of doctrinal practices and, on the other, forms of Christianity operating in the doctrinal mode and largely denuded of any full-blown imagistic dimensions. The two models of religious experience, codification, transmission, and organization stood quite starkly opposed. Since these divergent models are quite easily differentiated in Melanesia, it is hardly surprising that they have influenced and shaped patterns of religious innovation in the region in the directions they have.

Certain new religions, such as the Paliau Movement and the Pomio Kivung, draw heavily on both distinctively Melanesian and more generally Christian ideas. But, in their mainstream manifestations, these movements are modelled primarily on the transmissive and organizational principles of the doctrinal mode of religiosity, ultimately owing some of their inspiration to a religious revolution in sixteenth-century Europe. Conversely, localized 'cargo cults' and splinter groups may borrow heavily from both Christian and local religious traditions, but they tend to be modelled primarily on the transmissive and organizational features of the imagistic mode, indigenous to Melanesia. In such circumstances, the potentialities and limitations of both modes of religiosity have been relatively easy for religious innovators to recognize and therefore to exploit. Leaders such as Paliau and Koriam railed publicly against imagistic practices but were careful in practice to deal with them very sensitively, one might even say leniently. This may be attributable in part to the exceptional acumen of these particular Melanesian leaders who have, on the whole, shown considerable willingness to adapt theological principles to political realities. Many reformers in sixteenth-century Europe, and their missionary successors in Melanesia, were of quite another mind-set, much more rigidly attached to the doctrines they helped to disseminate and thus inclined to be intolerant of fundamental deviations, no matter how expedient and temporary.

8

Modes of Religiosity and Political Evolution

This volume has been concerned with the historical dynamics of modes of religiosity in Melanesia, including their entanglement with religious forms originating in Europe. The question of whether the imagistic/ doctrinal dichotomy might be applied to a much wider range of ethnographic examples around the world has been deliberately set aside. In part, this is because a considerable body of evidence is required to demonstrate the operation of modes of religiosity in any given case. Even limiting the discussion to Melanesia has involved focusing heavily on a small number of detailed case studies. Any attempt to generalize the approach to religions in other continents is likely to appear superficial and unconvincing, unless it is carried out in comparable detail, and then perhaps only by those with specialist knowledge of the ethnography. Even if general tendencies towards the coalescence of modes of religiosity in far-flung regions could be established, critics would immediately point to other cases where doctrinal and imagistic features are so thoroughly enmeshed that the distinction breaks down. It would, therefore, be necessary to explain why, in a wide range of cases, the elaboration of modes of religiosity is inhibited by factors that are regionally and historically particular. That too would be a massive task, well beyond the scope of the present volume.

So I will not conclude with a globe-trotting chapter, plucking out evidence for the coalescence of modes of religiosity in a range of ethnographic regions. The task of generalizing will be approached rather differently here, by considering how the theory of modes of religiosity might shed light on some broad trajectories in political evolution, starting with our earliest human ancestors.

It would seem that the imagistic mode of religiosity is very ancient, perhaps as old as our species. Among prehistoric hunter-gatherers, we do not encounter the problem that modes of religiosity can be entwined or enmeshed. Such populations, like the peoples of pre-contact Melanesia, had no experience of doctrinal practices. A major task is, therefore, to establish how and when the doctrinal mode was first elaborated, regardless of whether or how this encompassed, suppressed, or otherwise articulated with pre-existing imagistic practices. Such questions present a means of testing the explanatory power of the doctrinal/imagistic dichotomy, beyond the much narrower setting of recent Melanesian history.

It can hardly be contested that there are relatively 'simple' and relatively 'complex' societies, in technological and political terms, and that degrees of political complexity have to do with the scale on which the ends of government are achieved and common identities constructed, and the elaborateness of the institutional structures through which these processes are reproduced. It is clear that simpler forms of political organization are, broadly speaking, more ancient than the more complex forms and hence the development of the latter out of the former has sometimes been described, if only in a rather general sense, as a modality of 'evolution'. Among the many theories that have been proposed to account for aspects of this developmental process, those that make deterministic claims about literacy have particular relevance for this study.

A crucial question, for the most part implicit in the foregoing chapters, is whether literacy is a necessary condition for the independent invention of a doctrinal domain of operation. Largely non-literate leaders and followers of the Paliau Movement and the Pomio Kivung in Papua New Guinea were able to establish and sustain doctrinal traditions but not, one might suppose, in the absence of a model (in this case, missionary Christianity) thoroughly steeped in literate practices. After all, it would appear that the doctrinal mode of religiosity was unknown in Melanesia prior to the arrival of literate religious traditions. I argue in this chapter that literacy was a necessary, or at least a precipitating condition for the independent invention of doctrinal practices. Nevertheless, once exposed to the doctrinal mode of religiosity, other non-literate populations were capable of using it as a model for further religious innovation. Thus, the blossoming of doctrinal practices, if not their first appearance, has less to do with the sociological implications of writing technologies than with the establishment of new conditions of cultural transmission.

The Imagistic Mode in the Upper Palaeolithic

Any discussion of religious life in human prehistory starts from a somewhat limited data base. The archaeological record is unlikely to provide direct evidence of cosmology and ritual except where these take the form of materials capable of being preserved within the ground and of being interpreted correctly. Moreover, this volume is concerned not with just any information relating to prehistoric religions, but with evidence for the emergence of *modes of religiosity* over time, including styles of cognition, codification, and transmission that have seldom been fully investigated and documented even in contemporary ethnographic research based on detailed direct observation.

The situation is by no means hopeless, however. It is probably safe to assume, for instance, that Palaeolithic and Mesolithic hunter-gatherers did not possess large-scale, centralized, hierarchical socio-religious morphology. It is possible that some tendencies in this direction were activated under exceptional circumstances, but there is no evidence of this. The doctrinal mode of religiosity is therefore a relatively recent phenomenon, apparently becoming established first in Mesopotamia through the development of temple complexes, a process which began after 6,000 BC. This is not to say that our hunter-gatherer ancestors lacked religion and ritual.

Neanderthals probably performed a variety of rituals. They certainly buried their dead, in some cases along with foodstuffs, tools, and possibly flowers. But a much greater abundance of evidence relating to prehistoric religions comes from populations of anatomically modern humans, during the Upper Palaeolithic. During this period, there was a veritable explosion of artistic activity, especially the production of cave paintings and sculptures. Surviving examples of these artworks provide the first clear evidence for the coalescence of key features of the imagistic mode of religiosity.

In an extremely readable and informative monograph on the origins of art and religion, John Pfeiffer (1982) attempts to reconstruct at least some of the features of religious experience and practice during the Upper Palaeolithic. Focusing on evidence for ritual activity in natural caves and labyrinths, where most of the surviving artwork of this period has been found, Pfeiffer argues that cults of initiation probably involved the revelation of surprising imagery in conditions of extreme emotional and sensory arousal. Indeed, the inferences Pfeiffer draws suggest the development of religious forms remarkably like those of pre-contact Melanesia, where the doctrinal mode of religiosity was likewise unknown.

We can, of course, only speculate about the range and types of rituals carried out during the last Ice Age. Nevertheless, the discovery of ancient footprints in a number of cave systems suggests the performance of intitiation rites. In some cases, these prints were clearly made by groups of children in middle childhood, in others they were made exclusively by teenagers. There is evidence too that some groups of children were walking in a highly stylized fashion, on their heels, reinforcing the impression of ceremonial activity. Other footprints were apparently made by groups of children running in the caves (a dangerous manoeuvre, in a darkened environment with sharp, rocky projections and slippery surfaces). It is tempting to speculate that novices were induced to flee in terror from their initiators, as in the *embahi* ceremony of the Orokaiva (see Chapter 1).

At any rate, Pfeiffer argues that underground caves and labyrinths provided ideal environments for the transmission of traumatic and esoteric revelations. To begin with, these were naturally strange places, radically different from the familiar outside world. Temperatures were low and unchanging, in contrast with constantly fluctuating temperatures in the open air. Progress through the caves and tunnels required continuous descent, in contrast with the experience of moving through an undulating landscape outside. The dark and enclosing subterranean world contrasted with the bright and open surfaces above. Underground, people had to stoop, slide, and crawl, instead of walking. The familiar objects and surfaces of the outside world were replaced by strange textures and shadows. Sounds that would have been easily recognizable in the open produced odd acoustic effects down below. There is considerable evidence that the strangeness of the underground environment was made very much stranger through the production of subterranean artefacts and rituals.

Consider the visual imagery evoked by cave paintings, sculptures, and engravings. These often appear to have been placed deliberately in locations where they could be made to appear very suddenly out of the darkness. For instance, in some cases, these works of art could only be seen when illuminated from a particular spot (or from more than one spot). Thus, initiators would have been able to regulate the exposure of imagery through the manipulation of lamps and torches. Pfeiffer describes as follows his first experience of being shown two ancient clay sculptures in the famous caves at Tuc D'Audoubert, when his guide suddenly illuminated the figures with his torch: '[My guide] engineered a reenactment of something that must have happened in the rotunda on a number of occasions 10,000 to 15,000 years ago, an event designed deliberately to evoke a feeling of displacement, an unreal dreamlike setting, a shock of surprise . . . Under such conditions, probably intensified by other effects, people formed powerful associations and remembered for a lifetime what they heard and saw' (1982: 133). In other cases, visual imagery was produced in locations where they could only be viewed from a certain angle and distance, for instance, within very narrow tunnels which the observer would have had to squeeze into before being in a position to see the artwork. The element of surprise was also dramatically fostered through violent or grotesque imagery, for instance, the portrayal of animals with strange anatomies—distorted proportions, missing body parts, monstrously hybridized characteristics, and so on.

As well as cultivating a sense of secrecy and revelation through visual special effects, it is likely that underground religious rites bombarded the senses from all directions. The strange acoustics of cave systems provided ample opportunities for the production of unearthly noises, and evidence of a variety of ancient musical instruments has been uncovered in these labyrinthine galleries, including fragments of what appear to have been flutes, bullroarers, and a variety of percussion instruments. Surviving footprints in some caves indicate dancing, and it seems likely that this activity was accompanied by music, both choral and instrumental. As Pfeiffer observes:

Underground ceremonies must have been designed to take advantage of and shatter the silence as well as the darkness, to bombard the ear as well as the eye with a variety of sensations planned to arouse and inform . . . A song sung inside a tube-like corridor would not be heard until someone passed directly in front of the opening, directly across the sound beam . . . The playing of fragments of familiar melodies or entire melodies inside echoing spaces would correspond to displays of incomplete or distorted images respectively. Anamorphic music could be created as readily as anamorphic art—music recognizable from one position and taking on the shape of a known melody from another. (1982: 183)

Finally, Pfeiffer emphasizes the diverse opportunities, afforded by the subterranean environment, for the cultivation of intense emotion, especially states of terror. Caves and labyrinths are dangerous places, where the risks of slipping, gashing, drowning, suffocating, and becoming hopelessly lost were no doubt acutely felt by our sparsely equipped ancestors. Moreover, fears of evil spirits, enclosed spaces, and utter darkness could easily have been played upon with terrifying effect. Groups of novices, or unfortunate individuals, could have been abandoned in the inky blackness for periods of time, inducing hallucinations as well as extreme fear.

J. D. Lewis-Williams provides a rich body of evidence that much Upper Palaeolithic art represents imagery deriving from altered states of consciousness, generated within ritual settings (Lewis-Williams and

Dowson 1988; Lewis-Williams 1997). This argument rests on the universality of certain entoptic forms, and their interaction with hallucinated imagery, in altered states of consciousness, deriving from features of neurological functioning present in all humans (and possibly a range of other mammalian species). Entoptic forms consist of recurrent types of geometric visual percepts derived from the structure of the optic system, anywhere between the eye and the cortex. Hallucinated imagery, meanwhile, consists of 'iconic versions of culturally controlled items such as animals, as well as somatic and aural experiences' (Lewis-Williams and Dowson 1988: 202). On the basis of a series of detailed comparisons between the entoptic and visual forms generated by altered states of consciousness in a variety of unconnected cultures, Lewis-Williams attempts to demonstrate the underlying unity of such representations and their widespread recurrence in Upper Palaeolithic art. Although the contemporary ethnography used by Lewis-Williams included rituals that involve the use of hallucinogenic drugs, he suggests that such altered states in the Upper Palaeolithic were induced by sensory deprivation in underground labyrinths (Lewis-Williams 1997: 812).

Pfeiffer considers it most likely that hallucinatory experiences underground were ritually orchestrated, along with a range of revelatory traumas we can only begin to imagine. Putting together a range of evidence for ceremonial involving cognitive shocks, and extreme sensory and emotional stimulation, Pfeiffer suggests that subterranean rituals of the Upper Palaeolithic had distinctive mnemonic effects.

Pfeiffer's central thesis is that, during the last glacial peak, early humans adapted to a harsher environment by means of an information explosion (1982: ch. 8). This process of adaptation not only involved new forms of co-operation and patterns of communication and trade but also a closer investigation of natural resources, and methods of utilizing them. In the absence of systems of writing, there was a risk that hard-won information would be lost in the process of inter-generational transmission. Pfeiffer argues that subterranean ceremonial provided a solution to this problem, in the form of a set of mnemonic devices for the successful reproduction of a growing body of information:

One way of preparing people for imprinting has been known for a long time by tribes everywhere, modern as well as prehistoric: bring them into unfamiliar, alien, and unpleasant places ... This is designed to precede the imparting of information. Shaking an individual up, arranging to erase or undermine his everyday world as completely as possible, apparently serves as an effective preliminary to making him remember. Confused and uncertain about what is happening and what is about to happen, he becomes submissive, ready to listen and see and believe practically anything, or at least a good deal more than he would in a familiar setting (1982: 124).

In the 1970s, the standard explanation for the dramatic development of art and ceremonial at the height of the last Ice Age, was the desire to effect magical control over declining game. By producing images of wild animals in their paintings and sculptures, ancient artists hoped to effect ritual control over the fertility of these natural species and improve rates of hunting success. Pfeiffer points out a number of possible weaknesses of this approach. Firstly, the animals depicted in ancient cave paintings are often not the species figuring most highly in the diets of the artists. And, secondly, we have no clear evidence that earlier hunters, including Neanderthals, lacked the artistic capacities of Upper Palaeolithic peoples, and yet they did not go in for cave painting. Although by no means rejecting the standard explanation for the sudden profusion of cave art, Pfeiffer opens up a fresh line of argument, namely that religious and artistic innovation was an adaptation to the demands made on memory by an information explosion. Nevertheless, Pfeiffer's hypothesis is not without its drawbacks.

Firstly, Pfeiffer does not make it entirely clear how the paintings, sculptures, and engravings of the Upper Palaeolithic served to transmit information of practical value. His argument seems to rest on the assumption that, after various special effects had been used to produce a receptive frame of mind, information of a technical and practical nature was then orally transmitted. Unfortunately, we have no direct evidence of this. The only information that we know was transmitted was the surviving imagery which, in itself, seems to have had limited practical application. Secondly, Pfeiffer's discussion of the cognitive processes involved in these forms of religious transmission, although clearly implying the formation of enduring and vivid episodic memories, is psychologically naive, involving implausible mechanisms such as 'brainwashing', or inappropriate ones such as rote-learning, for which there seems to be no evidence in the cases at issue. Finally, Pfeiffer does not consider how cognitive and transmissive features inferred from the archaeological evidence might directly affect patterns of political association. An alternative approach would be to envisage the subterranean rituals of Upper Palaeolithic hunter-gatherers as imagistic practices. Viewed in this way, Pfeiffer's inferences about codification, transmission, and memory reveal more about the development of forms of sociality and inter-group relations than about the processing and reproduction of technical information.

For reasons which this volume has explored in some detail, the imagistic mode of religiosity entails the formation of highly cohesive ritual communities. In conditions of intensifying competition for natural resources, such practices would have conferred a palpable advantage on local groups. We have seen how, in pre-contact Papua New Guinea, the imagistic mode was crucial to the reproduction of groups of warriors. Similarly, in the Upper Palaeolithic, populations experimenting with the revelatory techniques of the imagistic mode would have formed potentially very effective hunting and warring groups. Populations lacking such groupings but competing for the same resources would have been quite easily wiped out. Interestingly, the massive proliferation of art and ritual around 17,000 years ago correlates with the development of new weapons, including the spear thrower and bow and arrow.[1]

Cultural-ecological explanations for warfare are well established in anthropology (e.g. Leeds 1963; Collins 1965; Divale and Harris 1976). But they are not the only explanations available. Aside from well-known innatist arguments (e.g. Lorenz 1966; Ardrey 1966) and structuralist hypotheses that envisage warfare as the converse of exchange (e.g. Mauss 1954; Lévi-Strauss 1969; Sahlins 1968), many rather more obscure explanations for warfare have been advanced. In a concise survey of the literature, Ferguson (1984) mentions attempts to account for warfare in terms of distributions of personality types and child-rearing practices, military preparedness, rules of marriage, residence, and descent, economic upheaval, and a variety of other variables. But by far the most common approach to explaining warfare in anthropology is to accept at face value the stated reasons of warring parties (e.g. the desire to exact revenge, to capture brides, slaves, trophies, or booty, to acquire spiritual powers or prestige, to obtain productive land, and so on). This last approach is concerned with accounting for warfare within narrowly defined ethnographic contexts, contributing little to a general theory of warfare.

Notwithstanding the diversity of these approaches, they have in common the fundamental assumption that the capacity of humans to wage war is naturally given. Only the innatists propose an explicit theory of this 'naturally given' capacity (i.e. that it is biologically rooted in aggressive drives). Against this view, it may be observed that feelings of

---

[1] Admittedly, however, there is no firm evidence that such technology was used in tribal warfare.

aggression are not a necessary condition for the waging of war. Other theories do not elaborate upon the naturalness of the human capacity to wage war, but simply take it for granted. Thus, they share with Thomas Hobbes the belief that in the absence of institutional means of imposing peace, humans will always be capable of waging war. Almost all theorists of warfare have in common this basic assumption, whether they focus on the specific material factors and cultural values that precipitate war or the political and economic arrangements that inhibit it.

This assumption, that the capacity of humans to wage war is naturally given, immediately loses its force when we stop to consider what war is, what defines it as a phenomenon. According to Ferguson: 'the basic underlying phenomena characteristic of war can be described as follows: organized, purposeful group action, directed against another group ... involving the actual or potential application of lethal force' (1984: 5). The problem is immediately clear: warfare is not possible without groups and, as far as I am aware, no anthropologist would seriously contend that any sort of human group may be regarded as 'naturally given'. On the contrary, groups are the product of complex processes of social and cultural transmission or 'reproduction', and it is these processes that we must first explain if we are to have anything resembling a general theory of warfare.

Crucial aspects of group formation in the Upper Palaeolithic appear to have been rooted in the imagistic mode of religiosity, and so it is to religion and ritual that we must look if we are to grasp the nature of intergroup violence in human prehistory. Somewhat surprisingly, the links between religion and warfare have been seriously neglected in anthropology. As Ferguson observes: 'Ritual commonly precedes, accompanies, and follows an engagement [in war] ... Despite the abundance of data on this connection, I could find no general theoretical study devoted to it. Perhaps that neglect stems from a prejudice that war and religion do not belong together' (1990: 46). Possibly Ferguson goes too far here, but the general point is well taken. Not only is it through rituals that military units are formed, but very often these rituals provide the main forum for the transmission of warlike values (e.g. self-sacrifice for the sake of the group, revenge, bellicosity, predation, etc.).

A rare example of an anthropologist who has taken seriously all these issues is Simon Harrison, in his recent monograph *The Mask of War* (1993).[2]

---

[2] The following summary of *The Mask of War* (Harrison 1993) was first published as part of a book review in the *Journal of the Anthropological Association of Ireland*, 3(2): 47–9 (Whitehouse 1993a).

This is a short and stimulating critique of the pervasive assumption in Western sociological thought that warfare results from the absence of a means of constraining or preventing it. In Hobbes's *Leviathan*, the state of nature is a state of 'Warre' which is only transcended when the right to use force is transferred from individuals to the state. According to Hobbes, however, between states warfare persists in the absence of effective mechanisms for its regulation. Other mechanisms for the prevention of Hobbesian 'Warre' are familiar: for Durkheim, it was social solidarity; for Freud, it was the super-ego; for Tylor, Mauss, Lévi-Strauss, and Sahlins, it was exchange.

Through an analysis of warfare among the Manambu and their neighbours, in Papua New Guinea, Simon Harrison seeks to overturn this traditional perspective. He maintains that warfare, among Sepik peoples and perhaps in Melanesia more generally, cannot be understood in terms of the absence of mechanisms for its prevention. Warfare is not the expression of something 'natural' to Melanesians which society fails to constrain; it is rather something in which they have to be induced to participate. Sociality premissed on peaceful co-operation and reciprocity has to be deliberately subverted in order to produce warlike behaviour. Warriors have to be made to kill by becoming something alien, by assuming a homicidal guise quite inimical to a 'natural' persona—in short, by wearing 'the mask of war'.

These observations are not consistent with cultural-ecological explanations for increased inter-group conflict, whether among modern or prehistoric populations. A crucial development in the Upper Palaeolithic was the reproduction of cohesive groups through processes of religious experimentation, culminating in the establishment of an imagistic mode of religiosity. In many cases, warfare itself must be regarded as a form of periodic, revelatory, traumatic ritual, as a set of 'rites of terror'. There is no reason to suppose, of course, that the proliferation of art and religion during the Upper Palaeolithic was motivated by the need to defend resources against interlopers. That these imagistic practices would have conferred a reproductive advantage on groups that adopted them need not have been explicitly recognized or used as a justification for the development or continuation of such practices.

The Doctrinal Mode and the Great Transformation

Whatever the difficulties in identifying the exact origins, distribution, and adaptive value of imagistic practices in human prehistory, it is clear that the doctrinal mode of religiosity became established much more recently. The first evidence of relatively large-scale, routinized religions, founded upon bodies of doctrine that were monitored and policed by a priestly hierarchy, probably dates back to the fourth millennium BC in Lower Mesopotamia. Similar processes occurred independently in North China, the Nile and Indus Valleys, Mesoamerica, and the Central Andes. The question of what triggered and shaped these processes has long been addressed by archaeologists in terms of a variety of ecological, techno-logical, demographic, and economic factors. In this process, the early insights of Fustel de Coulanges (1864), who attempted to account for the origins of centralization and hierarchy in terms of religious innovations, tended to be marginalized. According to Paul Wheatley, however, 'the combined testimony of archaeology, epigraphy, mythology, literature, representational art, and either extant or recorded architecture, leaves no room to doubt that religion provided the primary focus for social life in the immediately pre-urban period. In Fustel de Coulanges's straight-forward phrasing, "ce qui faisait le lieu de toute société, c'était un culte" ' (Wheatley 1971: 302).

There is clear evidence that settled agriculture, the production of surpluses, the establishment of large-scale work forces, changing ecolog-ical conditions, and patterns of military and commercial interaction regionally and over time, were among the many crucial factors that precipitated and shaped the great transformation. Nevertheless, these elements both contributed to, and were themselves shaped by the emer-gence of new religious forms. At the heart of the great transformation was the gradual emergence of a doctrinal mode of religiosity.

Among the crucial features of the doctrinal mode is a shift in styles of codification, from the multivocal imagery of collective ritual to the formulation of an argument-centred religious discourse. Such discourses are readily associated with the speech-acts of particular individuals and, as such, they open the way for the emergence of special forms of religious leadership, in which privileged persons become established as conduits for the divine. Whether such conduits are construed as kings, messiahs, prophets, or mediums, they constitute acknowledged authori-ties on matters of doctrine and practice, central nodes from which reli-gious orthodoxies are (or are assumed to be) promulgated. Once such arrangements have become accepted, the identity and integrity of a reli-gious tradition comes to depend upon the suppression of local distortions and innovations, whether deliberate or inadvertent.

The most obvious line of defence, for any emerging orthodoxy, is the establishment of an organized priesthood. Following a survey of regions of 'primary urban generation',[3] in both the Old and New Worlds, Wheatley concludes, 'the earliest foci of power and authority took the form of ceremonial centres, with religious symbolism imprinted deeply on their physiognomy and their operation in the hands of organized priesthoods' (1971: 303). The first priests were probably not easily distinguished from the sorts of ritual experts and masters of initiation found in imagistic traditions, in so far as their ceremonial functions may have been discharged only periodically. What was new was the standardization and expanded jurisdiction of their functions so as to encompass larger populations than ever before. Moreover, from about 3,000 BC in Mesopotamia, there is evidence of professional priesthoods, engaged in the reproduction of regional orthodoxies as a full-time job (see Wheatley 1971: 227–8).

The supervisory prominence of an organized priesthood may help to prevent local innovation and heresy, and concomitant fragmentation of a religious tradition, but the entrenchment of orthodoxy also requires methods of guarding against unintended innovation caused by memory failure. The principal solution to this problem, in all doctrinal traditions, is routinization. Although there may have been many reasons for the professionalization of priestly functions, the emergence of increasingly repetitive forms of ceremonial that presumably accompanied the establishment of full-time priesthoods would have facilitated the elaboration of standardized bodies of doctrine. Moreover, pressures towards the development of routinized institutional forms came from a number of other directions.

Settled agriculture, which notably preceded the consolidation of the first large-scale, centralized, religious traditions, is everywhere regulated by seasonal cycles. It has been suggested (e.g. Fairservis 1961) that the rise of ceremonial centres occurred at least partly in response to concerns about crop fertility and the uncertainty of seasonal harvests. Adams (1966) meanwhile has suggested that in Mesopotamia and Mesoamerica, where ecological conditions tended to be particularly unstable, early forms of worship were concerned with the propitiation of deities responsible for the reproduction of seasonal cycles (see Wheatley 1971: 304). Thus, the pace of ceremonial life may have speeded up in response to the seasonal rhythms of agricultural production, as compared with the more sporadic rites of prehistoric hunter-gatherers.

---

[3] According to Wheatley these regions consist of 'Mesopotamia, Egypt, the Indus valley, the North China plain, Mesoamerica, the central Andes, and the Yoruba territories of southwestern Nigeria' (1971: 9).

Very much shorter cycles of transmission would have been precipitated by the emergence of large-scale work forces, especially in the construction of temples and other religious monuments. The first ceremonial centres in both New and Old Worlds entailed the construction of architecture that must have required the co-ordinated labour of thousands of workers over many years. Such construction work involved highly sophisticated planning, leadership, and methods of implementation. It would, among other things, have entailed the division of time into convenient units, not only in order to facilitate long-term planning but also to enable the activities of teams of labourers to be co-ordinated on a daily basis. The construction industries of ancient cities were probably founded on heavily routinized regimes of labour, involving highly schematized tasks and large-scale, repetitive forms of ceremonial, encompassing leaders, supervisors, and assembled congregations of workers. The mobilization of labour in these ways would have provided the models for routinized worship more generally.

The above constitutes no more than a highly impressionistic account of how the doctrinal mode of religiosity may have come into being. The emergence of doctrine, the centralization of authority, the establishment of regional religious traditions and professional priesthoods, and the gradual shift towards routinized institutional forms, constituted a set of mutually reinforcing features, precipitated by a range of complex factors, many of which can only be partially and tentatively uncovered. But of all possible precipitating factors, at least in relation to the emergence of doctrine, one appears to have been especially prominent, namely the development of literacy. The explanation for this is twofold. First, the initial development of systems of writing tends to co-vary with the first appearance of centralized, hierarchical, large-scale, routinized religious traditions. Second, there are purely theoretical grounds for supposing that the advent of literacy may have been a necessary condition for the independent invention of doctrinal forms.

Literacy, Orality, and Modes of Religiosity

In *The Domestication of the Savage Mind* (1977), Jack Goody linked a dichotomy between the literate and non-literate world to a host of others, for instance, between myth and history, between magic and science, between primitive and modern, and so on. Goody argued that his own 'grand dichotomy' transcended the others by virtue of being able to encompass and account for many of them within the ambit of a single theory.

Central to Goody's argument was the claim that the writing down of laws, constitutions, genealogies, or religious doctrines produces a certain rigidity in these domains. It becomes very much harder to introduce significant changes in the realms of kinship, politics, and religion without having to acknowledge and defend these changes. By contrast, in non-literate societies, where cultural rules and norms are stored in memory, changes can occur without people necessarily realizing that things are changing. If somebody claims that the ancient and correct way of performing a ritual is to carry out a certain sequence of actions, then nobody can prove that it was not. People's memories might conflict, but the disagreement cannot be resolved with reference to objective, textual evidence. Goody thus argued that the institutional forms of oral societies were relatively plastic and flexible, continually adapting to changing conditions in a way that the more rigid institutions of literate societies could not. This also enabled Goody to account for the relatively ahistorical orientation of 'traditional' societies, whose members tend to assert that their institutions always have been the way they are now and have never changed.

Goody, however, identified other links between orality and the absence of well-developed historical discourses. The historian's concern with accuracy, consistency, and causal links between chronologically ordered events are all artefacts of literacy, according to Goody. In oral conditions, by contrast, representations of the past find their most elaborate expression in bodies of mythology. But myths typically present an impossible past, characterized by supernatural happenings; attempts are not necessarily made to compare different versions of myths, and to debate and iron out inconsistencies; moreover, the structuring of mythological events is often non-chronological, possibly involving non-durational (e.g. cyclical) representations of time. Genuinely historical representations only develop when the past is documented, when interpretations of these documents are themselves presented as texts that can be compared, debated, and checked against their sources. Thus, according to Goody, literacy is a necessary condition for the development of historical consciousness in society.

Goody proceeded to link the relatively ahistorical orientation of oral societies to objectively slow rates of institutional transformation. If laws, genealogies, rituals, and so on can be continually modified so as to create an illusion of stasis in the social system as a whole, then the objective pattern of change is likely to be gradual and incremental. In literate societies, by contrast, the system cannot be preserved so easily through continual tinkering. For instance, a corporate group that recruits members on the basis of descent must die out if the documented genealogical records show that its true descendants have declined in number to a critically low level. Whereas in oral conditions new members can be assigned to a dwindling lineage in such a way as to fudge the issue of *bona fide* descent from the founding ancestor, this becomes much harder in literate societies, where records of births and deaths present incontrovertible evidence of ancestry. Goody has made the same point in relation to a variety of institutional domains, as the following comments on the historical dynamics of religious traditions illustrate (Goody 1986: 9–10): 'In the literate churches, the dogma and services are rigid . . . If change takes place, it often takes the form of a break-away movement . . . the process is deliberately reformist, even revolutionary, rather than the process of incorporation that tends to mark the oral situation.' Thus, as in systems of descent, Goody envisaged patterns of sweeping and rapid transformation in scriptural religions rather than the gradual, incremental adaptations that are supposedly typical of oral traditions.

In addition, Goody has linked the advent of literacy to the development of individualism, and especially individual striving for a place in the historical record of a culture. Goody has argued that the celebration of individual authorship and historical achievement is an artefact of literacy. Whereas, for instance, the British have no difficulty linking the establishment of the Metropolitan Police Force to the individual efforts of Sir Robert Peel, the non-literate Trobriand Islanders had no comparable stories about the origins of the *kula* ring, or about the innovative acts of individuals responsible for its early development. Goody went so far as to argue that the very fact that individual effort is rewarded in literate societies by a kind of immortalization in history books encourages people to strive to change society, to achieve either fame or notoriety. In oral conditions, according to Goody, this motive is lacking: '[Where changes occur in non-literate societies] the individual signature . . . tends to get rubbed out, whereas in written cultures the very knowledge that a work will endure in time . . . often helps to stimulate the creative process and encourage the recognition of individuality' (1977: 14).

Nevertheless, a wealth of new research and theoretical debate in recent years has shown that generalizable deterministic arguments with regard to literacy are problematic (e.g. Heath 1983; Street 1984, 1988; Graff 1987; Finnegan 1988; Kulick and Stroud 1990; Besnier 1995). Most critiques of Goody's line of argument focus on the fact that literacy comprises an extremely heterogeneous set of practices, the 'consequences' of which vary enormously according to the social contexts in which literacy operates and the purposes to which it is put. Some of the scope and ambition of Goody's argument may be rescued, however, if we shift the emphasis away from the issue of literacy and orality, and focus instead on the crucial differences between doctrinal and imagistic modes of religiosity.

All the principal characteristics that Goody associated with literacy are in fact features of the doctrinal mode of religiosity, whether or not a tradition operating in this mode happens to utilize a system of writing. In fact, the literate/oral dichotomy is misleading because in either case we are dealing primarily with representations that are codified and transmitted in *language*, the dominant medium of the doctrinal mode of religiosity. Conversely, the characteristics that Goody attributes to non-literate societies are, on the whole, features of the imagistic mode of religiosity, in which religious transmission is focused on collective ritual performances.

According to Goody, the institutions of literate societies are rigid, their process of transformation relatively violent and sweeping, and the role of history, individual agency, and authorship is greatly emphasized. The literature on the Paliau Movement and the Pomio Kivung reveals that, despite the widespread absence of literacy among followers (and in many cases the leaders) of these movements, all the features that Goody associated with literacy appear prominently in the ethnography. Paliau's and Koriam's followers sustained elaborate and uniform historical representations relating to their respective movements: how they started; how their relations to various external agencies, including the national political arena, have developed over time; what processes led to the establishment of specific ritual forms, and in what sequence; and so on. Moreover, the followers of both movements frequently and elaborately describe many significant events in the careers of their leaders, especially Paliau and Koriam, and the effects of their actions on the political and social history of the region. These great figures in the history of the Paliau Movement and the Pomio Kivung are still remembered and venerated, even though they have since died. So movements of this type stress both the importance of history and of individual innovators.

At the same time, these movements exhibit precisely those forms of rigidity that Goody attributed to literate traditions. There has always been a striking uniformity in the expressed beliefs and ritual practices of Paliau's and Koriam's followers, an extreme conformity to orthodoxy, enforced and sanctioned at local level by a variety of means. Even minor infractions of the orthodoxy would have been readily recognized and opposed (unless they received endorsement from the highest level) and thus the situation was as rigid as in virtually any literate church. Followers of the Paliau Movement or the Pomio Kivung wishing to introduce innovations have always been obliged to recant, or else to leave the mainstream movement and set up a rival sect of their own.

Goody's point about the disruptive and far-reaching nature of change in literate conditions is likewise understandable in terms of the doctrinal mode of religiosity. Where religious ideas take the form of logically integrated arguments, any interference or innovation in these interconnected webs of ideation has profound consequences for the body of doctrine as a whole. One only has to imagine the effects of relatively minor innovations in Christianity, such as the dogma of predestination, or the ordination of women priests, to see how profoundly these issues have reverberated through the total body of theological representations in different churches. Thus, when changes occur in religions dominated by the doctrinal mode, whether or not these give rise to the establishment of competing sects, these changes tend to be far-reaching as the system reforms and adjusts to accommodate the modification. Here again, the presence or absence of literacy is not crucial. In the non-literate tradition of the Pomio Kivung, numerous examples could be given of how a minor change in one aspect of doctrine or practice has logical implications for all the surrounding webs of theological argumentation, totally altering the religious system as a whole.

The reason for these similarities between religions operating in the doctrinal mode and what Goody referred to as the 'literate churches', is that both regimes are highly routinized. Where the transmission of doctrines and ritual forms is extremely frequent and repetitive, these representations become standardized and fixed in memory, *regardless of whether they are also written down*. In both the Paliau Movement and the Pomio Kivung, one would not find massive discrepancies in people's understandings of the central tenets, policies, ritual procedures, and so on of the religion. In conditions of highly repetitive sermonizing and routinized ritual, religious representations become as rigid and incontrovertible as if they were printed on paper—more so, perhaps, because texts can be neglected, reinterpreted, and added to in ways that can significantly alter the orthodoxy over time and space, whereas Paliau's and Koriam's regimes were always centrally monitored and co-ordinated so that the independence of local sermonizers on matters of interpretation was minimized. The general point is that in establishing any orthodoxy, control of the social conditions of transmission[4] is always more important than determining the range of textual materials that should be regarded as authoritative.

Conversely, if one considers the features that Goody attributed to oral societies, these are clearly part and parcel of the imagistic mode of religiosity. The lack of interest in historical events and individual authorship is linked directly to the way in which representations are codified and transmitted in the imagistic mode. We have seen that in the Taro Cult, for instance, many followers had no idea how the movement started, who founded it, or how, when, and where it spread. Individual leaders were not significant because revelation occurred through collective ritual performance, and was not mediated by individuals speaking on behalf of the divine. In short, language was not the dominant medium of transmission, and so history (which is quintessentially language-based) had no place in the repertoire of religious representations.

In terms of objective patterns of institutional transformation, the imagistic mode is also distinctive, and here too resembles the situation that Goody linked more generally with non-literate conditions. Goody argued that objective rates of change in non-literate societies are gradual and incremental, involving the incorporation of new elements in such a way as to maintain the overall structure and coherence of the system. Nevertheless, if we recast the issues in terms of our two modes of religiosity, the picture looks rather more complex (and more interesting). Because of the logical integrity of the doctrinal mode, infractions of the orthodoxy have far-reaching effects on the religious system as a whole, as I have pointed out. By contrast, imagistic practices are founded on associational links rather than implicational logic. Ideological innovation largely consists of adding new iconic imagery to an existing set, or disregarding established imagery, but this does not have significant consequences for the total body of revelations. Iconic processes in the imagistic mode are relatively discrete and, although they ideally harmonize in the revelatory scheme, they do not depend one upon the other in strings of logical implication. For instance, the Baktaman initiation cult presents

---

[4] I include in these 'social conditions' the frequency with which the ideology, whether or not this is written down, is reviewed. In many Christian churches, great emphasis is placed on the reading of biblical materials in groups, and in many Islamic societies, worshippers are required to rote-learn and recite koranic texts. Such activities are important in shaping the uniformity and rigidity of doctrine in so far as transmission occurs very frequently, producing rigid representational models of the religious ideology. The mere presence of authoritative texts would not be enough in itself to reproduce the orthodoxy among worshippers.

numerous images of growth (fur, fat, dew, hair, etc.) but any of these could be dropped and/or replaced with a new image without affecting the ideological character of the cult as a whole (see especially Chapter 4). It is this that accounts for the gradual and incremental nature of institutional change in the imagistic mode and not the absence of literacy.

Nevertheless, the continuity of imagistic practices is greatly affected by the context of their reproduction. Imagistic practices evoke lasting revelations that do not bear substantial repetition. Thus, it would be nonsensical to undergo the same initiation rite twice, or to repeat exactly the activities of a previous ecstatic cargo cult. In the case of initiation, this is indeed a once in a lifetime experience (in the role of novice) and so there is no need to change the imagery for each successive generation. In practice, innovations may well be introduced but this is not essential to the success of the rites (and is almost always officially proscribed). But in the case of sporadic outbursts of cargo cult ritual, there is a genuine pressure to innovate because participants must experience fresh revelations during active periods. Thus, the Taro Cult did not precisely reproduce the ritual and imagery of the Baigona Cult: the trembling body of the *dutari* victim became the swaying body of the *jipari* victim, conveying the idea that the winds of prosperity had increased in power and intensity. Nevertheless, however important this innovation might have been from an experiential, revelatory viewpoint, the Baigona and Taro Cults were very much alike in ideological and organizational terms. It makes sense to view them as part of a single religious tradition, operating in the imagistic mode, analogous to the different phases of ritual action that mark the several degrees of initiation among the Baktaman. The principal difference is that the cargo cults in question, unlike the initiation cycles of inner New Guinea, are most unlikely to be reproduced as part of a process of inter-generational transmission. Thus, one may regard certain manifestations of the imagistic mode as fundamentally innovative and temporary in character, rather than as reconstructions of an ancient and relatively unchanging cultural tradition (as Goody's idealized notion of the non-literate institutional complex implied).

What is suggested by the foregoing observations is that the theory of modes of religiosity has greater flexibility and, perhaps, explanatory power than Goody's deterministic theory of literacy. This is not to deny, however, that literacy has been a crucial factor in triggering the elaboration of doctrinal practices, and it may be strictly necessary for their independent invention. Ernest Gellner, for instance, has suggested that literacy constituted a necessary condition for the invention of doctrine-based, logically integrated religious traditions.

> The truly crucial step in the cognitive development of mankind is the introduction of literacy, and its deployment in religion (i.e. scripturalism) . . . Writing makes possible the codification and systematization of assertion, and hence the birth of *doctrine* . . . The kind of ideology that makes its appearance with the religious use of writing . . . stands sharply contrasted with the community-oriented traditional religions which preceded it. They used ritual, not script, and were primarily concerned to underwrite and fortify communal organization and the rhythm of communal life. (1988: 71–5)

For Gellner, what I am calling the 'doctrinal mode of religiosity' constituted a significant advance on the 'imagistic mode', and a necessary condition for this advancement was literacy. Yet this is only the first of two crucial steps towards modernity. It is, Gellner asserted (1988: 79), the most dramatic and difficult. But it is not sufficient for the abolition of the 'argument of authority' and its replacement by a rational, democratic, scientific ethos. In short, it is not enough to produce Western modernity. The problem with the doctrinal mode of religiosity is that it is still a mode of 'being religious'. Deference is still commanded more substantially by *ideas* than by *facts*, a predicament which Gellner identified with Platonic philosophy.[5] In order for the miracle of modernity to occur, the logical rigor of the doctrinal mode must be applied to empirical facts in the natural world. Science, in other words, must triumph over religion in the inexorable process of secularization. This, argued Gellner, is the second and decisive step in the evolution of modernity.

The broad thrust of Gellner's argument is compelling. It helps to account for the fact that the earliest religious traditions dominated by the doctrinal mode of religiosity also possessed systems of writing. Nevertheless, once the doctrinal model had become established, literacy would not be necessary for the spread and innovation of doctrinal traditions, within connected populations. In those rare cases, such as the Incas of Peru, where doctrinal practices became established in the absence of writing systems, it would be necessary to assume that at least some gross features of the doctrinal model were acquired through exposure to another (e.g. more ancient) religious tradition. Alternatively, we might countenance a slightly diluted version of Gellner's argument, which

---

[5] The essence of 'Platonism' in this respect is the notion that 'Reality does not constitute a check on Ideas: on the contrary, *they* are the norms by which reality is to be judged and guided' (Gellner 1988: 76).

views literacy as a precipitating rather than a necessary condition for the independent invention of doctrinal practices. Either way, the advent of literacy has much less explanatory power than Goody has argued. Since systems of writing are not essential to the reproduction of doctrinal practices, once the models for such practices have been recognized, our attention must be directed to the social, rather than the technological, conditions for the transmission of ideas, a topic to which we now turn in greater detail.

Routinization, Communitas, and Modes of Religiosity

Victor Turner has argued for a distinction between ancestral/political cults and earth/fertility cults, corresponding respectively to particularistic and universalistic tendencies in West African religion: 'ancestral and political cults and their local embodiments tend to represent crucial power divisions and classificatory distinctions within and among politically discrete groups, while earth and fertility cults represent ritual bonds between those groups, and . . . tendencies towards still wider bonding. The first type stresses exclusiveness, the second inclusiveness. The first emphasizes sectional interests and conflict over them; the second disinterestedness and shared values' (1974: 185).

Turner was alluding here to a fundamental difference of orientation between particularistic and universalistic conceptions of humanity, both of which have their origins in forms of religious experience and action. On the one hand, there are rituals that evoke small, highly localized communities, pitted against each other in conditions of sectarian rivalry and opposition. Conceptions of humanity here tend to be restricted to the 'in group', outsiders being seen as non-human or less than human. Turner associated this sort of extreme parochialism with 'structure'— 'the bonds between members of tightly knit, multifunctional groups' (1974: 201). On the other hand, Turner identified rituals that evoke a sense of the 'brotherhood of man', the ' "community of feeling" that is tied to neither blood nor locality' (Turner 1974: 201). This sensation of the unity of humankind, the inclusive oneness of people regardless of cultural, historical, and genealogical differences, was captured by Turner in his notion of 'communitas'. Although the distinction between ancestral/political cults and earth/fertility cults was derived primarily from West African ethnography, the association of these two forms of ritual with the more general structure/communitas dichotomy enabled Turner to conceptualize the broad sweep of religious history in terms of a transition from parochial, 'structure'-dominated ritual communities towards more universalistic, communitas-dominated conceptions of humanity:

> Rituals . . . stressing the general good and inclusiveness, become more prominent in the so-called 'historical', 'higher', or 'universal' religions, such as Christianity, Judaism, Buddhism, Islam, Confucianism, and Hinduism, although they do not, of course, in any sense, replace the first type, the locally bounded religious congregations. In addition, individual responsibility is now extended from the domain of immediate kin and neighbourhood relations in localized normative systems to that of the generic human 'brother' and the 'neighbour' who might be anyone in the wide world but whom one should 'love'. The 'other' becomes a 'brother', specific siblingship is extended to all who share a system of beliefs. (Turner 1974: 186)

For Turner, the key to understanding the transition from parochial, small-scale, exclusive conceptions of the ritual community to the universalistic ideals of the 'historical' religions, lay in the phenomenon of the pilgrimage, which served to promote feelings of communitas among peoples of diverse origin, establishing forms of unity forever transcending localized group attachments and cultural differences. Turner proposed a specific developmental scheme, involving the sequential emergence of three types of communitas. Firstly, there is 'existential' or 'spontaneous' communitas, consisting of 'the direct, immediate, and total confrontation of human identities which tends to make those experiencing it think of mankind as a homogeneous, unstructured, and free community' (1974: 169). Turner argued, however, that over time this 'original existential communitas is organized into a perduring social system' (1974: 169). Somewhat in the spirit of Max Weber's (1947) notion of the 'routinization of charisma', Turner referred to this state of affairs as 'normative communitas'. Thirdly, Turner described the state of 'ideological communitas', referring to 'a variety of utopian models or blueprints of societies believed by their authors to exemplify or supply the optimal conditions for existential communitas' (1974: 169).

Turner's model has a number of drawbacks that I shall presently examine in detail. But let us focus initially on what is perhaps the most glaring defect of all, namely the mystical nature of Turner's conception of the origins of existential communitas. Turner seemed to believe that forms of liminality in the ritual process sparked off some kind of pan-human intuition of the oneness of mankind. Nevertheless, despite his voluminous writings on this topic, Turner never precisely defined the state of communitas, or described the cognitive processes that engendered it (see Morris 1987: 258–63).

In so far as communitas denotes a sensation of the unity and fraternity of humankind, it is particularly problematic that Turner saw the potentiality for this sensation in *all* religious traditions. For instance, Turner argued that communitas was engendered in the rites of passage of precisely those 'tribal' societies in which social groupings are small-scale, exclusive, and parochial—exemplifying, in short, the antithesis of communitas (Turner's 'structure'). Thus, in his analysis of tribal initiation rites, Turner argued that the instruction of novices 'dominantly through non-verbal, symbolic communication' and their isolation at sacred sites in a state of 'liminality' together instantiate a radical simplification of 'structure' in which 'generic rather than particularistic relationships are stressed' (1974: 196). Nevertheless, Turner's argument here is unconvincing. In the course of tribal initiation rites, novices do not experience a sense of the 'unity of humankind', or anything remotely resembling it. Even Turner's own ethnographic data on Ndembu initiation, in spite of its being the archetypal case and ostensible inspiration for his theory, fail to demonstrate the presence of existential communitas. Brian Morris has made a similar point: 'the circumcision rite among the Ndembu is, metaphorically, a "place of dying" ... I fail to see the "sentiment for humanity" expressing itself in some of the ordeals, nor can I see the "spontaneous, immediate, and personal nature" of these rituals' (1987: 260). In fact, the forms of cohesion and solidarity established through tribal initiation rites, including those of the Ndembu, instantiate pre-eminently particularistic ties. The universalistic conceptions that Turner associated with communitas can only arise through the development of the doctrinal mode of religiosity. Where imagistic practices provide the predominant forms of religious experience and revelation, conceptions of human unity do not extend beyond the ritual community, and the basic orientation to persons outside this community tends to be negative, if not openly predatory. In grasping the process through which the universalistic representations of communitas become thinkable, and (in the long-run) ideologically entrenched, Turner's model of the three forms of communitas provides a useful framework, although his depiction of the developmental sequence must be revised. But first, it is necessary to review some of the central arguments of the present volume in a much broader context.

For the greater part of human history, identification with a group has meant to align oneself to a set of actual, flesh-and-blood persons. The individual's social universe did not contain anonymous others—people like oneself, part of the human race, and yet conceptualized *in abstracto*. Relatively small groups of people, and the members of similar groups with whom communication and exchange took place, constituted the limits of humanity. Even where long-term processes of migration, conquest, and demographic expansion had led to the establishment of quite large populations speaking the same language and 'sharing' a fundamentally similar set of social and cultural institutions, tribal communities did not experience a conscious sense of identity with anonymous others, and frequently regarded strangers, though they may have spoken the very same dialect, as less than human. In order to identify with a category of imagined others, certain changes had to occur in the way a state of 'being human' was cognitively constructed.

In many tribal societies, the concept of humanity was produced through a very specific form of mental processing, engendered primarily in rites of terror and other imagistic practices. The cohesion instantiated through these sorts of rituals took the form of enduring episodic memories for revelatory events and, most importantly, for the actual persons who experienced them together. The identity between those who 'shared', or were presumed to share, such a set of memories could not easily be extended. Any outsider who came to be accepted (however partially and suspiciously) into the ritually manufactured circle of humanity, occupied a tenuous position. Over time, and through their participation in the ritual life of the community, they could be increasingly integrated into the in-group, but this essentially meant being located in a stock of salient episodic memories. In order to conceptualize humanity in more abstract terms, it was first necessary to modify the forms of remembering activated by identity-conferring rituals.

New ways of cognizing ritual became established with the advent of the doctrinal mode of religiosity, which seldom swept aside imagistic practices. In conditions of routinization, a significant sector of activity could no longer be remembered episodically. Highly repetitive rituals came to be conceptualized in a schematic form: 'first we do this, then that, and so on . . .' in a synchronic, rather than an historical, conceptual framework. Participants and functionaries in the rituals came to be envisaged as a set of anonymous agents, perhaps an amalgam of real persons but not a set of named individuals located in a specific web of social relations. In so far as ritual, and memories of ritual, provided the basis upon which common humanity was construed, this was a portentous transformation. Routinization made possible the conceptualization of an abstract community, composed of non-specified persons, with whom common identity was traced though commonalities, or presumed commonalities, in ritual performance.

Schema-based memories for human behaviour are obviously generated in all societies, and not only those in which religious life has become routinized. Many tribal societies sustain a repertoire of quite repetitive, non-revelatory rituals (magical spells, divinations, propitiatory rites, medical techniques, witchcraft practices, and so on) as well as numerous other technical procedures used in the daily round of subsistence activity. Schemas for these sorts of actions are activated in much the same way as I have described for the routinized rituals of the doctrinal mode of religiosity. But there is a crucial difference. The most sacred, revelatory, identity-forming rituals of tribal society are dominated by the imagistic mode; highly repetitive technical procedures (whether ritualized or not) are never seen as constitutive of the in-group and thus of 'humanity'. What is significant about the doctrinal mode is that its rituals and dogmas are constitutive of group identity, and are thus sacred and set apart from non-revelatory practices; however, these may be similarly repetitive. Thus, changes in the transmissive contexts of identity-conferring rituals made it possible for the first time to construe humanity in abstract, inclusive terms. As such, this was a truly revolutionary innovation. It facilitated the unification of large populations behind a wide variety of ideologies. But, for the moment, let us return to Turner's concept of communitas.

Our logical starting point is 'normative communitas', by which Turner associated universalism with routinization. As I have pointed out, Turner never explained the origins of communitas in general (except in terms of his apparently mystical assumptions) and still less did he connect its appearance to routinization. On the contrary, Turner believed that a spontaneous intuition of the generic unity of humankind preceded routinized expressions of it in the form of normative communitas. I suggest that it is the other way around: forms of political association premissed on abstract generic similarity only became possible in the first place in conditions of routinized identity-conferring ritual. The 'next step' was what Turner called 'ideological communitas', the allocation of conceptual unity to a specific ideological cause, whether the universalistic paradigm of the world religions (in which we all became, at least potentially, 'God's children'), or some more regionally confined programme addressing itself to a more exclusive (albeit large-scale, abstract, and 'imagined') community. The emergence of universalistic ideological programmes is directly linked to routinization. The revelatory power of repetitive ritual always lies in exegesis and in wider doctrinal discourse, the persuasiveness of which depends upon the logical rigor of the corpus of doctrine and the plausibility of the assumptions upon which it is based (see Whitehouse 1995: ch. 7). Non-verbal, iconic imagery cannot play a major role in rituals that are simultaneously repetitive and revelatory (see above, Chapters 3 and 5) and this is what motivates the elaboration of persuasive ideologies in the routinized religions.

The above developments must be seen as logically prior to Turner's 'existential' or 'spontaneous' communitas. There are several ways in which this direct, revelatory sensation of the oneness of humankind can be triggered. It may occur in moments of conversion or crowd hysteria, through solitary contemplation or persuasion from the pulpit. Another route to existential communitas is through the *interaction* of our two modes of religiosity. The doctrinal mode is a necessary development for communitas to become 'thinkable', but when the traumatic revelations of imagistic ritual are projected on to the wider community (as we saw in Chapter 6) a much more intense experience of the unity of the abstract community becomes possible. In so far as the cohesion established in localized ritual performances can be mapped on to cognitions of a wider (e.g. national or pan-human) community, this is what I think Turner was grappling with when he talked about 'the direct, immediate, and total confrontation of human identities' (1974: 169). Spontaneous communitas, the mystical starting point in Turner's theory, turns out to be the end-point of a much more complicated, but nevertheless intelligible, process.

Epilogue

It is all too easy to envisage religious practices where doctrinal models have not yet spread as the inventions of 'oral' or 'non-literate' cultures. But such cultures are no more (or less) 'oral' than those of contemporary Europe, and it is scarcely more instructive to characterize them as non-literate as non-space-travelling. The rituals of the Upper Palaeolithic and of pre-contact Melanesia were not, as has been suggested in connection with Muslim tribes, a set of 'audio-visual aids for the illiterate devotees' (Gellner 1969: 134). The same problem of negative labelling has long been remarked upon among political anthropologists working in so-called 'stateless' societies (e.g. M. M. Green 1964). Mass literacy and state formation cannot be regarded as normal attributes of human society, in relation to which other forms of social transmission and social organization should be character-ized. If anything, it should be the other way around, such that positive characteristics of more ancient transmissive forms may be seen as the norm, which complex societies have subsequently harnessed, moulded, or suppressed, but never successfully eliminated. All this may be so, and yet it is still the doctrinal mode of religiosity with which modern scholars of religion, including anthropologists, tend to be most intimately acquainted. Thus, of our two modes of religiosity, the imagistic is probably the least well understood in academic scholarship.

In Chapter 4, I argued that the contributions of Melanesianists to the anthropology of religion have been influenced, albeit inadvertently, by certain Western assumptions about what constitutes an intellectually respectable religious or cosmological tradition. This is reflected in choices of terminology, for instance, Juillerat's accounts of Yafar 'priests' and 'theology' or Worsley's discussions of Taro Cult 'doctrine', remarked upon in earlier chapters. This is by no means to dismiss such work as ethnocentric, still less the highly instructive findings of religious anthropology as a whole, which has struggled, with increasing inventiveness and reflexivity, to penetrate unfamiliar forms of religious experience. Nevertheless, it would be extraordinary if there remained no systematic biases in anthropological interpretation deriving from the fact that all anthropologists have, by definition, been socialized into doctrinal practices whereas their informants, for instance in parts of Melanesia, may not have been. In Chapter 7, I argued that missionary Christianity has been influenced, however indirectly, by values and practices originating in the European Reformation, but the same may be said of religious anthropology.

Looking back on the eighteenth and nineteenth centuries, Robertson-Smith famously observed, 'the study of religion has meant mainly the study of Christian beliefs, and instruction in religion has habitually begun with the creed, religious duties being presented to the learner as flowing from the dogmatic truths he is taught to accept. All this seems to us so much a matter of course that, when we approach some new or antique religion, we naturally assume that here also our first business is to search for a creed, and find in it the key to ritual and practice' (1907: 16). He went on, 'but in ancient religion . . . practice preceded doctrinal theory. Men form general rules of conduct before they begin to express general principles in words' (1907: 20).

Despite Robertson-Smith's cautionary words, however, the privileging of doctrine over rite, and discourse over image, continued into the first half of the twentieth century. As Leach put it (1954: 13), 'the classic doctrine in English social anthropology is that the rite is a dramatisation of the myth, the myth is the sanction or charter for the rite'—a viewpoint that was clearly committed to the principle that ritual imagery everywhere derives its meanings from ideas codified in language. Although critical of the functionalist aspects of this 'doctrine', Leach maintained that 'myth, regarded as a statement in words, "says" the same things as ritual regarded as a statement in action' (1954: 13–14). The details of Leach's perspective were, and remain controversial but even his most vocal critics have tended to concede that ritual symbolism may be regarded as language-like in important respects. Moreover, theoretical discourse in social and cultural anthropology during the last few decades has been dominated by perspectives originating in linguistics and literary criticism. This is not to deny, of course, that a substantial body of outstanding scholarship in the field of religious anthropology, many examples of which have been examined in this volume, has done much to transcend the logocentric biases within academic culture.

Nevertheless, the obstacles to a fuller understanding of imagistic practices are methodological as well as theoretical. The case for a theory of modes of religiosity ultimately depends on its explanatory value in relation to detailed ethnography. A first attempt at demonstrating this was made in *Inside the Cult* (Whitehouse 1995), and the present volume has sought to develop these arguments further in relation to exceptionally well-documented examples. But potential case studies are less widely available than might be supposed because ethnographers seldom publish the sorts of detailed data this kind of study requires. For instance, there are relatively few accounts of Melanesian religion in print that detail the frequencies with which various religious representations are transmitted, and none in which such data are systematically connected to differing patterns of cognitive processing. Investigation of the latter topic might involve the borrowing and development of methods practised in the psychological disciplines,[6] but it is also clear that the traditional methods of anthropological research would need to be applied somewhat differently if we are to develop a more complete description of the constituent features of modes of religiosity and the complex mechanisms by which they are reproduced.

A good deal of ethnographic research, as currently practised, is based upon relatively short periods of fieldwork. An ethnographer's first period in the field is typically the longest and later visits are likely to last no more than a few months at a time. As a result, the attention of anthropologists

---

[6] An example of recent innovative research of this sort is Hutchins's (1996) exemplary study of 'distributed cognition' within a tiny population of navigators on an American warship; nevertheless, we still have a long way to go before this sort of fine-grained analysis could be carried out in relation to complex ritual events.

tends to be focused on shorter cycles of social and cultural transmission. This is the main reason why, for instance, infrequent, fleeting, and localized Melanesian cargo cults, founded on imagistic practices, are often assumed to exert a marginal influence on religious sensibilities in the long term, and to be worthy of mention (if at all) only in brief footnotes. By contrast, most of the large-scale, routinized cargo movements, modelled on Christian churches and operating in the doctrinal mode, have been more extensively documented. Occasionally, anthropologists have happened to be in the right place at the right time and have detailed the activities of cargo cultists' imagistic practices (e.g. Williams 1928; Schwartz 1962; Whitehouse 1995). Those of us who experience this sort of good fortune have difficulty assessing the impact of imagistic practices during the long periods that separate ritual performances. If problems like these are to be overcome, at least some ethnographic research will need to be co-ordinated over much longer time periods, perhaps involving teams of successive researchers, novel patterns of research planning and funding, and a more collaborative approach to the construction and use of data bases.

In short, the theory of modes of religiosity is still embryonic, and further developments must be empirically driven. This is not to say that all further understanding of this topic requires fresh information, gathered specifically for the purpose. On the contrary, a massive amount of data already exists in the fieldnotes, publications, and (above all) the minds of ethnographers who have worked all around the world. The question is whether you, the reader, find that the hypotheses put forward here resonate with your experiences of religion and are worth investigating further.

REFERENCES

ADAMS, R. McC. (1966). *The Evolution of Urban Society: Early Mesopotamia and Prehispanic Mexico*. Chicago: Aldine.

ALLEN, M. R. (1967). *Male Cults and Secret Initiations in Melanesia*. Melbourne: Melbourne University Press.

ANDERSON, B. (1983). *Imagined Communities: Reflections on the Origin and Spread of Nationalism*. London: Verso.

ARDREY, R. (1966). *The Territorial Imperative*. New York: Atheneum.

BARKER, J. (1990a). Introduction: Ethnographic Perspectives on Christianity in Oceanic Societies. In J. Barker (ed.), *Christianity in Oceania: Ethnographic Perspectives*. Lanham: University Press of America.

—— (1990b). Mission Station and Village: Religious Practice and Representations in Maisin Society. In J. Barker (ed.) *Christianity in Oceania: Ethnographic Perspectives*. Lanham: University Press of America.

BARTH, F. (1975). *Ritual and Knowledge among the Baktaman of New Guinea*. New Haven: Yale University Press.

—— (1987). *Cosmologies in the Making: A Generative Approach to Cultural Variation in Inner New Guinea*. Cambridge: Cambridge University Press.

—— (1990). The Guru and the Conjurer: Transactions in Knowledge and the Shaping of Culture in Southeast Asia and Melanesia. *Man* (NS), 25: 640–53.

BATESON, G. (1936). *Naven: A Survey of the Problems Suggested by a Composite Picture of the Culture of a New Guinea Tribe Drawn from Three Points of View*. Stanford: Stanford University Press.

—— (1972). *Steps to an Ecology of Mind: Collected Essays in Anthropology, Psychiatry, Evolution, and Epistemology*. Northvale: Jason Armson.

BELSHAW, C. S. (1950). The Significance of Modern Cults in Melanesian Development. *Australian Outlook*, 4: 116–25.

BENEDICT, R. (1935). *Patterns of Culture*. London: Routledge & Kegan Paul.

BERGER, P. L. (1969). *A Rumour of Angels*. Harmondsworth: Penguin.

BESNIER, N. 1995 *Literacy, Emotion, and Authority: Reading and Writing on a Polynesian Atoll*. Cambridge: Cambridge University Press.

BIERSACK, A. (ed.) (1996). *Papuan Borderlands: Huli, Duna, and Ipili Perspectives on the New Guinea Highlands*. Ann Arbor: University of Michigan Press.

BLOCH, M. (1992). *Prey Into Hunter: The Politics of Religious Experience*. Cambridge: Cambridge University Press.

—— (1995). Mémoire Autobiographique et Mémoire Historique du Passé Eloigné. *Enquête*, 2: 59–76.

BODROGI, T. (1951). Colonization and Religious Movements in Melanesia. *Academia Scientiarum Hungaricae-Acta Ethnographica*, 2: 259–92.

BOHANNON, J. N. (1992). Arousal and Memory: Quantity and Consistency over

190   References

the Years. In E. Winograd and U. Neisser (eds.), *Affect and Accuracy in Recall: The Problem of 'Flashbulb' Memories*. New York: Cambridge University Press.

BOYER, P. (1993). Cognitive Aspects of Religious Symbolism. In P. Boyer (ed.), *Cognitive Aspects of Religious Symbolism*. Cambridge: Cambridge University Press.

BROWN, P. (1966). Social Change and Social Movements. In E. K. Fisk (ed.), *New Guinea on the Threshold*. Canberra: Australian National University Press.

BROWN, R., and KULIK, J. (1982). Flashbulb Memory. In U. Neisser (ed.), *Memory Observed: Remembering in Natural Contexts*. San Francisco: W. H. Freeman.

BRUNTON, R. (1980). Misconstrued Order in Melanesian Religion. *Man* (NS) 15: 112–28.

CAMERON, E. (1991). *The European Reformation*. Oxford: Clarendon Press.

CHINNERY, E. W. P., and BEAVER, W. N. (1915). Notes on the Initiation Ceremonies of the Koko, Papua. *Journal of the Royal Anthropological Institute*, 45: 69–78.

—— and HADDON, A. C. (1917). Five New Religious Cults in British New Guinea. *Hibbert Journal* 15: 448–63.

CHRISTIANSEN, S. A. (1992). Emotional Stress and Eyewitness Memory: a Critical Review. *Psychological Bulletin*, 112: 284–309.

—— and LOFTUS, E. F. (1991). Remembering Emotional Events: the Fate of Detailed Information. *Cognition and Emotion*, 5: 81–108.

COHEN, G. (1989). *Memory in the Real World*. Hove: Lawrence Erlbaum.

COLLINGWOOD, R. G. (1940). *An Essay on Metaphysics*. Oxford: Clarendon Press.

COLLINS, P. (1965). Functional Analyses in the Symposium 'Man, Culture, and Animals'. In A. Leeds and A. Vayda (eds.), *Man, Culture, and Animals: The Role of Animals in Human Ecological Adjustments*. Washington, DC: American Association for the Advancement of Science.

COLLINSON, P. (1997). From Iconoclasm to Iconophobia: The Cultural Impact of the Second English Reformation. P. Marshall (ed.), *The Impact of the English Reformation 1500–1640*. London: Arnold.

CONNERTON, P. (1989). *How Societies Remember*. Cambridge: Cambridge University Press.

CROOK, T. (1997). Growing Knowledge: Exploring Knowledge Practices in Bolivip, Papua New Guinea. Ph.D. Thesis, Cambridge University.

—— n.d. Rethinking Secrecy: A View from Bolivip, Papua New Guinea. Seminar Paper, Department of Anthropology, London School of Economics (May 1998).

CROZIER, W. R., and CHAPMAN, A. J. (eds.) (1976). *Cognitive Processes in the Perception of Art*. Cambridge: Cambridge University Press.

DIVALE, W. T., and HARRIS, M. (1976). Population, Warfare, and the Male Supremacist Complex. *American Anthropologist*, 78: 521–38.

DURKHEIM, E. (1915). *The Elementary Forms of the Religious Life*. London: Allen & Unwin.

—— (1952). *Suicide: A Study in Sociology*. London: Routledge and Kegan Paul.

EDELMAN, G. (1992). *Bright Air, Brilliant Fire: On the Matter of the Mind*. London: Penguin.

EPSTEIN, T. S. (1968). *Capitalism, Primitive and Modern: Some Aspects of Tolai Economic Growth*. Manchester: Manchester University Press.

FAIRSERVIS, W. A., Jr. (1961). The Harappan Civilization: New Evidence and more Theory. *American Museum Novitates*, 2055.

FEIL, D. K. (1978). Women and Men in the Enga Tee. *American Ethnologist*, 5: 263–79.

—— (1987). *The Evolution of Highland Papua New Guinea Societies*. Cambridge: Cambridge University Press.

FENTRESS, J., and WICKHAM, C. (1992). *Social Memory*. Oxford: Blackwell.

FERGUSON, R. B. (1984). Introduction: Studying War. In R. B. Ferguson (ed.), *Warfare, Culture, and Environment*. Orlando: Academic Press.

—— (1990). Explaining War. In J. Haas (ed.), *The Anthropology of War*. Cambridge: Cambridge University Press.

FESTINGER, L. (1957). *A Theory of Cognitive Dissonance*. Stanford: Stanford University Press.

FINNEGAN, R. (1988). *Literacy and Orality: Studies in the Technology of Communication*. Oxford: Basil Blackwell.

FORMAN, C. W. (1978). Foreign Missionaries in the Pacific Islands During the Twentieth Century. In J. A. Boutilier, D. T. Hughes, and S. W. Tiffany (eds.), *Mission, Church, and Sect in Oceania*. Ann Arbor: University of Michigan Press.

FREEMAN, N. H., and COX, M. V. (eds.) (1985). *Visual Order: The Nature and Development of Pictorial Representation*. Cambridge: Cambridge University Press.

FUSTEL DE COULANGES, N. D. (1864). *La Cité Antique*. Paris: Librairie Hachette.

GELL, A. (1975). *Metamorphosis of the Cassowaries: Umeda Society, Language, and Ritual*. London: Athlone Press.

—— (1980). Correspondence. *Man* (NS), 15: 735–7.

—— (1992). Under the Sign of the Cassowary. In B. Juillerat (ed.), *Shooting the Sun: Ritual and Meaning in West Sepik*. Washington: Smithsonian Institution Press.

GELLNER, E. (1969). A Pendulum Swing Theory of Islam. In R. Robertson (ed.), *Sociology of Religion: Selected Readings*. Harmondsworth: Penguin Education.

—— (1988). *Plough, Sword, and Book: The Structure of Human History*. London: Collins Harvill.

GODELIER, M. (1991). An Unfinished Attempt at Reconstructing the Social Process which may have Prompted the Transformation of Great-Men Societies into Big-Men Societies. In M. Godelier and M. Strathern (eds.), *Big Men and Great Men: Personifications of Power in Melanesia*. Cambridge: Cambridge University Press.

GOODMAN, N. (1976). *Languages of Art*. Indianapolis: Hacket.

GOODY, J. (1968). Introduction, in J. Goody (ed.), *Literacy in Traditional Societies*. Cambridge: Cambridge University Press.

—— (1977). *The Domestication of the Savage Mind*. Cambridge: Cambridge University Press.

—— (1986). *The Logic of Writing and the Organization of Society*. Cambridge: Cambridge University Press.

GRAFF, H. J. (1987). *The Labyrinths of Literacy: Reflections on Literacy Past and Present*. Lewes: Falmer.

GREEN, A. (1992). The Oedipus Complex as *Mutterkomplex*. In B. Juillerat (ed.), *Shooting the Sun: Ritual and Meaning in West Sepik*. Washington, DC: Smithsonian Institution Press.

GREEN, M. M. (1964). *Igbo Village Affairs: Chiefly with Reference to the Village of Umueke Agbaja* (2nd edn.). London: Frank Cass.

GUIART, J. (1951). Forerunners of Melanesian Nationalism. *Oceania*, 22: 81–90.

GUSTAFSSON, B. (1992). *Houses and Ancestors: Continuities and Discontinuities in Leadership among the Manus*. Gothenburg: Institute for Advanced Studies in Social Anthropology at the University of Gothenburg.

HALBWACHS, M. (1925). *Les Cadres Sociaux de la Mémoire*. Paris: Presses Universitaires de France.

—— (1950). *La Mémoire Collective*. Paris: Presses Universitaires de France.

HARDING, S. (1987). Convicted by the Holy Spirit: The Rhetoric of Fundamental Baptist Conversion. *American Ethnnologist*, 14: 167–81.

HARPER-BILL, C. (1996). *The Pre-Reformation Church in England 1400–1530* (rev. edn.). London and New York: Longman.

HARRISON, S. J. (1990). *Stealing People's Names: History and Politics in a Sepik River Community*. Cambridge: Cambridge University Press.

—— (1993). *The Mask of War: Violence, Ritual, and the Self in Papua New Guinea*. Manchester: Manchester University Press.

HEATH, S. B. (1983). *Ways With Words: Language, Life, and Work in Communities and Classrooms*. Cambridge: Cambridge University Press.

HENDERSON, G. C. (1931). *Fiji and Fijians, 1835–1856*. Sydney: Angus & Robertson.

HERDT, G. H. (1981). *Guardians of the Flutes: Idioms of Masculinity*. New York: Columbia University Press.

—— (ed.) (1982). *Rituals of Manhood: Male Initiation in Papua New Guinea*. Berkeley: University of California Press.

—— (ed.) (1984). *Ritualized Homosexuality in Melanesia*. Berkeley: University of California Press.

—— (1989). Spirit Familiars in the Religious Imagination of Sambia Shamans. In G. H. Herdt and M. Stephen (eds.), *The Religious Imagination in New Guinea*. New Brunswick: Rutgers University Press.

HERTZ, R. (1960). *Death and the Right Hand*, tr. R. and C. Needham. London: Cohen and West.

HEUER, F. and REISBERG, D. (1990). Vivid Memories of Emotional Events: The Accuracy of Remembered Minutiae. *Memory and Cognition*, 18: 496–506.

HIATT, L. R. and JAYAWARDENA, C. J. (eds.) (1971). *Anthropology in Oceania*. Sydney: Angus & Robertson.

HOBBES, T. (1968). *Leviathan*, C. B. Macpherson (ed.). Harmondsworth: Penguin.

HOGBIN, H. I. (1958). *Social Change*. London: Watts.

HUTCHINS, E. (1996). *Cognition in the Wild*. Cambridge, Mass.: MIT Press.

ITEANU, A. (1990). The Concept of the Person and the Ritual System: An Orokaiva View. *Man* (NS), 25: 35–53.

JEUDI-BALLINI, M. (1998). Entre le clair et l'obscur: les transformations de l'histoire. *L'Homme*, 28: 237–51.

JUILLERAT, B. (1980). Order or Disorder in Melanesian Religion? *Man* (NS) 15: 732–4.

—— (1992). *Shooting the Sun: Ritual and Meaning in West Sepik*. Washington, DC: Smithsonian Institution Press.

—— (1996). *The Children of the Blood: Society, Reproduction, and the Imaginary in New Guinea*. Oxford: Berg.

KITTELSON, J. M. (1985). Luther the Educational Reformer. In M. J. Harran (ed.), *Luther and Learning: The Wittenberg University Luther Symposium*. London and Toronto: Associated University Presses.

KOIMANREA, F., and BAILOENAKIA, P. (1983). The Pomio Kivung Movement. Religious Movements in Melanesia Today, 1(2). Goroka: Melanesian Institute, 171–89.

KOSKINEN, Aarne A. (1953). Missionary Influence as a Political Factor in the Pacific Islands. *Suomalaisen Tiedeakatemian Toimituksia Annales Acad. Scie. Fenn.*, 78: 1–163.

KÜCHLER, S. (1994). Landscape as Memory: The Mapping Process and its Representation in Melanesian Society. In B. Bender (ed.) *Landscape: Politics and Perspectives*. Providence, RI: Berg.

KULIK, D., and STROUD, C. (1990). Christianity, Cargo, and Ideas of Self: Patterns of Literacy in a Papua New Guinea Village. *Man* (NS) 25: 286–303.

LANTERNARI, V. (1963). *The Religions of the Oppressed: A Study of Modern Messianic Cults*. New York: Mentor Books.

LAWRENCE, P. (1971). *Road Belong Cargo: A Study of the Cargo Movement in the Southern Madang District. New Guinea*. Prospect Heights, Ill.: Waveland Press.

LEACH, E. R. (1954). *Political Systems of Highland Burma*. London: G. Bell & Son.

LEEDS, A. (1963). The Functions of War. In J. Masserman (ed.), *Violence and War, with Clinical Studies*. New York: Grune and Stratton.

LÉVI-STRAUSS, C. (1966). *The Savage Mind*. London: Weidenfeld and Nicolson.

—— (1969). *The Elementary Structure of Kinship*. London: Eyre & Spottiswoode.

LEWIS, I. M. (1971). *Ecstatic Religion: A Study of Shamanism and Spirit Possession*. London: Routledge.

LEWIS-WILLIAMS, J. D. (1997). Agency, Art, and Altered Consciousness: A Motif in French (Quercy) Upper Palaeolithic Parietal Art. *Antiquity*, 71: 810–30.

—— and DOWSON, T. A. (1988). The Signs of All Times: Entoptic Phenomena in Upper Palaeolithic Art. *Current Anthropology*, 29: 201–45.

LINDENBAUM, S. (1984). Variations on a Sociosexual Theme in Melanesia. In G. H. Herdt (ed.), *Ritualized Homosexuality in Melanesia*. Berkeley: University of California Press.

LORENZ, K. (1966). *On Aggression*. London: Methuen.

MCARTHUR, M. (1971). Men and Spirits in the Kunimapia Valley. In L. R. Hiatt and C. J. Jayawardena (eds.), *Anthropology in Oceania*. Sydney: Angus & Robertson.

MCCAULEY, R. N. (1999). Bringing Ritual to Mind. In E. Winograd, R. Fivush, and W. Hirst, (eds.), *Ecological Approaches to Cognition: Essays in Honor of Ulric Neisser*. Hillsdale, NJ: Erlaum.

MACFARLANE, A. (1970). *Witchcraft in Tudor and Stuart England: A Regional and Comparative Study*. London: Routledge & Kegan Paul.

MCGRATH, A. E. (1993). *Reformation Thought: An Introduction* (2nd edn.). Oxford: Blackwell.

MALOAT, PALIAU (1970). *Histori bilong mi taim mi bin na i kamap tede*. M. W. Ward (ed.), *The Politics of Melanesia*. Canberra and Port Moresby: The University of Papua New Guinea and the Research School of Pacific Studies, Australian National University.

MASCHIO, T. (1994). *To Remember the Faces of the Dead: The Plenitude of Memory in Southwestern New Britain*. Madison: University of Wisconsin Press.

MAUSS, M. (1954). *The Gift*. London: Routledge & Kegan Paul.

MAY, R. J. (ed.) (1982). *Micronationalist Movements in Papua New Guinea*. Canberra: Australian National University Press.

MEAD, M. (1956). *New Lives for Old: Cultural Transformation—Manus, 1928–1953*. New York: Mentor Books.

—— (1964). *Continuities in Cultural Evolution*. New Haven: Yale University Press.

MEGGITT, M. J. (1974). Pigs Are Our Hearts: The *te* Exchange Cycle among the Mae Enga. *Oceania*, 44: 165–203.

MODJESKA, N. (1982). Production and Inequality: Perspectives from Central New Guinea. In A. J. Strathern (ed.), *Inequality in New Guinea Highlands Societies*. Cambridge: Cambridge University Press.

MOELLER, B. (1971). Piety in Germany Around 1500. In S. E. Ozment (ed.), *The Reformation in Medieval Perspective*. Chicago: Quadrangle Books.

MORAUTA, L. (1972). The Politics of Cargo Cults in the Madang Area. *Man* (NS), 7: 430–47.

—— (1974). *Beyond the Village: Local Politics in Madang, Papua New Guinea*. London: Athlone Press.

MORRIS, B. (1987). *Anthropological Studies of Religion: An Introductory Text*. Cambridge: Cambridge University Press.

MUNN, N. D. (1973). Symbolism in Ritual Context: Aspects of Symbolic Action. In J. J. Honigmann (ed.), *Handbook of Social and Cultural Anthropology*. Chicago: Rand McNally.

—— (1995). An Essay on the Symbolic Construction of Memory in the Kaluli *Gisalo*. In D. de Coppet and A. Iteanu (eds.), *Cosmos and Society in Oceania*. Oxford: Berg.

NEISSER, U. (1982). *Memory Observed: Remembering in Natural Contexts*. San Francisco: W. H. Freeman.

—— (1988). Time Present and Time Past. In M. M. Gruneberg *et al.* (eds.), *Practical Aspects of Memory: Current Research and Issues, 2: Clinical and Educational Implications*. Chichester: John Wiley.

—— and Harsch, N. (1992). Phantom Flashbulbs: False Recollections of Hearing the News about Challenger. In E. Winograd and U. Neisser (eds.), *Affect and Accuracy in Recall*. Cambridge: Cambridge University Press.

—— WINOGRAD, E., BERGMAN, E., SCHREIBER, C., PALMER, S., and WELDON, M. S. (1996). Remembering the Earthquake: Direct Experience versus Hearing the News. *Memory*, 4: 337–57.

NOY, P. (1969). A Revision of the Psychoanalytic Theory of the Primary Process. *International Journal of Psycho-Analysis*, 50: 155–78.

—— (1979). Form Creation in Art: An Ego-Psychological Approach to Creativity. *Psychoanalytic Quarterly*, 48: 229–56.

OTTO, T. (1992). The Paliau Movement in Manus and the Objectification of Tradition. *History and Anthropology*, 5: 427–54.

PANOFF, M. (1969). Inter-Tribal Relations of the Maenge People of New Britain. *New Guinea Research Bulletin*, 30: 1–62.

PFEIFFER, J. E. (1982). *The Creative Explosion: An Inquiry into the Origins of Art and Religion*. New York: Harper & Row.

POOLE, F. J. P. (1982). The Ritual Forging of Identity: Aspects of Person and Self in Bimin-Kuskusmin Male Initiation. G. H. Herdt (ed.), *Rituals of Manhood: Male Initiation in Papua New Guinea*. Berkeley: University of California Press.

REDFIELD, R. (1955). *The Little Community: Viewpoints for the Study of a Human Whole*. Chicago: Chicago University Press.

ROBERTSON-SMITH, W. (1907 [1889]). *Lectures on the Religion of the Semites*. London: Adam and Charles Black.

ROWLEY, C. D. (1965). *The New Guinea Villager: A Retrospect from 1964*. Melbourne: F. W. Cheshire.

SAHLINS, M. (1968). *Tribesmen*. Englewood Cliffs, NJ: Prentice-Hall.

SCHACHTEL, E. G. (1947). On Memory and Childhood Amnesia. *Psychiatry*, 10: 1–26.

SCHWARTZ, T. (1962). The Paliau Movement in the Admiralty Islands, 1946–1954. *Anthropological Papers of the American Museum of Natural History*, 49: 210–421.

—— (1976). The Cargo Cult: A Melanesian Type-response to Change. In G.

DeVos (ed.), *Responses to Change: Society, Culture, and Personality*. New York: Van Nostrand.

SCHWIMMER, E. (1973). *Exchange in the Social Structure of the Orokaiva: Traditional and Emergent Ideologies in the Northern District of Papua*. London: Hurst.

SCRIBNER, R. W. (1989). Oral Culture and the Transmission of Reformation Ideas. In H. Robinson-Hammerstein (ed.), *The Transmission of Ideas in the Lutheran Reformation*. Dublin: Irish Academic Press.

SCRIVNER, E., and SAFER, M. A. (1988). Eyewitnesses Show Hypermnesia for Details about a Violent Event. *Journal of Applied Psychology*, 73: 371–7.

SMITH, M. F. (1980). From Heathen to Atheist: Changing Views of Catholicism in a Papua New Guinea Village. *Oceania*, 51: 40–52.

SPERBER, D. (1975). *Rethinking Symbolism*. Cambridge: Cambridge University Press.

SPRIGGS, M. (1991). Bougainville Talks may offer a Chance for Peace. *The Canberra Times*, 23 August.

STEINBAUER, F. (1979). *Melanesian Cargo Cults: New Salvation Movements in the South Pacific*. London: George Prior.

STRATHERN, A. J. (1971). *The Rope of Moka*. Cambridge: Cambridge University Press.

—— (1992). Exegesis, Comparison, and Interpretation. In B. Juillerat (ed.), *Shooting the Sun: Ritual and Meaning in West Sepik*, Washington, DC: Smithsonian Institution Press.

STRATHERN, M. (1992). The Mother's Brother's Child. In B. Juillerat (ed.), *Shooting the Sun: Ritual and Meaning in West Sepik*, Washington, DC: Smithsonian Institution Press.

STREET, B. V. (1984). *Literacy in Theory and Practice*. Cambridge: Cambridge University Press.

—— (1988). Literacy Practices and Literacy Myths. In R. Säljö (ed.), *The Written Word: Studies in Literate Thought and Action*. Berlin: Springer-Verlag.

TOVALELE, P. (1977). The Pomio Cargo Cult—East New Britain. In R. Adams (ed.), *Socio-Economic Change—Papua New Guinea*, Lae: University of Technology.

TROMPF, G. W. (1984). 'What Has Happened to Melanesian 'Cargo Cults'? Religious Movements in Melanesia Today, 3(4), Goroka: Melanesian Institute, 29–51.

—— (1990a). The Cargo and the Millennium on Both Sides of the Pacific. In G. W. Trompf (ed.), *Cargo Cults and Millenarian Movements: Transoceanic Comparisons of New Religious Movements*. Berlin: Mouton de Gruyter.

—— (1990b). Keeping the *Lo* under a Melanesian Messiah: An Analysis of the Pomio Kivung, Papua New Guinea. In J. Barker (ed.), *Christianity in Oceania: Ethnographic Perspectives*. Lanham: University Press of America.

—— (1991). *Melanesian Religion*. Cambridge: Cambridge University Press.

TULVING, E. (1972). Episodic and Semantic Memory. In E. Tulving and W. Donaldson (eds.), *Organization of Memory*, New York: Academic Press.

TURNER, V. W. (1967). *The Forest of Symbols*. Ithaca, NY: Cornell University Press.

—— (1974). *Dramas, Fields, and Metaphors: Symbolic Action in Human Society.* Ithaca, NY: Cornell University Press.

TUZIN, D. F. (1980). *The Voice of the Tambaran: Truth and Illusion in Ilahita Arapesh Religion.* Berkeley: University of California Press.

—— (1982). Ritual Violence among the Ilahita Arapesh: The Dynamics of Moral and Religious Uncertainty. In G. H. Herdt (ed.), *Rituals of Manhood: Male Initiation in Papua New Guinea.* Berkeley: University of California Press.

—— (1992). Revelation and Concealment in the Cultural Organization of Meaning: A Methodological Note. In B. Juillerat (ed.), *Shooting the Sun: Ritual and Meaning in West Sepik.* Washington, DC: Smithsonian Institution Press.

VAN GENNEP, A. (1965 [1908]). *The Rites of Passage.* London: Routledge & Kegan Paul.

WAAGENAAR, W. A. and GROENEWEG, J. (1990). The Memory of Concentration Camp Survivors. *Applied Cognitive Psychology* 4: 77–87.

WAGNER, R. (1992). The Imagery Keeps Its Scale: An Obviation Model of the Yafar Yangis. In B. Juillerat (ed.), *Shooting the Sun: Ritual and Meaning in West Sepik.* Washington, DC: Smithsonian Institution Press.

WANEK, A. (1996). *The State and its Enemies in Papua New Guinea.* Richmond, Surrey: Curzon Press.

WEBER, M. (1930). *The Protestant Ethic and the Spirit of Capitalism.* London: George Allen and Unwin.

—— (1947). *The Theory of Social and Economic Organization.* Oxford: Oxford University Press.

WEINER, A. B. (1992). *Inalienable Possession: The Paradox of Keeping-while-giving.* Berkeley: University of California Press.

WEINER, J. F. (1991). *The Empty Place: Poetry, Space, and Being among the Foi of Papua New Guinea.* Bloomington: Indiana University Press.

WERBNER, R. P. (ed.) (1977). *Regional Cults.* London: Academic Press.

WETHERELL, D. (1977). *Reluctant Mission: The Anglican Church in Papua New Guinea 1891–1942.* St. Lucia: University of Queensland Press.

WHEATLEY, P. (1971). *The Pivot of the Four Quarters: A Preliminary Enquiry into the Origins and Character of the Ancient Chinese City.* Edinburgh: Edinburgh University Press.

WHITEHOUSE, H. (1992a). Leaders and Logics, Persons and Polities. *History and Anthropology*, 6: 103–24.

—— (1992b). Memorable Religions: Transmission, Codification, and Change in divergent Melanesian Contexts. *Man* (NS), 27: 777–97.

—— (1993a). Review of S. J. Harrison (1993), *The Mask of War: Violence, Ritual, and the Self in Papua New Guinea. Journal of the Anthropological Association of Ireland*, 3: 47–9.

WHITEHOUSE, H (1993b). Review of B. Juillerat (1992), *Shooting the Sun: Ritual and Meaning in West Sepik. Journal of the Anthropological Society of Oxford (JASO)*, 25: 213–17.

—— (1994). Strong Words and Forceful Winds: Religious Experience and Political Process in Melanesia. *Oceania*, 65: 40–58.

—— (1995). *Inside the Cult: Religious Innovation and Transmission in Papua New Guinea*. Oxford: Oxford University Press.

—— (1996a). Apparitions, Orations, and Rings: Experience of Spirits in Dadul. In J. M. Mageo and A. Howard (eds.), *Spirits in Culture and Mind*. London: Routledge.

—— (1996b). From Possession to Apotheosis: Transformation and Disguise in the Leadership of a Cargo Movement. In R. Feinberg and K. A. Watson-Gegeo (eds.), *Leadership and Change in the Western Pacific*. London: Athlone Press.

—— (1996c). Jungles and Computers: Neuronal Group Selection and the Epidemiology of Representations. *Journal of the Royal Anthropological Institute* (NS), 1: 99–116.

—— (1996d). Rites of Terror: Emotion, Metaphor, and Memory in Melanesian Initiation Cults. *Journal of the Royal Anthropological Institute* (NS), 2: 703–15.

—— (1998). From Mission to Movement: The Impact of Christianity on Patterns of Political Association in Papua New Guinea. *Journal of the Royal Anthropological Institute* (NS), 4: 43–63.

WILLIAMS, F. E. (1928). *Orokaiva Magic*. London: Humphrey Milford.

—— (1930). *Orokaiva Society*. London: Humphrey Milford.

WINOGRAD E., and KILLINGER, W. A. (1983). Relating Age at Encoding in Early Childhood to Adult Recall: Development of Flashbulb Memories. *Journal of Experimental Psychology: General*, 112: 413–22.

WORSLEY, P. (1957). *The Trumpet Shall Sound: A Study of 'Cargo Cults' in Melanesia*. London: MacGibbon & Kee.

—— (1996). Foreword in A. Wanek, *The State and its Enemies in Papua New Guinea*. Richmond, Surrey: Curzon Press.

WRIGHT, D. and GASKELL, G. D. (1992). 'The Construction and Function of Vivid Memories. In M. A. Conway, D. C. Rubin. H. Spinnler, and W. A. Wagenaar (eds.), *Theoretical Perspectives on Autobiographical Memory*, Netherlands: Kluwer Academic Publishers.

YOUNG, M. W. (1983). *Magicians of Manumanua: Living Myth in Kalauna*. Berkeley: University of California Press.

INDEX

secrecy (*cont.*):
  and memory 57
  and revelation 36, 117–18
  and solidarity 31
Smith, M. F. 41 n.
Sperber, D. 25
splinter groups:
  political impact of 52–3, 129
  and recodification of dogma 129, 130,
    142–3
  suppression of 99, 129, 148, 159
  and tedium effect 44–6, 143, 148
  see also cohesion; emotion; iconicity;
    imagery; initiation; leadership;
    revelation; routinization
Spriggs, M. 48
Steinbauer, F. 42 n., 44, 56
Strathern, A. J. 20 n., 87
Strathern, M. 85
Street, B. V. 174
Stroud, C. 174
structuralism, *see* binary opposition; digital
    codes

Taro Cult:
  compared with the Noise 131, 132–3,
    134, 136, 138
  dissemination of 72, 77–80
  and emotion 109–10
  and memory 100
  political impact of 123–4, 126–8
  practices 66–7
  ritual imagery in 67–72, 178
  see also cohesion; iconicity; imagery;
    initiation; multivocality; Orokaiva;
    revelation
tedium effect 44–6, 115, 142–3, 148, 155;
  see also leadership; routinization;
    splinter groups
Tovalele, P. 54 n.
Trompf, G. W. 19, 45, 48, 54 n., 73
Tulving, E. 5, 113
Turner, V. W. 3, 16–17, 180–5

Tuzin, D. F. 21–2, 28–30, 32, 86
Tylor, E. 169

universalism:
  and communitas 180–5
  and Melanesian religious movements
    43, 99–100, 112, 114, 144
  and missionization 40–1
  and semantic memory 9–10, 122

Van Gennep, A. 20

Waagenaar, W. A. 91
Wagner, R. 89
Wanek, A. 48, 53, 56, 74, 76, 102
warfare:
  and colonization 127
  and localism 31, 148
  and ritual imagery 22, 27
  theories of 167–9
  see also cohesion; Orokaiva
Weber, M. 3, 4, 181
Weiner, A. B. 20 n.
Weiner, J. F. 19
Werbner, R. P. 1
Wetherell, D. 37–9, 44, 70 n., 123
Wheatley, P. 170, 171
Whitehouse, H. 3, 8, 18 n., 34 n., 41,
    43–4, 45, 46, 48, 51, 54 n., 58, 62, 80,
    84 n., 99, 100, 113, 115, 119, 123 n.,
    128, 129, 135, 139, 143, 145, 146,
    168 n., 185, 187, 188
Wickham, C. 5 n.
Williams, F. E. 23, 25, 30, 66, 67–9, 70, 71,
    78–9, 103, 109, 110, 123, 131, 134,
    188
Winograd E. 119, 121
Worsley, P. 47, 57, 70, 95 n., 123, 186
Wright, D. 7–8, 120–2

Yali 56, 75, 76, 79, 128
Young, M. W. 37, 90